NON-STANDARD LANGUAGE
IN ENGLISH LITERATURE

THE LANGUAGE LIBRARY

EDITED BY DAVID CRYSTAL

N. F. Blake

〰〰〰〰〰〰〰〰〰〰〰〰〰〰〰〰〰〰〰〰〰〰〰〰〰〰

NON-STANDARD LANGUAGE IN ENGLISH LITERATURE

〰〰〰〰〰〰〰〰〰〰〰〰〰〰〰〰〰〰〰〰〰〰〰〰〰〰

Exclusive distributor for U.S. and Canada:

WESTVIEW PRESS
5500 Central Avenue
Boulder, Colorado 80301

ANDRE DEUTSCH

First published 1981 by
André Deutsch Limited
105 Great Russell Street London WC1

Copyright (c) 1981 by N. F. Blake
BT 1764-83   9/24/82
Printed in Great Britain by
The Thetford Press Limited, Thetford, Norfolk

British Library Cataloguing in Publication Data
Blake, N.F.
Non-standard language in English literature.
-(Language library)
1. English literature-History and criticism
2. English language-History
I. Title
820'.9   PR83

ISBN 0-233-97311-7
ISBN 0-233-97422-9 Pbk
Distributed in the United States of America and Canada by Westview Press,
5500 Central Avenue, Boulder, Colorado 80301

PR
P3
B4185

In memoriam
SIMEON POTTER

CONTENTS

🔯🔯🔯🔯🔯🔯

PREFACE

𝕊𝕊𝕊𝕊𝕊𝕊

WHEN I WAS A LECTURER in Professor Simeon Potter's department, we sometimes talked about the need for a book about non-standard language in literature because it is a subject that has been neglected so far. When he became editor of the Language Library he suggested that I might like to do a book on that topic. I was unable to follow up his suggestion at the time, but I promised to tackle it one day. Unfortunately his death has prevented him from seeing the result, but I have wished to dedicate the volume to his memory because of his interest in the subject and in gratitude for his generous assistance to me at Liverpool. I am sorry for his sake that the book is no better than it is. I am grateful to his successor as editor of the Language Library, Professor David Crystal, for welcoming the book when I mooted the topic with him, and I would like to thank him for his help.

This topic is one which arises in conversation with colleagues, friends and students from time to time and I know that I have benefited from the ideas discussed even though it is difficult to recognize now from whom some of them originated. Several students who have studied for higher degrees under my supervision have tackled stylistic studies of various writers in English and their representation of non-standard language has been a part of their work. They are Dr F. Mooti, Mr A. Megalli, Miss S. Latif and Mr O. Adejare. I should like to thank them in particular for the many discussions we have had.

Finally I would like to thank Miss Natasha Horlov, Mrs Sandra Burton and my wife for their help in preparing the typescript and in reading the proofs.

INTRODUCTION

᪥᪥᪥᪥᪥᪥

TO THE AVERAGE READER it may appear that there are few problems in using non-standard language in a work of literature, and the absence of any critical work in this area might be interpreted as confirmation of that view. Nothing could be further from the truth, however, for the use of non-standard language is so full of pitfalls that any false step can readily destroy the tone of a work. Unfortunately for the author, not all readers react to non-standard language in the same way, and this makes his task of using it all the more perilous. There are many people who find historical novels impossible to read because they detest the falseness of the artificial archaisms with which many examples of that genre abound. Other people may react by feeling that some distancing of language in the dialogue is essential to create the sense of the past in a novel, for they will feel equally cheated if the language is too modern for their taste. Similarly many of us respond differently to the use of regional dialects in a novel or play, and so a writer has to consider carefully the advantages and disadvantages of non-standard language before he embarks on its use.

The standard language is a written language, and all varieties of speech are subsumed within it for the purposes of written communication. What that standard is changes from one period to the next and hence what is non-standard will naturally vary as well. Today it is no longer obligatory to write 'compared with' as against 'compared to', and few would consider the latter non-standard. Indeed only a few purists are even likely to notice the latter – a sure sign that a form has become standard to all intents and purposes. Similarly the insistence on absolute standards of spelling is less stringent now than it used to be, so that most readers would perhaps pay no attention to 'can not' or 'can't' rather than 'cannot' and would certainly not regard these forms as non-standard.

The importance of non-standard English is that it tells us something about the standard and its limits, for only what is clearly marked as non-standard will have any impact upon the reader. The limits of tolerance in the standard will be reflected in what is considered non-standard. It is possible that a fastidious writer today might try to discriminate between one speaker who used 'can't' and another who

11

used 'cannot', but he would be in danger of this distinction being overlooked by all but the most discriminating of his readers unless he himself drew attention to it. The non-standard language must be marked sufficiently for the average reader to grasp that it is non-standard and hence an author is unlikely to use as non-standard those features of language which are on the boundaries between the standard and non-standard. This means, in effect, that in literature non-standard language is that language which is clearly marked as different from the rest of the language in the work in question. If, for example, both the narrative and the dialogue of a novel are written in pidgin English (as I believe is true of some novels written for less educated people in some former British colonies), one could not say that the dialogue in that novel was non-standard for there would be nothing against which it was marked within the confines of that novel. If, however, a novel is narrated in standard English and all the dialogue is in pidgin, there is a contrast within the novel between two types of language. It would be clear that the speakers in the novel did not conform to the standard of the author and his readers, and the dialogue would be marked. More often it is only some speakers in a novel who will use non-standard English and their language will be contrasted with that of other characters. For the purposes of this book it is the contrast between one form of language and another within a work of literature which will categorize one form as non-standard. This is an important criterion to remember, because a writer is using language to achieve a particular effect and the contrast between two forms of language will be important for him in this aim.

What effects, then, can be gained through the use of non-standard language? When we meet a stranger for the first time we notice two things about him immediately – his speech, and his habits, such as the clothes he wears, particularly if they are different from our own. They help to distinguish him from us and our other acquaintances, though as we become more familiar with him his peculiarities, such as his speech, become less noticeable precisely because they no longer seem so strange. Their strangeness will emerge into prominence again only if a third party is introduced into the group and reacts to the difference of the stranger, or if the group for some emotional or defensive reason closes ranks against outsiders. In literary works, it will be important to use non-standard language most fully when a character who uses it is introduced, since that helps to categorize him, or at moments of stress, since that draws attention to his difference which may be one of the causes of the stress. For the rest of the time the non-standard language will probably be played down. Another reason for this method of writing is that non-standard language is not easy to write without it becoming a caricature, and so writers do not want to continue it at full stretch for any length of time. Furthermore, too extended a use of non-standard language could lead to incomprehension on the part of the reader since it is inevitable that the character will eventually have to resort to less familiar words and phrases. Because non-standard language is not usually used extensively, it is often given to minor characters, such as taxi-drivers, who naturally have little to say in the work as a whole. Since the standard language is an educated language, non-standard language has almost always been regarded as uneducated and unsophisticated. It is only in the twentieth century that upper-class speech which deviates from the standard has been introduced into literature. Because literature has until the recent present been written by the educated, it is not unnatural that non-standard language has been widely looked down on as being the appropriate language for the lowly born, the foolish and the ignorant. Hence non-standard language has been a marker of class and of comedy, for we are generally sufficiently self-satisfied to laugh at those who cannot match our own educational attainments and who reveal this through the way they speak. It is only since people in the lower classes have been endowed with other virtues in the eyes of the educated that some modification of the role of non-standard language has developed.

When, in a literary work, a character speaks in a non-standard way he will immediately be contrasted with those characters who use the standard. To those who speak the standard, the way in which others speak may be regarded as comic because it may sound to them as though such people are mangling the language in an attempt to speak in a standard manner. Those writers interested in comedy will increase the number of misunderstandings that can arise from this use of two languages. Thus a Welshman might be allowed to say *pig* for 'big'. Non-standard language will therefore often signal comedy, because the serious matters will be handled by the major characters. If those matters need some comic relief, minor characters can be produced to provide it. Otherwise non-standard language will indicate class. At first this was largely the rustic poor, but with the Industrial Revolution it increasingly became the urban working class. It is rare for the non-standard language to be part of the character portrayal of a character for it is too blunt an instrument for that. The contrast between standard and non-standard only draws attention to gross differences such as class, though such differences may be part of a wider political or moral statement. It may, as more recently, be political in showing that the aspirations of people who speak like that are real and have to be accommodated; or it may be moral in that it underlines that a man should not be dismissed as stupid simply because he speaks in an unusual way. An accent is no guide to a man's character, though people may make assumptions on that basis. Generally, too, scene-setting is at best a subsidiary feature of the use of non-standard language. The dialect that individuals use in literature can rarely be localized sufficiently for it to paint the atmosphere of a place. Nevertheless, it may well be that some readers accept that the language is evocative of a place simply because they are ignorant of different forms of language, and will take the author's representation as accurate if it fulfils their own rather generalized expectations.

The point should perhaps be emphasized that linguistic realism is not attempted in literature. Sociolinguistics has shown us that we each possess a multitude of languages which we use in the different social situations which we meet daily. Literature cannot accommodate that variety and in general each character is given one language to use. Occasionally he may adopt a different language as a type of disguise, as it may be suggested Prince Hal does in Shakespeare's *Henry V*. He uses comic prose in the taverns as a disguise of his real nature, but he reverts to poetry when he speaks to his father and other members of the court. Even if a character develops in a novel, his language will remain largely unaltered, because he will be cast as a standard or a non-standard speaker. Similarly a non-standard speaker will use the same language whoever he is addressing, whereas he might readily in real life try to modify his accent when speaking to a more educated person. There is, one might say, only one standard language, but there are a myriad of non-standard ones. In literature this variety of non-standard language is reduced to a limited number of stereotypes drawn to contrast with the standard. Furthermore, narration is almost invariably in the standard and it is only dialogue which is non-standard. This in turn helps to underline the role of the standard and emphasizes the deviant nature of the non-standard; it is after all *non*-standard. There is in literature no room for the many varieties of language we each have and so there is a polarization between standard and non-standard. A speaker uses either one or the other; one is not, as in real life, sometimes formal and sometimes informal in one's speech.

An author can use one of the several constituents of language to indicate non-standard speech: spelling (to indicate variation in pronunciation), vocabulary and syntax. Of these the former is the most important. The problem with vocabulary is that it is difficult to tell which words are considered non-standard. Many words are informal or colloquial, but that does not necessarily make them non-standard. Certainly types of vocabulary like cant or jargon may well be non-standard, but the problem with them is one of comprehension. The cant of thieves will not be known to the average honest citizen and so a writer cannot afford to introduce many words of this nature in his work. Every unusual vocabulary item has to be explained. Either the narrator can do it in a novel or in poetry, or else one of the other characters can ask what it means and have it explained. This approach is naturally the major one in drama. It is not one, however, which can be used too often for it will tend to impede the action. If the vocabulary does not help to place a character without elaborate explanation then it is not very useful. Nevertheless, some words and phrases have become associated with certain people: *look you* is a sign of Welshness and *sure* of an Irish speaker. Syntax is also fluid and so may be difficult to use. As we have seen some differences in syntax are not marked, such as *different from* as opposed to *different to*, and others are colloquial and so difficult to use as a marked feature of non-standard language. The syntax may not be distorted too far in an effort to create non-standard language for then the result will be considered either unintelligible or poetic. Certain types of syntax are found frequently in non-standard portrayals. They include archaisms which are no longer part of the standard, such as double negatives, and faulty congruence, such as a singular verb with a plural subject.

The most important aspect of non-standard language in literature is the use of spelling to suggest a deviant pronunciation. This is instantly recognizable as non-standard precisely because spelling has been standardized for so long. In a written context, *cum* instead of 'come' immediately stands out as marked. Furthermore, it is possible to corrupt spelling a little so that the word is still understood, although its non-standard nature is never in doubt. Here the apostrophe is the most useful item in the writer's armoury precisely because it alerts the reader to the absence of some letter that he expects through his conditioned response to the formal stylized medium of writing. The writer will use the apostrophe to mark a form as non-standard and he will not mind being inconsistent in its use. Generally one non-standard marker per word will be enough. A non-standard speaker who drops his initial *h*'s as in *'ave* and his final *g*'s as in *speakin'* may be represented as keeping one or the other where both occur in the same word. Consequently one may expect to meet this speaker saying *'unting* or, less likely, *hun-*

tin' rather than *'untin'*. The reason is that the more non-standard features a word has the less likely a reader is to understand it. For the writer it will be sufficient to signal to his readers that a character speaks in a non-standard way; he is not intent on any exact representation of the language. That would in fact be impossible in the Roman alphabet we use, and even if it were possible the result would be total lack of communication between author and reader. The writer must choose certain features, and this has led to some features being traditionally included in non-standard portrayals. He for the most part borrows his non-standard language from other writers rather than going out into factories or farms to record the exact language. The corruptions are merely markers. This can be seen most clearly from certain spelling corruptions which are almost without significance as far as pronunciation is concerned. English spelling is so archaic that the spelling of many words today bears little resemblance to their actual pronunciation. Often in non-standard portrayals such words will be given a more 'phonetic' pronunciation. 'What' may be spelt *wot* and 'fellow' *feller*. These spellings suggest a deviant pronunciation because they are deviant spellings. But in so far as the spellings can be interpreted phonetically they represent the pronunciations that most standard speakers would use in ordinary conversation. They are non-standard in writing alone.

There has grown up a tradition of non-standard spelling, though not all writers adhere to it. The fall of final consonants is one fairly regular feature. The substitution of *ow* for *ou* or *ol* as in *howse* or *owd* 'old' is also quite common. In the sixteenth and seventeenth centuries the use of *ch* forms for the first person singular of the personal pronoun was a traditional feature. It is immaterial whether such features actually appear in the dialect the writer is supposedly portraying; the important point is that the reader recognizes it as non-standard and has some vague idea as to what it might mean. But, in fact, because writers borrow their non-standard language from each other, most of them probably have little idea what sounds they are trying to reproduce, and there is never a key to what these symbols represent. The American stories about Brer Rabbit are supposedly told by an American negro. There is nothing in the word *brer* which could lead an educated Englishman to know what the negro sound was which this spelling represents. Indeed the average English person pronounces this word in a way which bears little resemblance to its negro original, though most understand that it is meant to be a black American pronunciation.

Because of the problem of comprehension for the reader most non-standard spellings are confined to very common words. If 'rile' were represented as *roil* in a text which spells 'time' as *toim*, it is probable that many readers would fail to realize what it meant. The pull of the standard is strong. It is for this reason that most representations of non-standard language have one or two regular features, such as dropping a final consonant, to which other features may be added from time to time. The elisions and syncopations found in non-standard representations are known to most of us because many may be used by us in less formal talk, and they provide a constant reminder to the reader that the speaker is non-standard. Despite this normal procedure in representing non-standard speech, modern scholars have often tried to suggest that authors were indeed trying to create a realistic non-standard speech and that they had a good ear to catch the various tones. Chaucer, Emily Brontë and Dickens, to name but a few, have all been praised in this way. They can be made to appear competent phonetically because a scholar can always interpret their spellings in accordance with what he knows of the dialects they are trying to represent. But the accuracy of their dialect portrayals may well be exaggerated in this way. While I would not wish in any way to diminish these writers' achievements or to imply that they might not have had a good ear for variant pronunciation, it nevertheless needs to be emphasized that it was neither desirable nor necessary for them to portray a dialect accurately.

It may seem surprising how few variant dialects there are in English literature. The explanation is to be found in what has already been noted in this introduction: writers borrow from other writers and so non-standard representations become traditional. There was no need for a multiplicity of dialects as far as literature is concerned: it might almost be said that for literary authors one non-standard variety is as good as another. The first dialect to emerge was the rustic dialect which remains with us today. It has persisted in being a mainly southern language with such features as the voicing of initial *f* and *s*, though it is today regarded as more a south-western variety. It arose in the sixteenth century and it has so coloured our attitude towards country people that many people today who hear a northern farm-worker speak would not consider him really a rustic. Examples of the northern dialect arise in the seventeenth century, and for the most part they have not been specific to given localities in the North. Even the language of the North Midlands is usually portrayed as a northern variety without much distinction from other northern types. It was only in the nineteenth century that this variety became common, for it was then that authors began to be interested in the industrial urban class. The language was needed because the people portrayed were so different from the rustics and their language was associated with harshness and squalor. The Cockney dialect also emerged in the nineteenth century. As attitudes towards the country changed as a result of the Romantic movement, a new comic dialect was needed and it was this need which Cockney filled. Because it is a London dialect it has always been associated with the poor and uneducated. For as the standard language is based on the London dialect, it follows that any educated Londoner will use the standard. Since the northern dialect has been employed when writers have tried to ennoble and dignify the working classes, Cockney has rarely been used for anything else than comedy. Particularly associated with this dialect has been the faithful, but pert, servant. Beyond England, the Welsh and Irish dialects, though they are more variant pronunciations than dialects, have almost invariably been linked with humour, the latter, of course, particularly with a charming incompetence. The Scots, on the other hand, have been more earnest and their dialect has been more serious and respected. This is in part the result of the separate Scottish kingdom which lasted so long and in part the result of an important Scottish literature. There is no Welsh equivalent to Burns or Sir Walter Scott. Even long before then, however, as for example in Shakespeare's *Henry V*, it is the Scot who is the more serious dialect speaker; the Welsh and the Irish are more humorous.

When it occurs, cant is particularly associated with thieving. This is because so much literature has dealt with the conflict between the rich and the dispossessed. Thieves' cant helps to suggest a separate culture which is in direct opposition to the standard morals of the average citizen. It was also needed for safety, and so its use is often that of the code, to keep outsiders in ignorance. Slang, however, is more associated with the young, particularly the idle young. It too has become a kind of passport – a sign that one has acquired the trimmings of fashion, for slang is much more temporary than cant. More recently it has been used to draw a contrast between the young and the old, for the latter remain more staid in their linguistic usage. Jargon and cliché hardly appear as such in non-standard descriptions. It is only when special situations are depicted, such as a boarding school, that jargon may appear, for the boys will have their own language. But in general, cant, slang, jargon and cliché have not been much exploited in literary works. This is because they are expressed through vocabulary, and, as we have already seen, the use of a specialized vocabulary poses real difficulties for a writer.

Although non-standard language appears first in a poem in English, in Chaucer's *Canterbury Tales*, poetry has not been a rich ground for it in our literature. Chaucer used it because his *Canterbury Tales* is a dramatic work that has much in common with plays and novels. It is long and has many characters, who need to be distinguished as they interact with one another. For the most part, longer poems have tended towards the epic or heroic, and naturally non-standard language would not be appropriate to the tone of such works. Occasionally, archaisms may be used to enrich the poetry, but that is a rather specialized form of non-standard language. It is only when poetry turns to satire that we find much use of non-standard language, for it may often be used to draw the contrast between what is and what should be. It was soon being used in drama, and it is there that it had the greatest development in the sixteenth and seventeenth centuries. Drama is a slightly different medium from poetry and the novel in that it is performed, and in a performance an actor can assume an accent whether it is signalled in the text or not. For instance, Hotspur, in Shakespeare's *Henry IV part I*, may be given a northern accent and Owen Glendower a Welsh one. The use of non-standard language in drama may therefore seem to be greater than is actually the case. It is mainly used to expose affectation or hypocrisy, to effect a disguise, or to indulge in clowning. In the nineteenth and twentieth centuries there have been fewer examples of non-standard language in drama. Its place has in that respect been taken by the novel and so in the latter part of this book the novel bulks very large. Because the novel is longer than the average play, it contains more characters and consequently often includes more minor roles. The novelist can explain the language of his characters in the narrative sections and so he is more free than the dramatist to experiment with different varieties of non-standard language. Its use in the novel is usually less ambiguous because the novelist provides a more detailed context. The novel becomes an important medium only in the eighteenth century, and at first the non-standard varieties used are those which had been found in drama. Comedy is all important, but gradually non-standard language is woven into the serious moral of the novel, and its role changes. Those that speak it are no longer mere rustics or buffoons; they become the major participants. They are seen to be as sensitive and intelligent as any standard speaker. As its use in comedy decreases, so the use of non-standard language diminishes, for it is not every novelist that wants to use it seriously or has a plot in which it would be of assistance.

This book is concerned with the mainstream of English literature; it does not tackle non-literary writings, essentially those which were not intended for publication. Likewise it is not concerned with dialectal writings. Particularly in the nineteenth century there was a spate of writings in some dialects, and even today organizations like the Yorkshire Dialect Society promote dialect writing. Such works are normally entirely in dialect and the dialect is thus the standard. They consequently have no place in this book which is concerned only with those varieties of language which are introduced into a work in contrast with its standard variety. Similarly I have concentrated on works written in Great Britain, though I have looked at a few twentieth-century works written abroad. I have not attempted to cover non-standard language in America for it is too large a subject and many of the works written there in the nineteenth century have not become well known in England. Since the average writer is little concerned with the exact phonetic realization of the language he portrays as non-standard, I have not concerned myself too much with identifying the sounds he might have had in mind. The approach is historical, and, on the whole, general, in that I have tried to look for the motivations behind the use of non-standard language, the different varieties that have been used and the marriage of tradition with innovation.

Chapter 1

CHAUCER AND HIS
PREDECESSORS

𝔊𝔊𝔊𝔊𝔊𝔊

THE MEDIEVAL PERIOD in English literature is a long one, stretching
as it does from the beginnings of written English in the seventh century to the end of the fifteenth century. In this period it is not until the
fourteenth century that any author starts to make use of different
linguistic registers in his portrayal of his characters, and the main focus
of this chapter will necessarily fall on that author, Chaucer. Yet it is
important to understand why no earlier authors did so by surveying
the period as a whole, for even Chaucer made only a small beginning
in the use of non-standard language.

The Anglo-Saxons arrived in England in the fifth century and
gradually conquered and settled the country. The language spoken by
these invaders, who were made up of different tribes, was not identical
and after the settlement different dialects emerged throughout the
country. Various geographical and historical factors contributed to a
further distinction among some dialects at least. The Danish invasions
from the eighth century onwards led to many northern dialects
assimilating Danish words and sounds, thus accentuating existing differences between northern and southern speech. Although there must
have been a multiplicity of dialects, the written sources enable us to
trace only four major ones: Northumbrian, Mercian (in the Midlands),
West Saxon and Kentish. Documents are written in all these dialects.
For the most part no one dialect was considered as standard in this
period, in that a man living in Northumbria would not set out to write
a book in the Kentish dialect because he felt that it had more status
than his own. Writing was taught to the Anglo-Saxons by the Christian missionaries, who were familiar with the Roman alphabet.
Presumably they learned first to write in Latin and then adapted what
they had learned to the writing of their own speech. Since there was no
tradition of writing in English they naturally tried to represent their
own spoken forms in writing; a man in Northumbria would thus write
different English from a man in Kent.

21

There was, however, one time in the Anglo-Saxon period when there was a trend towards the establishment of a uniform written language. In the tenth century the West Saxons gradually reconquered the Danelaw, that part of England which had been settled by the Danes. There, many of the monasteries in which writing flourished had been destroyed or abandoned so that the ability to write was no longer to be found. This, at least, is what King Alfred implies in his preface to his translation of the *Cura Pastoralis* by Pope Gregory the Great. Naturally the reintroduction of writing in these areas was the work of those who still knew how to write, and that meant for the most part scribes trained in Wessex since that area had not been ravaged by the Danes. When they taught the northerners how to write again they did so by teaching them how to write English rather than Latin, since the knowledge of Latin had somewhat decayed and since there was now, unlike the earlier period, a tradition of writing in English. But the English of these teachers was the West Saxon dialect, so that people throughout the country started to write in this dialect. Thus West Saxon acquired the status of a written standard for the tenth and the first half of the eleventh century. This development was halted by the Norman Conquest, which reduced English to the status of a second language. As English sank in esteem, the various parts of the country relapsed into writing their own forms of English, which meant that writing once again approximated more closely to speech. This effect of the Norman Conquest is important for us since it interrupted the development of a written standard; literary works began to appear again in a variety of dialects. When that happens people do not value one dialect more than another and so are unable to contrast non-standard forms with those in the standard dialect, for there is no standard. The variants that are available are simply treated as variants and not as indicators of social or cultural differences, as we shall see later.

The continuation of the variety in dialects is attributable also to certain other factors. As we have seen, writing was introduced by Christian missionaries and it was taught in clerical establishments. Gradually monasteries were set up and became the home of schools and the places where books were copied. These monasteries were scattered throughout the country and owed allegiance to no central English authority. Hence, as far as writing was concerned, there was at this time no centralizing tendency which would promote the adoption of one dialect as a standard. Instead of a national standard there were a multitude of local standards, each depending on its own teaching centre or monastic foundation. Even locally uniformity can never have been insisted upon and was rarely achieved becuase English was not a subject of instruction. The aim of education was to teach a boy how to read and write Latin, not to write English. Hence there was little incentive to standardize English to make it more suitable as an end of instruction. Clerks were the writers and were consequently employed in the civil service, but this was attached to the organs of government, which, as they depended upon the king, accompanied him round the country on his visitations. There was no established civil service permanently resident in London which might have encouraged the development of a uniform writing system. Hence the educated men of the country either lived in various ecclesiastical establishments throughout the country or travelled round in the king's entourage. There was little in this situation which promoted a standardized system of writing.

Another feature of writing in the Middle Ages needs to be remembered: when texts were multiplied they were copied by hand. Printing was unknown in England, and printing encourages the creation of a standard since all copies of a book are practically identical. What is printed in London, for example, will be sold throughout the country and so needs to be acceptable to a wide range of buyers. When a text is copied by hand it can be adapted to the language of the recipient. Why should a man in Newcastle have to read a text copied in the Liverpool dialect? The scribe may just as easily make it suitable for him by changing the language of the text into his own dialect, for each copy is made individually and so need not be identical with the next one. This fact has important implications for the language of the texts. If, for example, a man in Manchester wanted to characterize the speech of someone outside his area, he could presumably choose the dialect of a neighbouring place such as Sheffield. But if this manuscript was then copied in the South, the average southern scribe might not have been aware of the differences between the two dialects to notice the different forms of speech. Thus when he copied it into his own dialect, the distinctions might have become blurred or totally lost. Even if he was aware of the differences, it might be difficult for him to keep them in a southern environment. For when a text was transferred from one dialect into another, it was never done completely. The result was usually a mixed dialect consisting of elements from the original and the second dialect. In the average manuscript it would take a fine sense of speech to detect differences between original dialects that had existed in the first copy. This feeling that the copying of manuscripts robbed them of their individual linguistic indices probably inhibited writers from trying to use variations in regional dialects as markers of social or regional origin.

In this connection we must remember that spelling itself was flexible at this time. Even today there is no academy or government agency which lays down what is the correct spelling for any word, and consequently there are acceptable alternatives. The ending *-ize* is often spelt *-ise*, and many words of classical or foreign origin exist in more than one spelling. Some prefer *tiro* to *tyro* or *gipsy* to *gypsy*. For the most part, convention, which has been dictated by education, printing and the ready availability of dictionaries, has created the feeling that each word has a correct spelling. At earlier periods, and this applies beyond the medieval period which is our principal concern at the moment, the absence of an educational standard and of complete wordlists of English meant that no one could tell what the correct spelling of any particular word was. No one could say that *do* was more correct than *doe* or *doo*, though naturally many had their individual preferences. Without this background of regularity the indication of non-standard forms is difficult because there is no standard against which such forms can be evaluated. Today the spelling *tuppence* is indicative of an informal level of style only because *twopence* is accepted as the standard spelling of the word; the former spelling is marked. In a situation where there was no standard spelling and when most texts were written in a mixed spelling, this type of variety would not be marked and hence could not be used by authors to indicate a particular level of style.

In the Middle Ages and beyond, the modernization and adaptation of texts was a standard procedure. No one thought that a text should be preserved in precisely the same form as it left the author's pen. A text was a living thing, which could be adapted, added to or extracted from according to the needs and inclinations of those who wanted to make use of it. Copyright did not exist and once an author published his work he lost control over it; it became public property. Today we have become obsessed with the idea of accuracy and authenticity: newspapers are even prepared to include a learned correspondence as to whether a particular poet meant to include a comma in a certain line or not. This sense of total faithfulness to the author's copy did not exist at earlier periods. Scribes in the medieval period felt free to rewrite words or even sentences if they felt it appropriate to do so. Even later, the four folios of Shakespeare are witness to a progressive modernization of his language. In such modernizations, differences of language which might have been exhibited by choice of vocabulary or even spelling would not survive. This fact meant that authors did not indulge in that kind of linguistic variety as a marker of character or situation.

In the Old English period (up to the Norman Conquest), the use of non-standard language was further discouraged by the type of literature current. Prose works consisted mainly of chronicles, saints' lives and moral treatises, and poetic ones of heroic and religious poems. There was no drama, in which confrontation among people from different classes and the need to reveal character and attitudes through speech both encourage variety in language. There were no literary genres built around repartee, informality or scatology through which a different register of usage might have found expression. Opportunities for dialogue do occur in poetry and prose, but the elevating tone of the poetry and the alliterative style make it difficult to distinguish dialogue from narrative. An indication of the similarity between the two is provided by the Old English elegies, *The Wanderer* and *The Seafarer*. These two poems occur in the manuscript known as the Exeter Book from *c.* 1000 AD, and, in common with other contemporary works, they are written without the use of inverted commas (which had not anyway been developed by that time). In the manuscript there is no overt indication of what is direct speech and what is narrative. It is generally agreed that there is at least one speaker in each poem, mainly because such words as *said* and *spoke* in their Old English forms occur in the poems. What is less clear is whether there is only one speaker and, if so, how much of the poem is the direct speech of this character. Modern editors put their inverted commas in different places. That the editors cannot tell direct speech from narration indicates that there are no linguistic markers which separate the one from the other. In passages in which the personal pronouns or related forms do not occur, the language could as easily be narration as dialogue. They tend therefore to be moral comments or gnomic utterances which could as easily be authorial as put in the mouth of a character. Poetry encouraged stylistic embellishment, and that appeared as much in speech as in narrative.

There were naturally opportunities for dialogue of different levels, though these were not exploited linguistically. In *The Battle of Maldon* the retainers of the English leader Byrhtnoth make a series of speeches after his death in which they announce their devotion to him and their determination to avenge his death on the invading Danes. Several of them come from different parts of the country, one being for example a hostage from Northumbria. Others seem to represent different levels of society, for one is described as an *unorne ceorl*. Although the meaning of this phrase is not clear, it is widely accepted that it indicates a lower status than that of the other retainers, for *ceorl* is the ancestor of Modern English *churl*. Yet in no instance is the language varied on a geographical or social basis: each retainer speaks in exactly the same way as the next one. Before the battle starts Byrhtnoth has an altercation with the messenger from the Vikings across the river. In this exchange there is considerable vituperation, but it is not expressed in a different style from that found in the rest of the poem. There are no personal insults or derogatory expressions; there are no colloquialisms or asseverations. The message and the retort are delivered in the normal high style of alliterative poetry. This stylistic elevation as part of a moral and heroic poetry influenced the representation of the people who appeared in it. The characters are cast in a heroic mould which leans towards grand posturing and declamation. In *The Later Genesis*, which describes the fall of the angels and their subsequent attempt to gain their revenge by corrupting mankind, Satan is portrayed in the traditional heroic terms. He is the leader of a band of retainers who sets a fine example of courage and initiative and is rewarded with the loyalty of his followers. This is in sharp contrast with many later medieval portrayals where Satan became a grotesque figure of fun who indulged in shameless speech. The Satan of the Old English poem speaks in the same way as any other hero and cannot be distinguished from them in his attitudes and their expression.

With the arrival of the Normans and their followers in 1066 the linguistic situation underwent an important transformation. French became the language of the upper classes, though there can never have been sufficient native French speakers to make it likely that French would become the spoken language of the country. It naturally influenced English in that French words and constructions were adopted. Hence the more French a person's English was, the higher up the social scale he was likely to be; the advent of French terms provided a means of social differentiation through language. As it happens this possibility was slow to be exploited in literature. In part this was because at first relatively little literature was written in English, for French, as the prestige language, was more commonly used for literary works. In part also the literature that was written dealt with aristocratic people and their ideals. It was not appropriate in works of this nature that the courtly and chivalric tone should be undermined by the use of non-standard English. Romances deal with noble people who follow elevated ideals. In addition many of them were either translated from French or were based on French models and so naturally they aped the French language in speech as much as in narration. The courtly nature of this style inhibited the use of colloquialisms such as oaths. A few poems in other genres are found, but they also rarely make use of different styles. *Dame Sirith*, a *fabliau*-type poem involving seduction, is so short that it has insufficient space to develop different linguistic registers. Even the longer *The Owl and the Nightingale*, a vigorous debate between two birds, contains little that might be called colloquial though the birds are relatively acerbic. Their anger is expressed more through description in the narrative passages than through the birds' own language.

Poetry in the traditional alliterative style is found rarely in the early Middle English period. It was revived in the fourteenth century, but then it had been influenced in its attitude and language by French literature from which many of its subjects are taken. Nevertheless its revival did open up the possibility of a contrast between poetry in the alliterative style, which was more usually found in the North and West, and that in the French romance style which was associated with London and the South-East. At first, however, the difference between the two styles was not so much one of social class as one of subject matter. Warfare and battle were regarded as fit subjects for the alliterative style, as Chaucer reveals in his *Knight's Tale*.

Although there is little evidence of it in literary dialogue, consciousness of linguistic differences did grow in the Middle English period. In the early thirteenth century Ranulph Higden, a monk of Chester, mentions in his Latin work *Polychronicon* that many men teach their sons French so that they can ape their betters and pass them off as men of birth. He also comments on the differences among the dialects of the North, Midlands and South, to the detriment of the first. When John Trevisa translated this text into English in 1387 he expressed the latter comment in this way:

> Al þe longage of þe Norþhumbres, and speciallich at Ʒork, is so scharp, slitting, and frotynge, and vnshape [*sharp, piercing, rasping and formless*] þat we Souþerne men may þat longage vnneþe [*hardly*] vnderstonde (I. 59).

Dialect prejudice was beginning to emerge and language was now available as a marker of social class and of humour. All it needed was for someone to take hold of the possibilities and to exploit them in literature.

Chaucer used two forms of non-standard English in his poems: the first was dialect and the second a variety of indicators to express an informal or low-class language. He used a recognized regional variety of English in an extended way only in one work, *The Reeve's Tale*, even though many of the other tales in *The Canterbury Tales* are carefully localized in different parts of the country or even abroad. In *The Reeve's Tale* two Cambridge undergraduates are said to come from a place 'fer in the north' (1:4007) called Strother, which may well be a fictitious name since it has defied modern attempts at identification. It may have been imagined by Chaucer as being in the Tyne-Tees area, for in this story the two undergraduates speak in a language which some scholars have identified (not absolutely convincingly) with that area. Briefly the story is as follows. A miller at Trumpington has been stealing corn from a Cambridge college. Two undergraduates from the college persuade their Warden to let them take the next bag of corn to the mill so they can ensure none of it is stolen. On arrival there they tie up their horse and watch the machinery while the corn is ground. The miller slips out and unties the horse's bridle. When the undergraduates realize their horse has run off, they set out to catch it which proves difficult. The miller takes this opportunity to steal much of their corn. They retrieve their horse so late at night that they are forced to stay the night at the miller's house. This is so small that they have to sleep in the same room as the miller's family, which consists of the miller himself, his wife, a daughter of twenty and a six-month baby boy. In the course of the night the undergraduates contrive to seduce the miller's daughter and wife. When the miller discovers this, he tries to exact revenge, but the undergraduates merely beat him up. As they leave they reclaim their stolen corn, whose whereabouts was revealed to them by the daughter, and thus they have a complete revenge on the miller.

Before we discuss the representation of the dialect, it is important to ask why Chaucer used it at all. It has usually been assumed that he did so to poke fun at the undergraduates by emphasizing their provincial background. Although, as we have seen, uncomplimentary remarks were made by Trevisa and others about northern speech, to regard its use here as satiric may be a modern way of interpreting the occurrence of dialect speech. Of the characters in the tale the undergraduates are the ones highest up the social and educational ladder, whereas one might expect dialect to be put into the mouths of those who were ignorant and rustic. The miller is perhaps more provincial and certainly more boorish than the undergraduates. They may be headstrong and arrogant, but they give little indication of provincial mannerisms and attitudes. Indeed the miller makes no reference to their speech and we are not led to believe that because of their speech he treated them differently from the way he would have treated other undergraduates who spoke London English. When the miller does poke fun at them, he does so in their role as undergraduates and not as northerners. Thus when he excuses the cramped accommodation he has to offer he says that clerks, who can naturally handle logic and dialectic, have no difficulty in making small places seem large. Such comments serve only to emphasize the undergraduates' learning and to play down any northern unsophisticated ways they may have. Furthermore the story ends with the clerks victorious over the grasping miller, so that if their speech was meant to be satiric it is difficult to place that satire within the meaning of the tale as a whole. It may be more satisfactory to discount the idea of mocking provincial prejudice and to assume that Chaucer added the dialect simply to add to the rumbustious comedy of the tale. He may have been experimenting with dialect to see to what uses he could put it. The tale is a *fabliau*, a short, humorous and often bawdy story. Many *fabliaux* found in Middle English are translations or adaptations of French versions, as is true with those in *The Canterbury Tales*. In the French examples it is customary to use dialect or linguistic quirks as a source of humour and Chaucer may have imitated this French tradition in his use of the northern dialect. We should remember that in England this is the first example of the use of regional dialect in a literary work. Audiences may have been prepared to accept it as comic without yet realizing that it could be used to satirize provincial attitudes.

How then did Chaucer represent this dialect in passages which amount to just over one hundred lines of text? He selected different features, phonological, grammatical and lexical, for the speech of the undergraduates. These features do not occur regularly in the earliest manuscript, the Hengwrt manuscript, which may be taken to represent most faithfully what Chaucer wrote. Lexical items are difficult to identify as northern with confidence because we are uncertain about the geographical distribution of many words. Thus *capil*, one of the words used for 'horse' by the undergraduates in this section, is also used by the Summoner, Friar, Host and Reeve elsewhere in *The Canterbury Tales*. As it is found most frequently in alliterative poetry, largely restricted in Middle English to the North and West of the country, it is often identified as a northernism in the speech of the undergraduates. However, its occurrence in poems not in the alliterative tradition makes its status as a northern word doubtful. The same applies to *daf* 'a fool' which is also found in alliterative poetry and occasionally elsewhere. In many other instances it is collocated with *dote* 'to be stupid', though Chaucer avoids that association. It might be thought that Chaucer was influenced in his choice of northern vocabulary by the words commonly found in alliterative poetry, but this does not seem to be the case. He is careful, for example, to avoid alliteration in the speech of the undergraduates. The connection between northern and alliterative words in this dialect passage is probably fortuitous.

Many words used by the undergraduates are Scandinavian in origin. They are thus found in any part of England settled by the Danes, the Danelaw which also embraced East Anglia, and cannot be related to a particular part of the North. Such words include *hail* 'luck' and *il-hail* 'bad luck', *heythen* 'hence', *hethyng* 'scorn', *ymel* 'among' and *til* 'to'. Three words of Scandinavian origin, *lathe* 'barn', *swayn* 'servant' (ON *sveinn*, cf. OE *swān*) and *wight* 'active', are found elsewhere in Chaucer's work or in Middle English romances and may thus have been part of the literary language even though more common in the North. The form *thair* 'their' instead of *hir* is also of Scandinavian origin and was at that time a northern word, though it was quickly to become part of the standard language. Some words of Anglo-Saxon origin may have been limited to the North at that time. They include the archaic *sel* 'good fortune' and the very rare *wanges* 'teeth, molars', though *werkes* 'aches' was of wider distribution. The vocabulary contains words which were exclusively northern or which were northern in origin and were making their way southwards. The area in which these words were found is hard to delimit and so the evidence they provide is of somewhat uncertain value. Furthermore many of the words may have been more distinctively informal than northern. The word *capil* is a good example. Chaucer avoids putting a literary or French-based vocabulary in the mouths of the undergraduates and he may have been aiming at a more informal kind of discourse suitable to the occasion. After all they had only gone to the mill to have a bit of fun.

Among phonological features Chaucer used, the most important was the reflex of Old English *ā*. Already, in about 1200, this long vowel had been raised in the South and it is normally represented in southern texts by *o* or *oo*. However, north of a line from the Ribble to the Humber, this sound either kept its Old English value or was fronted; in writing the *a* was preserved. Chaucer has many examples in the undergraduates' speech like *ra* 'roe deer', *swa* 'so' and *twa* 'two'. This *a* is found also before the consonantal groups *-ng* in *sang* 'song', but not before the group *-ld* where the form is *told* not *tald*. Another feature is the representation of the final consonant group in words like *which* and *swich* 'such' (Chaucer's usual spellings) as *whilk* and *swilk*. These words came from Old English *hwilc* and *swilc*. The *-lk* forms, which may have been influenced by cognate Scandinavian words, were typical of northern dialects. The undergraduates also regularly use *sal* for *shal*. These phonological features used by Chaucer were among the most common and noticeable differences between northern and southern dialects. As such they were probably familiar to most people.

Verbal inflections provide the most frequent examples of grammatical features. In the third person singular of the present indicative *-es, -s* is found for southern *-eth, -th* as in *findes, bringes* and *wagges*. As for the plural the southern *-e, -en* is replaced by *-es* twice in the present indicative (*fares* and *werkes*) and once in the imperative (*spedes*). However, these *-(e)s* forms were making their way southwards and in the singular were found occasionally in Chaucer's other writings, though they were still basically northern. In the past participle, southern dialects generally kept initial *y-*, but lost the ending *-(e)n*. Chaucer represents the northern dialect by omitting the *y-* and for the so-called strong verbs keeping the *-(e)n*, as in *born, stoln* and *shapen*. As it happens such forms do occur in Chaucer's other poems and their value as evidence is uncertain. In addition Chaucer uses forms like *is* for the first and second persons singular of the present indicative of the verb 'to be' instead of *am* and *art*. In the plural he uses *ar* for the more typically southern *been*.

Some idea of this northern dialect spoken by the undergraduates can be gained from the following passage:

> 'It shal be doon,' quod Symkyn, 'by my fay.
> What wol ye doon whil that it is in hande?'
>   'By god, right by the hoper wol I stande,'
> Quod Iohn, 'and se how the corn gas in.
> Yet saw I neuere by my fader kyn
> How that the hoper wagges til and fra.'
>   Aleyn answerde: 'Iohn, wiltow swa?
> Thanne wol I be byneth by my crown,
> And se how that the mele falles down
> Into the trogh. That sal be my desport.
> For, Iohn, in faith I may been of youre sort,
> I is as ille a millere as ar ye.'   (1: 4026-37)

31

In this passage the speech of Symkyn, the miller, is in Chaucer's normal language, whereas John and Aleyn, the two undergraduates, use a northern form. Questions that must now be asked are how many people recognized the northern qualities of this language and how accurately it reflected northern speech. It has often been suggested that Chaucer exhibits an ear for dialect which was remarkably accurate for his age and that consequently most of his readers or listeners would not have appreciated more than the commonest details of his representation. As a general principle we may think it unlikely that an author will use a dialect or register which is unfamiliar to the majority of his audience. Even today this is largely true – and it was even more so of the medieval period. The situation is complicated in Chaucer's case by the various readings in the many manuscripts of *The Canterbury Tales* that have survived. Editors have assumed that the northernisms which Chaucer put into the text were converted into southernisms by the scribes. Consequently all the northernisms found in diverse manuscripts have been attributed to Chaucer with the result that his assumed original is full of many recondite northern forms. It has therefore been easy to claim that Chaucer's knowledge of the northern dialects was far superior to that of any of his London contemporaries and that the corrupt southernisms in the text were the work of the scribes who were ignorant of the northern dialect forms. This method of reasoning is unjustified. It is widely agreed now that the Hengwrt manuscript (Hg) is the earliest extant manuscript of *The Canterbury Tales* and that it contains the best text of the poems. While we cannot be certain that it contains an exact representation of what Chaucer wrote, we may be reasonably confident that it represents his original more closely than any other manuscript.

If we take Hg as our base we soon realize that the representation of the northern dialect by Chaucer is rather more general than has hitherto been assumed and that many of the other manuscripts have introduced new northernisms not found in Chaucer's original. These additions include typically northern spellings such as the initial *qu-* for Hg's *wh-*, both of which derive from Old English *hw-*. Thus we find *qua* (Hg *wha*), *quat* (Hg *what*), *quilk* (Hg *whilk*) and *quistel* (Hg *whistle*). Similarly in some manuscripts the spelling *is* is replaced by *es*. Northern forms of words are also inserted in later manuscripts, such as *boes* (Hg *bihoues* 'is fitting') and *howgates* (Hg *how*). Even words and idioms were changed occasionally. Thus one Cambridge manuscript has *gar vs haue* for Hg's *Get vs som*, in which *gar* from Old

Norse *gøra* 'to make' is a typically northern word. All of these examples show that although there may have been examples in some manuscripts of the substitution of northernisms by southernisms, there was also a deliberate attempt by some copyists to increase the number of northernisms in the text. Once many of them realized that Chaucer was trying to depict a northern dialect, they exercised their scribal prerogative of improving their original. Whether this means that Chaucer's knowledge of northern forms was less profound than that of an average scribe is difficult to say, though it is not unlikely. After all, scribes were frequently presented with northern texts which they copied in a southern language and so were used to replacing northern with southern forms. They would hardly find it difficult to reverse this process and replace southern forms with northernisms since they would be only too familiar with the linguistic features which corresponded in the two dialect areas. However, Chaucer may have been more familiar with the northern dialects than the speech of the undergraduates suggests since he may have intended to give only a general flavour of a northern dialect so that his audience would readily understand what he included. The scribes may have gone beyond what Chaucer intended more through ignorance of his intentions than from a greater knowledge of the northern dialects. All we can say definitely is that Chaucer gives a portrayal of northern language which is so generalized that it cannot be localized with accuracy, though it may be located north of the Ribble-Humber line. At the same time it is clear that many scribes knew more about the northern dialects than Chaucer included in the speech of the undergraduates and so modified their speech accordingly. If we can take their knowledge as representative of the time, we may conclude that Chaucer's audience had no difficulty in understanding what the undergraduates said. Chaucer was not as exceptional as some scholars have imagined.

Chaucer's other type of non-standard language, the use of items indicating low-class speech, occurs throughout *The Canterbury Tales* and arises in part from the nature of the poem, which describes how people from different walks of life band together to form a travelling party to Canterbury. Some of the pilgrims are sophisticated and genteel, others are boorish and crude. It is natural that Chaucer should seek to reflect this difference in the way they speak. Furthermore many of the tales also contain characters from different social classes, as we have already seen of *The Reeve's Tale*. Such tales could also use different registers to reflect the differing social standing of the characters in them. In fact within the tales, as compared with the prologue and epilogue of the framing story, the use of non-standard linguistic features occurs less frequently than one might have expected, perhaps because their protagonists are rather more distanced than the pilgrims in the framing story.

When we come to consider this type of non-standard language, we are faced with the difficulty of deciding what it constitutes. The problem arises naturally enough because what is standard is still relatively undefined at this time. Consider, for example, these lines from *The Miller's Tale*:

> This man is falle with his astromye
> In som woodnesse or in som agonye. (1: 3445-6)

They are spoken by the carpenter who is an honest artisan of little education or social pretension. He uses the word *astromye*, for 'astronomy', here and once elsewhere. It is often claimed that this form of the word is non-standard and hence that it is employed in these two instances to underline the carpenter's illiteracy. Is this really so? Chaucer himself does not use the word often enough for us to tell whether he regarded one form of the word as more standard than the other. Even if he should have preferred one form, it is clear that others would not necessarily have responded to or shared his preference.

When one is faced with a form like *astromye* it is possible to interpret it as a copying mistake which should be emended, as an illiterate form, or as an acceptable alternative in the language which carried no stigma. The first is unlikely since the extra syllable of *astronomye* is not required by the metre and since no scribe in any of the more than fifty manuscripts that survive bothered to correct the form. That this is so makes it unlikely that *astromye* is a non-standard form, as though it were a malapropism, for if it were one might have expected at least a few officious scribes to correct the form. No scribe evidently found any difficulty with the reading. The problem is that if it is a malapropism how was the audience to realize this, because there are many such variant forms in *The Canterbury Tales*. Thus in *The Friar's Tale* the old woman falsely accused by the summoner uses the form *procutour* for *procuratour* at 2: 1570. This form, which is also found in almost all manuscripts, is frequently emended in modern editions, presumably on the grounds that editors do not think the old woman would have indulged in malapropisms. But how would a fifteenth-century reader know in these cases that *astromye* was a marked form and *procutour* was a copying mistake? Is it not more likely that both are acceptable variants at that time? Modern editors may be interpreting Chaucer in a modern way. After all, many such variants are found throughout his work. These may be either variants in the quality of sound as in *swete/swote/soote* or variants in the number of syllables as in *benedicitee/bendiste, parauenture/paraunter* and *taketh/tath*. It is not reasonable to select one pair of variants where so many exist and say one form is standard and the other non-standard and hence marked. We must therefore accept that *astromye* is an acceptable variant in the fourteenth century of *astronomye* and that its use carried no overtones of illiteracy or substandard speech. The one form was used in preference to the other when the metre demanded one syllable more or less.

If it is difficult to use variant forms of a word as markers of non-standard usage, the same applies to syntactic structures. This is important to bear in mind because today deviations from accepted syntactic arrangements are often used to assist in the portrayal of particular characters. In *The Knight's Tale*, Arcite, one of the two lovers, speaks the following sentence:

> And now I am so caytyf and so thral
> That, he that is my mortal enemy,
> I serue hym as his squyer pourely. (1: 1554-6)

In this sentence the *he that is my mortal enemy* is syntactically isolated in that the *he* looks as though it will be the subject of the subordinate clause after *that*. In fact the subject turns out to be *I*, and the *he* is understood as a kind of loose apposition to *hym*. This failure of grammatical concord would today be regarded as a solecism which in a literary work is likely to be put into the mouth of a character without much formal education. Such an assumption would be quite unfounded for Chaucer, for such constructions were common enough in the fourteenth century. The regulation of English syntax did not occur till much later, and until it occurred status was not attributed to one grammatical structure rather than another.

Consequently, writers were forced to rely on lexical rather than syntactic markers for non-standard language. These features may be considered in two groups. The first consists of malapropisms. In view of the earlier discussion it must be appreciated that a malapropism had to be a corruption of one word into another word which was unsuitable and even grotesque in the context in which it was found. It was not possible for a more common variant to be replaced by a less common one or even for a word to be corrupted into a meaningless form. In the latter case scribes and modern editors would simply emend the meaningless form into something intelligible. Examples of malapropisms are not frequent, no doubt partly because there was as yet no great interest in words for their own sake, and consequently readers were not trained to expect them or writers to include them. A possible example occurs in *The Miller's Tale*, where John the carpenter calls the Flood *Nowels flood* (1: 3512) instead of 'Noah's flood'. Since in the same tale the clerk Nicholas refers to *Noe* 'Noah' correctly, there seems to be a confusion in the carpenter's mind between Noah and Nowel. This confusion might well have been regarded as ludicrous by a contemporary audience, who would attribute the mistake to the carpenter's ignorance. Other examples are found in the host's language, for he is portrayed as a man of blunt and indecorous language. Often these malapropisms occur in oaths or expletives. Thus the host uses *cokkes bones* (11: 9) instead of 'God's bones', the confusion possibly seeming nothing short of grotesque to a contemporary audience, particularly as such hypocritical characters as the pardoner touted animal bones around to pass off as saintly relics. That the corruption occurs in such expletives is understandable since they would be very familiar expressions in which a mistake would show up most clearly. It is for the same reason that the host also makes mistakes in Latin tags, though in such cases the corruptions did not need to produce meaningful aberrations. People came across Latin mostly in set religious formulae and it was characteristic enough that such formulae should be garbled by the uneducated and the indifferent. Thus the host corrupts *corpus domini* into *corpus dominus* (10: 435).

The second group consists of oaths and expletives. The status of some words in this group may be considered dubious since many are more colloquial than non-standard, though the boundary between the two is often hard to draw. When, in *The Reeve's Tale*, Aleyn calls John a *swyneshed* (1: 4254) we may doubt whether the word was non-standard as such, though its use in this context may have been. Some of the words like *avoy* (10: 2880) in *The Nun's Priest's Tale* were borrowed from French and may not have been part of the spoken English language at all. It may be a literary borrowing from a language where it was colloquial. Nevertheless many oaths, such as those which refer to Christ's body, his passion and so on, were regarded as unacceptable, as we can see from the criticism which they frequently receive, for example in the sermon within *The Pardoner's Tale*.

Many of the low words used in the poem, particularly by the host,
lie on the boundary between standard and non-standard. When, at
the end of his tale, the pardoner invites the host to offer to his relics,
the host responds in a very blunt, crude way:

> Thow woldest make me kisse thyn olde breech
> And swere it were a relyk of a seint
> Thogh it were with thy fondement depeynt.
> But by the croys which that seint Eleyne foond
> I wold I hadde thy coylons in myn hond
> In stide of relikes or of seintuarie.
> Lat cutte hem of: I wol thee hem carye.
> They shul be shryned in an hogges toord. (9: 946-53)

Here the language is typical of the low style. Some of the words might
not occur frequently in the high style, though most could occur there.
The words themselves were not marked out as particularly non-
standard but it is the combination of many low words together and the
subject matter which makes this passage what it is. The words in isola-
tion are not significant.

There are some words in the poem whose meaning is uncertain and
which may belong to a non-standard level of speech. In *The Miller's
Tale*, Absolom goes to the smith, and the latter teases him for being
up so late at night in this way:

> Som gay gerl, god it woot,
> Hath broght yow thus vpon the viritoot;
> By seinte Note ye woot wel what I mene. (1: 3761-3)

The last line suggests that the meaning of to *bring upon the viritoot*
was not well known, and that it was part of the slang of the day.
Modern scholars remain uncertain of its meaning for it seems to have
no parallels, again suggesting that the phrase belonged to a less polite
level of speech. A few other words belong to this category in the poem
but they are not numerous.

We have seen that up to Chaucer's death there were few examples of
non-standard English in literary texts and that Chaucer himself made
little use of this variety. His early poems are largely courtly in tone and
so have no need for a non-standard level of language. It was only
because *The Canterbury Tales* depicted different levels of fourteenth-
century society in interaction with one another which led him to ex-

periment with different varieties of language. For the most part he seems to have taken his cue from the French *fabliaux* upon which he modelled his bawdy stories, for in them a certain realism contributes to the humour. In contrast, the courtly stories remained idealistic and hence used a high style for the most part. But the innovation made by Chaucer, even if it was only tentative, was an important one which was to be developed further by his successors.

Chapter 2

FROM CHAUCER TO SHAKESPEARE: THE NON-DRAMATIC TRADITION

🔟🔟🔟🔟🔟🔟

CHAUCER'S REPUTATION in the two centuries following his death took two forms. To some, especially his imitators in England and Scotland, he was the great rhetorical poet of high style who had enriched English poetry. To some Elizabethans, however, he was very much the poet of bawdy. Thus in Middleton's *The Family of Love* Gerardine, after making a scatological pun, comments 'which I in Chaucer-style do term a jest' (III.i.800). Writers interpreted Chaucer in whichever way they wished, and they could do so because there is in *The Canterbury Tales* a mixture of the elevated and the coarse not only among the various characters, but also within the language of an individual pilgrim. Chaucer did not differentiate his characters sharply into two groups, the ideal and the churlish; some fall into both. The wife of Bath can indulge in bawdy reminiscences and yet tell an idealized romantic story. The host addresses some pilgrims in terms of fawning politeness, but he can also indulge in frank obscenity with others. This mixture was unacceptable to later writers who preferred to separate the two into self-contained groups.

The beginning of this can be seen in the work of John Lydgate. Perhaps following Chaucer's example he indulges in portrayals of low-class life, especially in his *Ballade on an Ale-Seller*. Nevertheless Lydgate was unable to find the necessary vocabulary to describe the female ale-seller in the poem, and so we get the rather bizarre situation of a low-class woman being described in language which does not seem to fit the way the woman is pictured. The use of non-standard language in such a situation was clearly not something which came easily to writers at the time, for there was little guidance for them in earlier literature.

When Lydgate came to write his *Siege of Thebes* he included a prologue in which he, John Lydgate, joins the pilgrims of *The Canterbury Tales* on their pilgrimage to Canterbury so that his story about Thebes becomes his tale on that journey. Naturally this means that Lydgate, as a pilgrim, and the host have a conversation in which Lydgate is questioned about himself and finally asked to tell his story. Although in Chaucer's poem the host was polite and blunt in turn, in Lydgate's poem he is merely rude. The language he uses, however, rarely employs non-standard features except for some that he borrowed directly from Chaucer like *by kokkis blood* (126). Lydgate's treatment is interesting in highlighting several important points. The first is that a tradition of non-standard language had not yet developed and English writers clearly found it a problem to know how to represent blunt and churlish language. The second is that as far as possible they took their lead from Chaucer, which in effect resulted in the growth of what one might call a non-standard tradition. In other words writers would look to previous writers for the forms they would use in such situations rather than take examples from speech. Often earlier works would provide a model of the type of form to be adopted, even if they did not provide the actual form. The third is that from this time there developed a dichotomy between standard and non-standard English which led to a specialization in their different uses. The low-class characters and the comic scenes began to be given the non-standard forms with the result that low-class people tended to be portrayed solely in comic situations.

Further development is found in the work of John Skelton (*c.* 1460-1529). A learned poet, Skelton was made poet laureate by the University of Oxford, and about 1496 he became tutor to the young Prince Henry. At first he was associated with the court, though he became rector of Diss, Norfolk, about 1503. Apparently in later life he returned to live at Westminster. In Skelton's courtly poetry we find rhetorical language at its most elevated and the vocabulary is not mixed with non-standard forms. The prologue of *The Bowge of Court* is written in a highly rhetorical style which imitates the opening of the *General Prologue* of *The Canterbury Tales*. There are many foreign loan-words, parallel phrases and clauses, long sentences, figures from classical mythology and all the other attributes of high style.

Skelton employed the low style, however, for quite separate works. He wrote a collection of poems entitled *Dyuers Balletys and Dyties Solacyous*, many of which were parodies of one kind or another. Since in these poems there is a contrast between the ideal language of courtly love and the realities of human sexual behaviour, the latter is portrayed in a down-to-earth language. Thus one of the poems in this collection ends with this stanza:

> What dremyst thou, drunchard, drousy pate?
> Thy lust and lykyng is from the gone;
> Thou blynkerd blowboll, thou wakyst to late;
> Behold, thou lyeste, luggard, alone!
> Well may thou sygh, well may thou grone,
> To dele wyth her so cowardly:
> Iwys, powle hachet, she bleryd thyne I! (22-8)

Several typical features of this type of language appear here. The first is a general name-calling through words indicating disapproval, such as *drunchard*. Particularly frequent in this period are words ending in *-ard*. Not all the words are necessarily non-standard, though many are, and certainly when grouped together as here the effect is intended to be one of linguistic disapproval. Some of the words and expressions like *powle hachet* are of uncertain meaning and this suggests that they may have been taken by Skelton from a non-standard variety of speech. Here, then, we have words of a more traditional nature like those ending in *-ard* linked with more colloquial items. The second interesting feature is the use of alliteration which here is clearly understood to indicate a non-standard literary style. It should not be imagined that non-standard speakers used more alliteration than others, but simply that writers at this time felt that alliteration was non-courtly and hence vulgar and provincial. This attitude is associated with the development of the London standard and of taste in literary style which we shall return to consider.

It is possible that Skelton's *The Tunnyng of Elynour Rummyng* was written in imitation of Lydgate's *Ballade on an Ale-Seller*, but if so there is a great change in the type of language employed. In the first place Skelton used the rhyming metre now referred to as skeltonics, in which two or more short lines (usually with only two stressed syllables per line) rhyme together. This metre itself creates a humorous effect as well as producing a demand for many rhyming words. This can be seen by looking at the opening lines:

> Tell you I chyll,
> If that ye wyll
> A whyle be styll,
> Of a comely gyll
> That dwelt on a hyll;
> But she is not gryll,
> For she is somwhat sage
> And well worne in age,

> For her vysage
> It woldt aswage
> A mannes courage. (1-11)

In this poem Skelton does not seek to avoid the use of neutral or even elevated words, for the words rhyming in *-age* are all of French origin. But the opening rhyming sequence is different. The first line has the word *chyll* which is a south-eastern dialect form for 'I will' (cf. OE *ic wylle*) though it became used simply for 'will'. It is difficult to tell whether Skelton used the form for variation, because he did not want to repeat *will* in the first two lines, or to act as a marker of parody of the traditional minstrel opening in a poem. As the south-eastern dialect was suffering a decline in status at this time, the latter is quite possible. However, no other dialect or unusual forms are used in the poem, unless *woldt* is meant to be significant in this way. The word *gyll* is probably part of non-standard usage as well. A shortened form of the name *Gillian*, it occurs in the sixteenth century in contexts which suggest it is a term of disparagement for a woman. The word is not dialectal, but low. Skelton needed many such words since his poem dealt with women of doubtful morals and most that he used probably came from the same low variety of English. Some like *gyb* (99) are not attested in this meaning in earlier sources; others like *dant* (515) are loan-words, in this case from Dutch. Whether its origin from a language such as Dutch was a factor in its status is unknown; it is not recorded elsewhere in English. Another word of Dutch origin in the opening passage is *gryll* which may also have been of a low variety, though in this case the word is found in Middle English. Yet other words like *fysgygge* (538, from *fizz* and *gig*) may have an onomatopoeic origin.

Many of these words emerge here in English literature for the first time, though some were to occur not infrequently in other sixteenth- and seventeenth-century works. There would seem to be little doubt that Skelton took them from the low or colloquial speech of his time. When the reference is to a particular sort of person such as a prostitute or drunk, there is good reason to suspect that the word in question is non-standard if it is not found earlier. If, however, the meaning of the word is more general, as with *gryll* 'fierce', the status of the word is more difficult to gauge. *Gryll* was found in Middle English texts and was apparently dieing out at the beginning of the sixteenth century, though its imminent demise need not signify that it had sunk in status. Nevertheless, the way in which some words are introduced into the poem indicates that they were felt to be colloquial or non-standard.

> He calleth me his whytyng
> His mullyng and his mytyng,
> His nobbes and his conny,
> His swetyng and his honny. (223-6)

Here the 'calleth me' and the long list of terms of endearment suggest a colloquial level. Some of the words are found in love lyrics of the fifteenth century, but others are not. Some may have been given this meaning by Skelton himself for *whytyng* and *mytyng* are small fish referred to in his *Against Garnesche*, or they may have been taken by him from colloquial levels of discourse.

In addition to these words Skelton also uses idiomatic expressions in *The Tunnyng of Elynour Rummyng* which may have become proverbial and hence acquired a second, less respectable, meaning. *Symper-the-cocket* (55) is a case in point; it had the traditional meaning 'with affected airs'. As Skelton uses it to describe Elynour it may have developed a secondary meaning as well. The same is true of *prycke-me-denty* (582), used of a 'dandy'. Skelton's is the first example in English of its use, and the reference to a client in the ale-house and the inclusion of *prick* in the idiom suggest that a *double entendre* is involved. Some of these proverbial expressions remain difficult to interpret, which may itself indicate that the meaning intended was vulgar. Thus the *peny cheke* (415) brought by mad Kyt may literally be some kind of chicken, though it may represent something less salubrious. Besides such idioms there are many lines reported from songs or poems. These may be genuine or fictitious, though the latter is more likely. They were probably invented to create the atmosphere of licentiousness in the ale-house. Chaucer himself may have given Skelton his lead here since he introduces snatches of songs into *The Canterbury Tales*. The words used are rarely non-standard, though they may have had vulgar connotations.

A typical kind of verbal exuberance in this poem was the use of reduplicating forms in which the second element changes a single vowel or, occasionally, consonant of the first. The employment of this type of word became very common in the sixteenth and seventeenth centuries, though examples tend to occur in particular contexts. Often, as here, they are used by low people, or else they are used to imply something which is worthless or of little value. Their status is apparently that of a colloquial word, though it is quite possible that some were literary rather than spoken colloquialisms. Thus in

> With a whym-wham
> Knyt with a trym-tram (75-6)

both examples of reduplication are found here for the first time, though both occur again in other sixteenth-century writers. Whether they took the words from Skelton or from speech is impossible to decide. *Trym-tram* was in fact used by Sir Thomas More and was no doubt accepted as a colourful word for 'something of little value'. There was a vogue for words of this type and it is likely that it affected the spoken as much as the written language. The form *cawry-mawry* (150) is found earlier than Skelton in *Piers Plowman*, which suggests that such reduplicating forms had existed at the spoken level for some time though they had rarely emerged into literary works before the sixteenth century. That there is a vogue for this kind of verbal play is indicated by the way Skelton can vary the type. In

> With theyr naked pappes
> That flyppes and flappes,
> It wygges and it wagges (135-7)

the reduplication occurs in separate words rather than within a word. One example, *tyrly-tyrlowe* (292), which seems to refer to some kind of song or tune, is perhaps a Skelton invention. He also used it in *Collyn Clout* (950).

There are occasions when Skelton did invent words, often when forced into doing so by his rhyming metre. Mostly they occur in humorous situations and are therefore understood to be comic rather than elevated. In his description of Elynour's customers he writes:

> In came another dant,
> With a gose and a gant:
> She had a wyde wesant,
> She was nothynge plesant:
> Necked lyke an olyfant;
> It was a bullyfant,
> A gredy cormerant. (515-21)

The word *bullyfant* is not found elsewhere and as it is polysyllabic it could at this time have been considered by some as a learned word. It is no doubt invented by Skelton and suggests a cross between a bull and an elephant – certainly something large and unpleasant. The context shows it is a comic word. The meaning and status of *gant* are less certain. It usually meant a 'gannet', though that meaning is hardly appropiate here. No doubt the rhyme caused him to create this as a comic variant of *gander*. His favourite means of invention is to add a suffix, usually -*y* but sometimes -*ell*/-*ill*, giving the word the status of an endearing diminutive. Typical examples are

> Angry as a waspy
> She gan to yane and gaspy (330-1)

and

> 'This ale,' sayd she, 'is noppy;
> Let us syppe and soppy
> And not spyll a droppy,
> For so mote I hoppy,
> It coleth well my croppy.' (557-61)

Innumerable examples occur and although some may have been current colloquially it is better to think that the majority are Skelton's own literary creations, especially as it is not a feature of other texts of the time. But the diminutive *fonny* (229), from *fonne* 'a fool', is possibly a colloquialism since several words from this base were used then. Not all such words are new, either. In

> Her eyen gowndy
> Are full unsowndy (34-5)

gowndy is a word found from Middle English onwards with the rather technical sense of 'emitting matter from the eyes'. But its partner, *unsowndy*, would appear to be a Skelton invention based on the more common *unsound*. Examples of suffixes in -*ell*/-*ill* are rare in comparison, but *bybyll* (550) from *bib* 'to drink', is made to rhyme with *Sybbyll*. The existence of such words as *tipple* suggests that *bibble* may also have existed colloquially though it is not found elsewhere.

That Skelton deliberately chose this type of language in *The Tunnyng of Elynour Rummyng* is indicated by the fact that although he used skeltonics in other poems he did not use the same type of vocabulary, probably because they did not deal with such low subjects.

Indeed none of Skelton's other works, with the possible exception of his play *Magnificence*, which is best reserved for the discussion of other dramatic texts, exhibits the same number of non-standard forms. However, the same type of non-standard forms do occur elsewhere, but not with the same frequency. In *Against Garnesche*, Skelton's vigorous reply to an attack upon him, there is a great deal of name-calling. Garnesche is called *manticore, malapert, Sir Wrig-Wrag* and *Harvy Hafter*. The same applies to the *Duke of Albany*, a poem glorying in the Scottish retreat from the Tweed after Albany's invasion of 1523. The Scots are called *puant pisspots*, and the Duke himself is a *palliard, skirgalliard, poltroon* and *coistrown*. Otherwise these two poems contain little of interest to us. It is only *Collyn Clout* which contains a wider range of linguistic items. Among them are such words as *bloder* (66), a variant of *blather, blether,* found in this form for the first time in English, and *noddy* (1244) 'foolish', also a first occurrence in English. Both are probably colloquial words. There are idiomatic usages with vulgar connotations such as *fucke sayle* (397) and several proverbial name types usually involving *Jack*, such as *Jacke-a-Thrum* (282), *Jacke-of-the-Nocke* (322) and *Jacke and Gyll* (96). There are reduplicating forms like *hoder-moder* (69), *tyrly-tyrlowe* (950) and even *tot-quottes* (563). The last form is an anglicization of a Latin phrase. Several other cases of corrupt Latin are found in the poem for it deals with the ignorance and corruption of the clergy. There are also new suffixes as in

> And you wyll be stylla,
> You shall have your wylla! (260-1)

In addition there are the usual opprobrious epithets for worthless scoundrels.

Skelton is an important writer in that he is the first person in English to introduce non-standard forms in any major way. His forms are taken from colloquial speech or invented by him to create the desired humorous effect, and the types of form he uses fall into well-defined categories. They are lexical rather than syntactic, though idiomatic and proverbial expressions are also exploited. Some of the humour is decidedly literary and learned, though the absence of malapropisms is worthy of remark.

In the fifteenth and sixteenth centuries the influence of the London dialect grew stronger and it came increasingly to be accepted as the national standard. It thus influenced the way people wrote, though it is not so easy to tell how far it influenced their speech. The letters and papers of John Shillingford, Mayor of Exeter, in the middle of the fifteenth century, already show the penetration of London features in the dialect of the South-West. Other letter collections of the period, such as that of the Pastons, present less certain evidence in that many members of these families spent considerable periods of time in London and the families lived closer to London. At this time, in any case, the London dialect underwent important modifications. Originally it had been a basically south-eastern dialect. Thus such Kentish features as the representation of OE *y* as *e* had extended in the early fourteenth century through London into Herefordshire and some contiguous parts of East Anglia. Chaucer himself has several Kentish features in his writings: he uses *seke* 'sick' (OE *sēōc*) whereas most other Middle English dialects represent this vowel as *i*. However, in the fourteenth century there was extensive immigration into London from the East Midlands and East Anglia, and this influx of people speaking an East Midlands variety of English caused the London dialect to assimilate many features characteristic of that area. Naturally this trend can be detected from written records only; we have no means of knowing how the speech of individuals was affected. It is not unlikely that speakers in the London area came increasingly to fall into two major groupings with the upper levels of society using an East Midlands dialect and the lower a south-eastern variety. This would inevitably lead to the two groupings attracting to themselves different status according to the type of people who characteristically spoke either variety. Hence south-eastern English would generally decline in status as those who spoke it in London came from inferior social positions. This development was no doubt expedited by the attitude of Londoners towards Kent. Today the county is regarded as idyllic and pastoral. In the fourteenth and fifteenth centuries (and even indeed beyond) its reputation was quite the reverse. It was an area which included the forbidding forest of the Weald and which bred unrest and disturbance. Many of the popular uprisings, such as the Peasants' Revolt of 1381, had either started or gained considerable support there, and the citizens of London had every reason to regard the South-East with a mixture of trepidation and contempt.

The first indication of this attitude towards the Kentish area and its dialect comes from *Peter Idley's Instructions to his Son* which was probably composed about 1445-50. In the poem Idley comments

And thoughe myn Englysshe be symple to your entent,
Haue me excused – I was born in Kent. (II. 1425-6)

Although Kent is an area of low-class, or at least inelegant, language, there is no attempt by the author to recreate the dialect in writing. He simply uses his Kentish origin as an excuse for his lack of linguistic refinement in the traditional humility formula, so beloved of authors at this time. In fact there is a strong probability that Idley was not born in Kent at all, since his family came from Oxfordshire. If that is so, it suggests that to be born in Kent had acquired proverbial status indicative of provincial origins. William Caxton, at the end of the century, was to make similar use of Kent's bad reputation in his own example of the humility formula in his *History of Troy* (1473), the first book printed in English. There he uses his birth in Kent together with his long residence abroad to explain his linguistic shortcomings. Perhaps about the same time the character Amen in *A Mery Geste how the Plowman lerned his Pater Noster*, printed by Wynkyn de Worde about 1515, is characterized 'It semed by his langage that he was borne in Kente' (148). In none of these works is there any attempt to represent any features of the Kentish dialect, though in the last example there is a clear inference that the language spoken in Kent was provincial and lacking in status.

It was not long, however, before an actual representation of Kentish speech occurred. In his *Pastime of Pleasure* Stephen Hawes made Kent the home of the foolish dwarf, Godfrey Gobylyve. The dwarf says:

'Sotheych,' quod he, 'whan I cham in Kent
At home I cham though I be hyther sent.
I cham a gentylman of moche noble kynne
Though Iche be cladde in a knaues skynne.' (ch. 29)

In this example 'I am' appears as *I cham* and 'I' by itself as *Iche*; and the word *sotheych* is a reflex of the early Middle English *soþlich* which in late Middle English usually appears as *soothly* and was by now becoming a little archaic. This is not extensive, but it does reveal an awareness of the differences between dialects and a willingness to exploit them. Dialect forms were now available in written English which would automatically brand a person as vulgar and low-born.

At first its development affected only the Kentish dialect even though the standard was associated with London and its immediate environs. Inevitably dialects lieing some distance away would come in time to be regarded as provincial. Thus, in Middleton's *The Family of Love*, Dryfat remarks 'What! Art thou a Welch carrier or a northern landlord, th'art so saucy?' (IV.ii.1275-6) with the clear implication that those from such distant places are comic bumpkins who have no knowledge of how to behave and speak. But in general no attempt was made to portray any other dialect speech consistently. The Kentish dialect was close to London and probably in certain features identical with low-class London English, hence attracting most attention as far as dialect divergence was concerned. For once one dialect attracted to itself the characteristic of boorish, peasant language, there was no need for other dialects to be employed for this purpose since writers had a ready-made tool to hand. The south-eastern dialect became the peasant dialect par excellence and this left other dialects available for comic situations without necessarily involving the implications of boorishness. Indeed any attempt to use another dialect for the representation of peasants might merely have caused confusion in the minds of readers.

The development of the London dialect as the standard went hand in hand with the acceptance of Chaucer as the founder of a cultivated English literary style. Chaucer wrote in a variety of London English, though it was not that variety which was to become the standard. Nevertheless the two were sufficiently alike for the two developments to assist each other: Chaucer's work helped popularize the standard, and the standard encouraged the growth of Chaucer's reputation. The result was that literary writing gradually became concentrated in London and its immediate environs and that literary writers looked back to Chaucer as the model they should imitate in their compositions. Courtly style became characterized by certain traits which we have already isolated in Skelton's poetry. Inevitably non-London dialects fell into gradual disuse for literary works, and certain styles, such as the alliterative style which was regarded as non-courtly, were increasingly regarded as unfashionable and hence discarded. This change happened more quickly in poetry than in prose and drama, for drama in particular continued to receive encouragement from the clergy and it took place in those centres where it had been traditionally performed. It was only in the sixteenth century with the dissolution of the monasteries and the performance of plays in noblemen's houses or in purpose-built theatres that London came to be the centre of dramatic production as well. Until then the Church and local nobles continued to foster productions in different parts of the country.

The change which had been gradually developing during the fifteenth century came to a head in 1476 when Caxton introduced the printing press into England. For though he had his press at Westminster, his books sold throughout the country. People in counties far from London would thus be readily able to see what people were reading in London and in what sort of language it was written. Caxton was faced with several problems resulting from this situation. The first was the question of which form of a word to use. He comments in his prologue to *Eneydos*:

> And that comyn Englysshe that is spoken in one shyre varyeth from another. In so moche that in my dayes happened that certayn marchauntes were in a shippe in Tamyse for to have sayled over the see into Zelande. And for lacke of wynde thai taryed atte forlond and wente to lande for to refreshe them. And one of theym named Sheffelde, a mercer, cam into an hows and axed for mete and specyally he axyd after eggys. And the goode wyf answerde that she coude speke no Frenshe. And the marchaunt was angry for he also coude speke no Frenshe, but wolde have hadde egges; and she understode hym not. And thenne at laste another sayd that he wolde have eyren; then the good wyf sayd that she understod hym wel. Loo! what sholde a man in thyse dayes now wryte, 'egges' or 'eyren'? (36. 45-58)

The one form, *egges*, was northern and the other, *eyren*, was southern. In this instance the standard language has adopted the northern form, which was Caxton's own preferred form. The scene painted by him is instructive in showing that variation in speech could lead to humour and misunderstanding at this time. People were beginning to be so sensitive about language that writers commented upon this new preoccupation.

In the same prologue to *Eneydos* Caxton introduces other aspects about the changing language of his time. People were increasingly aware of change as a phenomenon in language. This was partly the result of a comparison of English with Latin, which as a dead language did not change, and partly due to the growth of Chaucer's reputation. It was felt that Chaucer had written so admirably that he ought to be read in the very words that he himself had written. This meant that as the language itself developed there would be a gap between the language that Chaucer had used and the language used by his readers in their everyday life. It was difficult to adjust to this for there was still a convention that the language of older authors should be modernized every time their works were reissued. When Caxton printed Trevisa's translation of Higden's *Polychronicon* he claimed that he had altered 'the rude and old Englyssh, that is to wete certayn wordes which in these dayes be neither usyd ne understanden' (86 (b) 16-17). When he printed his second edition of *The Canterbury Tales* he mentioned that a gentleman had complained about the quality of his first edition which 'was not accordyng in many places unto the book that Gefferey Chaucer had made' (11. 42-3), and so Caxton had issued a corrected version. He did not indicate, however, in what ways his text had been deficient or what corrections he made, and it may be that the gentleman had complained only about the order of the tales rather than the words used. But there was at all events a different attitude towards Chaucer from that which prevailed for other authors; for instance Trevisa was 'rude and old' and yet Chaucer had to be preserved in his original form.

Many of the prose texts printed by William Caxton consisted of translations which he himself had made from the French, for it was part of his publishing policy to sell works in the Burgundian fashion of the day. Hence many of the originals which he used were written in an elaborate French style, which was transferred as far as possible into the English versions. The impetus that Chaucer had given to the imitation of French affected prose as much as poetry, and this development created a contrast between courtly prose in the Chaucerian style and the traditional alliterative style. At first there was, however, some controversy over the desirability of imitating this elaborate style. In his prologue to *Eneydos* Caxton wrote

> And whan I sawe the fayr and straunge termes therin, I doubted that it sholde not please some gentylmen whiche late blamed me sayeng that in my translacyons I had over-curyous termes whiche coude not be understande of comyn peple and desired me to use olde and homely termes in my translacyons. (36. 26-31)

However, his own sympathies lay very much with the new elegant style, for he claimed his book was intended 'not for a rude, uplondyssh man to laboure therin ne rede it, but onely for a clerke and a noble gentylman' (36. 69-70). The terms, *uplondyssh*, *rude* and *unconnynge*, are frequently introduced into his prologues and epilogues to refer to those who have no appreciation of fashionable style, but they are not used of a particular alternative style. However, it was natural that any writing which did not meet with the approval of a courtly audience would come to seem suitable only for uncultivated boors and hence be deemed non-standard.

The effect this situation had on the production of texts can be appreciated by a consideration of Caxton's edition of Malory's *Le Morte Darthur*. Malory completed his version in 1469/70 and Caxton printed it in 1485. Despite the short gap between the completion of the one version and its printing there are many changes made in the printed text. It is widely accepted that Malory used as a major source the alliterative poem *Morte Arthure*, which is one reason why his prose is so full of alliterative words and tags. This applies particularly to the *Tale of Arthur and Lucius* (which was to become book 5 in Caxton's edition) since that tale is the one most indebted to the poem. When Caxton printed his edition it contained two levels of linguistic change. In what became his book 5, he completely modernized the language by introducing French or romance-type words for the traditional vocabulary and for alliterative forms. Thus *haynxman, torongeled, werlow* and *grekynge* are replaced by *page, rugged, deuyll* and *spryngynge*. Often, indeed, he introduced longer French words instead of shorter common English ones: Malory's 'asked hir why she sate sorowing' became 'demaunded of her wherfore she made suche lamentacion' (p. 200). For Caxton there was clearly a difference between the two types of vocabulary, and that difference carried with it implications of status and prejudice. In the other books of Malory's work Caxton probably made no changes himself though the two versions show many differences. The reason is that there was a tendency among compositors to normalize the language of their copy – a tendency that would grow stronger with time. Spellings were altered, inflexions changed and punctuation increased. Sometimes these changes were towards greater consistency if not necessarily towards modernity, for individual compositors had their own preferences. Nevertheless the changes inevitably produced greater uniformity in time so that printed matter came increasingly to show much more consistency than any other form of writing. Spelling, and the other accidentals of writing, would gradually become more important in distinguishing standard from non-standard usage. This end was not achieved in Caxton's time, but the introduction of the printing press laid the foundation for this process to be accomplished.

Alliteration retained a more central role in Scottish poetry in the fifteenth and sixteenth centuries though even there it assimilated new associations. Whereas in England regional poetry ceased to be written in the fifteenth century because of the growing stranglehold of London over literary life, in Scotland there remained a vigorous poetic tradition fostered to some extent by the existence of an independent monarchy. Consequently, in this period, there were two centres of poetic activity, Edinburgh and London, within Great Britain, while other parts of England and Wales ceased to be productive. Even the Scottish output received a check when James VI of Scotland became James I of England and moved south to London. Nevertheless the survival of this Scottish tradition has been important for the Scottish dialect, and has meant that it has escaped the worst prejudicial attitudes which have afflicted most other English dialects.

Even so the Scottish poets were not unaware of events in England. They accepted that Chaucer was the 'rose of rethoris all' and set about introducing his stylistic attitudes into Scotland, loading their poems with aureate diction just as John Lydgate and the other English Chaucerians had done. But whereas the English Chaucerians neglected and scorned the alliterative style, the Scottish poets tried to assimilate that style as well. In general, though, they used alliteration for special purposes. In the fourteenth century alliteration was associated principally with the North of England, and when the polarization between London and Edinburgh took place it is not surprising that alliteration should have moved north over the border. In the fifteenth century the alliterative style is used for romances and for farcical and fantastic poems which may have been more popular in tone. From this usage there developed the conception that alliteration was suitable for satire, burlesque and that most typical of all Scottish poems, the *flyting*, in which abuse is hurled by a poet at an adversary. Indeed James VI specified in his treatise on poetics, *Ane Schort Treatise, Conteining some Revlis and Cautelis to be obseruit and eschewit in Scottis Poesie* (1584), that alliteration was especially suitable for the '*Tumbling* verse of flyting'. In addition he recommended that the poet should use 'corruptit, and vplandis wordis' in such poems. The result was that the Scots produced a poetry rich in alliteration, heavy with substantives and concrete in reference. The language is full of energy – an energy which springs to some extent from the range of lexical inventiveness. For where Skelton introduced new words here and there in his poems, the Scottish poets revelled in linguistic bravado and innovation. Many words were no doubt created for the purpose and may have puzzled even some of the poets' contemporaries, but others were taken from non-standard speech. The contrast between the aureate diction with its rhetorical elaborations and the alliterative style with its lexical exuberance is very marked, but it should not be considered that one style was 'poetic' and the other 'popular'. The poets who wrote the scurrilous poems were professional poets who laboured to achieve the effects they were after. We today may regard such works as childish or even lavatorial, but this was not the view of those who admired them. It is significant, too, that both types of poem were written for the court.

Indeed the flyting poems of the fifteenth century were often rather literary in their vocabulary. In *The Cursing of Sir John Rowll*, in which the poet anathematizes those who have stolen some geese from his yard, the invective consists of many literary words, many of which were of Latin origin.

> All tymes in thair legasie
> Fyre, sword, watter, and woddie,
> Or ane of thir infirmateis
> Off warldly scherp adverseteis,
> Povertie, pestilence, or poplecy,
> Dum, deif, or edroposy,
> Maigram, madness, or missilry,
> Appostrum or the perlocy,
> Fluxis, hyvis, or huttit ill,
> Hoist, heidward, or fawin ill,
> Kald, kanker, feistir, or feveris,
> Brukis, bylis, blobbis, and bleistiris. (39-50)

It is only with masters of this type of invective like William Dunbar (*c*. 1460-1521?) that the language was extended into non-standard areas. A good example is his final stanza in *The Flyting of Dunbar and Kennedie:*

> Mauch muttoun, byt buttoun, peilit gluttoun, air to Hilhous;
> Rank beggar, ostir dregar, foule fleggar in the flet;
> Chittirlilling, ruch lilling, lik schilling in the milhous;
> Baird rehator, theif of natur, fals tratour, feyindis gett;
> Filling of tauch, rak sauch, cry crauch, thow art oursett;
> Muttoun dryver, girnall ryver, yadswyvar, fowll fell the;
> Herretyk, lunatyk, puspyk, carlingis pet,
> Rottin crok, dirtin drok, cry cok, or I sall quell the. (145-52)

Here one must admire first the sheer technical accomplishment of the poetry. There is alliteration and internal rhyme within the lines as well as rhyme joining the lines together in the stanza. It was therefore not unnatural that this metre should pose considerable restraints upon the poet who would have to search around for the necessary vocabulary. It is not possible to go into detail over the words used in this last quotation. The origin and exact meaning of some of the words like *chittirlilling* are uncertain and thus they may have come from a colloquial level of language. Some phrases are idiomatic and others slang. Dunbar was a master at piling up defamatory words and at exploiting the differences in tone between Latinate and alliterative vocabulary so as to create an effect of the grotesque.

It is not worth lingering over the Scottish Chaucerians for they had little influence on later English literature. Because Scotland remained an independent kingdom until the union in 1603 the Scots dialect maintained a certain prestige which perhaps saved it from becoming an object of ridicule in English writings. The existence of the fifteenth- and sixteenth-century Scottish writers contributed to the literary survival of Scots and thus allowed it to re-emerge in later periods as a literary medium when all other dialects had virtually disappeared. In the South, on the other hand, three features are important during the sixteenth century in the developing attitude to non-standard language: the growth of jest books, the increasing recognition of low-class speech and the growing influence of London as a standard.

Jest books may be said to start in England with the publication in 1484 of Caxton's translation of *Æsop's Fables*, since in that edition he included some fables from Alphonso and Poggio which were more in the nature of short comic stories or witty remarks. Most jest books, like Caxton's *Æsop's Fables*, were translations from French, Dutch or Latin, though *A Hundred Mery Talys*, printed by John Rastell in 1526, is a notable exception. The jest books often turn on a pun, a funny incident, the worsting of a simpleton or similar events. They often have a colloquial feel to them for the high style is avoided and most are told in an informal manner. Nevertheless, many of the stories have a long history. As with most jests, there is usually a character against whom the joke is told, and it is natural that he should be represented as naive and incredulous since that adds to the humour. In *A Hundred Mery Talys* and later jest books this role is often filled by someone from outside London or even from abroad. In Great Britain, Wales and the North figure frequently as the homes of these people, for presumably such places were not considered to be as sophisticated as London.

The importance of the jest books for the growth of non-standard English lies in three factors. The first is that they bring a variety of characters from outside London into their jokes, for the most part treating them as simpletons. Since the jests are brief the authors do not necessarily have recourse to dialectal or other linguistic traits to sketch in their characters, but the inclusion of these people is a reflection of the attitude to provincials and foreigners which was growing at the time. The second is that different forms of language are used from time to time in the jest books, and these forms helped to develop attitudes to certain linguistic types. Dialect is the easiest linguistic type to recognize and perhaps also the easiest to represent now that the spelling of English was becoming rather more stable. In *A Hundred Mery Talys*, Welshmen are frequently made to say *By Cot's bloot* or *blut* with *c* and *t* representing *g* and *d* respectively. The precise significance of *u* is more difficult to determine, though it is possible to suggest that spelling was now sufficiently stable for it to be considered a marked form. But at this time it is easier to use variations in consonantal than vocalic sounds, precisely because the former have been more consistently represented in orthography. Similarly a northerner is made to say *By God's sale I is heart* (p.149) in which the word developed from the Old English *sawol* 'soul' has a medial *a* rather than an *ou* or *o* which were used in the South. The form *I is* for 'I am' was also characteristically northern. In the *Merry Tales made by Master Skelton* (1567), Skelton tricks a man from Kendal into believing he is sick. The man says *By the misse, Ise wrang! I bus goe till bed* 'By the mass I am sick, I had better go to bed'. Later he adds *In gewd faith do see, and Ise bay for you scot to London* 'Truly do so and I will pay for your whole journey to London' (p.328). When Skelton had 'cured' the man they both rode off to London. Occasionally a south-western dialect form is found, though the background of the speaker is in these instances not often noted. Thus in *Tales and Quick Answers* (c. 1535), a 'blunt fellow' says *by mass, chadde as liefe drink water* 'By the mass I would as soon drink water' (p.312), where *chadde* is a variant of *ich hadde*. In the *Merry Tales made by Master Skelton* a cobbler of Diss, Norfolk, where Skelton was the parish priest, says *I will see how Ich shall be ordered* (p.339), where *Ich* is a variant of *I* more usually associated with the South-West. These forms occur only sporadically in the tales in question.

These last examples show some of the problems of using dialect. The *ich* and *chadde* forms are characteristically south-western, though they may also have developed a more general non-standard association. They occur in semi-proverbial utterances which may have been linked with country lore rather than with a particular district. The examples of northern dialect are not complete for both *till* and *to* are used, and *goen* is found where one might expect *gan*. The use of *bay* for 'pay' is a corruption rather than a northern form. But the examples are able to provide a smattering of dialect material and this was the intention of the author. Northerners were dialect speakers and hence, also by this token, liable to make all kinds of mistakes in English.

The third important aspect of the jest books is their use of vocabulary and idiomatic phrases which is not found so much, or at all, in more elevated writings. Many of these may have been taken from a colloquial level of language. In some respects this 'low' vocabulary is also found in some Middle English works but was in danger of being ousted from literature by the fashion for aureation characteristic of the fifteenth century and later. The jest books ensure the continuation of proverbial and folk idiom by preserving in written English many examples which may have been familiar at the spoken level. The words include *cover knave* 'hat', *musket* (i.e. *muskrat*) 'mistress', *peak* 'sneak', *pickthank* 'sycophant' and *poller* 'confidence trickster'. The expressions include *mine eames peasen* 'at peace with the world' and *ka me ka thee* 'tit for tat', the former of which already has an archaic form by the sixteenth century. These words and idioms do not necessarily occur for the first time in English in the jest books, but they are used frequently there. More importantly the jest books helped to create a climate which accepted the use of such words in literature and which recognized that the bizarre and grotesque should be expressed in an appropriate language.

The increasing recognition of low-class speech was caused by the growth in the number of people in the underworld and by the impact they had on other sections of society. There was a particularly large underworld population in London, and the rise of London as the centre of literary culture meant that many writers were familiar with those in that social milieu. Indeed many writers spent much of their life on the fringes of the underworld because their financial rewards were so limited, and many wrote books describing how people in these walks of life survived. The sixteenth century witnessed the dissolution of the monasteries, the rise of capitalism and the burgeoning of the protestant work ethic, and all these contributed to the rise in the numbers of vagrants and unemployed. Society had not yet developed means to cope with these social outcasts and the problems they created. Many sections of the underworld developed their own jargon, and writers recorded it as part of their account of the way such people lived.

Greene's *The Art of Conny-Catching* and Dekker's *The Gull's Horn-Book* are two of the better known examples. Tracts such as these give us some understanding of various levels of language such as thieves' cant, which has such terms as *apple-squire* 'pimp', *cleym* 'sham sore', *gilks* 'skeleton keys', *mort* 'woman' and *queer-ken* 'prison'. We shall come across this type of language again in discussing the drama of the period.

In the meantime London English was being increasingly accepted as the standard for written language. Puttenham gives particular expression to this attitude in his *The Arte of English Poesie* (1589):

> Our maker therfore at these dayes shall not follow *Piers plowman* nor *Gower* nor *Lydgate* nor yet *Chaucer*, for their language is now out of vse with vs: neither shall he take the termes of Northern-men, such as they vse in dayly talke, whether they be noble men or gentlemen, or of their best clarkes all is a matter: nor in effect any speach vsed beyond the riuer of Trent, though no man can deny but that theirs is the purer English Saxon at this day, yet it is not so Courtly nor so currant as our Southerne English is, no more is the far Westerne mans speach: ye shall therefore take the vsuall speach of the Court, and that of London and the shires lying about London within lx. myles, and not much aboue. (III.4)

The whole chapter, which cannot be quoted here, shows that good language was associated with the upper-class speakers and although such speakers could be found in all parts of England they were particularly to be found around London. The implication is that this educated speech was also used by noblemen, whether they came from London or not. At the same time it is clear that although some old authors were still read, their works were now archaic because the language had developed so much since the early fifteenth century. Their language should not be imitated, for it was now considered non-standard, and this opened the way for archaism to be used in literature as a non-standard feature.

That dialect consciousness was growing can be seen from the use of dialect in different types of writing. There exists in broadside form from 1552 a debate in verse between Thomas Churchyard and Thomas Camell, in which each attacked the other and accused him of stupidity. After a time the amusement pales and so the author introduces additional characters who speak in dialect. Possibly these additional characters are meant to be of a more humble social standing than the principals. Most speak the south-western dialect which was becoming the stage comic dialect; but one in particular speaks a different type of English which may be an attempt to represent a class rather than a regional variety. He uses expressions like *yeery day* 'every day', *yeery whit* 'every whit', *hyt peeres* 'it seems', *yo bin nod speasde* 'you are not displeased', and *bout fortye moyle be yend* 'forty miles around'. He represents *v* by *w* internally and *f* initially in *awisement* and *fengeaunce*. He has *wooder* for 'other' and *whorne* for 'horn'. The reflex of ME [a:] is *o* in *lost* 'last' and *nome* 'name'. It must be confessed, however, that these features do not add up to a consistent variety of English; it is a hodge-podge of features used to create a non-standard effect. Furthermore, there is no real indication that the speakers of this or the south-western forms are illiterate or rustic. It would appear that the different forms were used to increase the humour of the broadside rather than to imply any social comment. Dialect was used here more for humour than as a class-marker.

Edmund Spenser was the first English poet to use archaisms and dialect forms extensively. As an innovation it met with a cool response from his contemporaries; Sidney dismissed the speech of *The Shepheardes Calender* (1579) as 'an old rustick language'. It is indeed the poem of Spenser's which presents most examples of non-standard language. An important point to notice is the difficulty in distinguishing between Spenser's archaic and dialect forms. This is largely because he did not draw his examples from living dialect speakers; he took them from earlier writers, particularly Chaucer, Malory, Langland, Lydgate and Skelton. From Malory, a particular favourite of his, he borrowed many northern words which were archaic by the sixteenth century as far as the London standard was concerned. Because he drew his vocabulary from previous authors he did not use the stock comic dialect based on south-western speech. Whether this was intentional or not we cannot tell, but it did mean that his 'rustick language' is idealized and not comic or low. The peasants of *The Shepheardes Calender* live in an idyllic pastoral; they are not from a vulgar and boorish environment.

Not everyone welcomed Spenser's innovations and many did not understand them. For this reason 'E.K.' had to offer an apology for Spenser's language at the beginning of the printed edition and provide a gloss of hard words after each eclogue. E.K. claimed that Spenser was to be complemented on reviving many 'good and naturall English words' which had fallen out of use, but for the most part his archaisms revive words which had been replaced by others and to that extent they were unnecessary. They helped Spenser create his individual style, but they could hardly be adopted widely since they filled no felt need. Not all the words glossed by E.K. were unfamiliar to a sixteenth-century reader, though many were. For the most part he does not give information about the origins of a word, although occasionally he mentions from which earlier author a word is borrowed. The glosses are to words and phrases rather than to inflexional endings. Among those found in the April eclogue are: *gars thee greete* 'causeth thee weepe and complain'; *dight* 'adorned'; *medled* 'mingled'; *yfere* 'together'; *soote* 'sweete'; *behight* 'called or named'; *forswonck and forswatt* 'ouerlaboured and sunneburnt'; and *yblent* 'Y, is a poeticall addition. Blent blinded'. Anyone familiar with Chaucer will recognize most of these words, though the first phrase is northern and is taken from Malory.

Spenser thus produced an uncolloquial and unidiomatic language which is interesting merely for showing that archaisms and dialect forms could be used in high poetry. In general he was more attracted to archaism, for in English archaisms tended to elevation whereas dialect forms tended to colloquialism.

Spenser's example was followed by William Warner in his *Albion's England* (1586), for in book V, chapter xxiv, he introduces 'a simple Northerne-man' who expresses in a northern dialect the views of the common people about the monks and other religious characters. The language is not a thorough representation of the northern dialect, for Warner has simply followed certain orthographic and linguistic adjustments whether the resulting form is truly northern or not. He has a few northern words like *garre* 'make', *gang* 'go' and *ille* 'evil'. He replaces *o* with *a* in *fra* 'from', *na* 'no', *strang* 'strong', *sa* 'so' as well as *lard* 'lord', *dares* 'doors' and *warse* 'worse'. He has *u* for *o* in *gud* 'good' and *bukish* 'bookish', and *k* for *ch* in *syke* 'such', *kirk* 'church' and *ylke* 'each'. He uses the forms *gif* 'if' and *sal* 'shall'. Among the verbs there occur *I is* 'I am' and *Iis* 'I will', and the third person singular present indicative is always in -*(e)s* as in *gyles* 'beguiles' and *guds* 'benefits'. Elision is introduced as a characteristic element of the dialect with such forms as *een* 'even', *liell* 'little', *ery* 'every', *member* 'remember' and *purpoe* 'purple'. To Warner this northerner seems to represent the true Englishman who is not corrupted by the effete manners of the South, and there is nothing comic about the fourteen stanzas he is given. A similar attempt to represent the northern dialect, though this time more for verisimilitude, is found in William Bulleyn's *Fever Pestilence*

(1564). These two examples may have produced some of the dramatic representations of the northern dialect early in the seventeenth century, though they appear not to have been as well-known or as influential as Spenser's work.

The last author to be considered in this chapter is Thomas Deloney whose *Jack of Newbury* was registered in 1597. Deloney was influenced by the jest books and by contemporary drama. His novel has much in common with plays since so much of it was given over to dialogue. Jack of Newbury's father- and mother-in-law speak the stage rustic dialect, for they are described as poor people from Aylesbury in Buckinghamshire. Their speech contains the following elements from that dialect: forms of the personal pronoun like *che* 'I' and *cham* 'I am'; *thicke*, presumably from ME *thilk* 'this, that'; the voicing of the velar stop in *thong* 'thank'; and the voicing of initial *s* and *f* in *zee*, *vaith*. These features are inserted in what is otherwise standard London English. In addition the father-in-law has many malapropisms in his speech, such as *exclamation* for 'reputation'. His use of *vice* for 'voice' may be comic, but it can hardly be part of his rustic dialect since the sound could be heard in London English at the time. The following is a good example of the mixed language which resulted from the use of comic features with the standard:

> thicke I will bestowe, you shall haue with a good will: because che heare very good condemnation of you in euery place, therefore chill giue you twenty Nobles and a weaning Calfe, and when I dye and my Wife, you shall haue the reuelation of all my goods. (28:28-31)

The primary purpose of this representation is comedy rather than accuracy. The same applies to the Italian merchant who speaks in 'broken English'. His language can be represented by this passage:

> Mettressa *Ione*, be mee tra and fa, mee loue you wod all mine heart, and if you no shall loue mee againe, mee know me shall die, sweete Mettressa loue a mee; and by my fa and tra you shall lack nothing: First me will giue you de silke for make you a Frog. Second de fin Camree for make you ruffes, and de turd shall be for make fin hankercher, for wipe your nose. (61:23-28)

In this Italian's language there is a strong element of obscene grotesqueness, as in *turd* and *beshit*. There are features that one might expect from an Italian speaker such as the use of *d* for initial *th*, but other features are quite unrealistic such as *wod* 'with' and some of the syntactic abbreviations. Deloney was clearly intent on coarse humour rather than on any attempt at a reasonable representation of an Italian speaking English. His use of these non-standard types was not followed up, because there were to be no other novels for some time in English literature. The use of this type of language becomes largely confined to drama, which we must now consider.

Chapter 3

FROM CHAUCER TO
SHAKESPEARE: DRAMA

𝕘𝕘𝕘𝕘𝕘𝕘

WITH THE DRAMA we must go back to the medieval period, though
we need not enquire into its origins. We may distinguish two types of
drama, the mystery plays which survive in cycles from such places as
York and Chester, and the non-cycle plays which in medieval times included particularly moralities and interludes. It was the latter type
which had most influence on the future development of drama in
England, perhaps because plays of this type were performed more frequently in London; so first we must consider briefly the cycle plays.
Here we are faced with a difficulty, for the dates at which the cycle
plays were written cannot be determined with any accuracy. Indeed it
is possible that many plays exist in a revised form so that an original
date of composition may not be very meaningful as far as the language
of the extant texts is concerned. Early in our own century the fourteenth century was regarded as the probable period of composition,
but more recently the fifteenth century or even later has been propos-
ed as more likely.

Certain characteristics of the cycle plays militate against the use of
non-standard language despite the fact that drama might seem to encourage its use because of the need to differentiate characters. The
plays are essentially didactic in intention since they portray human
history from the creation to doomsday. The characters that appear are
idealized, representing human or divine types rather than individuals,
and so no attempt is made to distinguish the particular differences
among the participants. There is a division between good and evil, but
the distinction between upper and lower class is hardly marked if only
because so many of the good people belong to the lower echelons of
society. The plays are written in poetic metres which may have encouraged elaboration in accordance with the tenets of medieval
rhetoric rather than colloquialism or informality. In any case the type
of stage and arena used for performance may have encouraged
declamation rather than intimacy. Although the cycles themselves are

lengthy, the individual plays which go to make them up are relatively brief; they hardly provide sufficient scope for variation among characters, many of whom appear in only a single play. The plays that survive come from outside London and were written in a modified form of the local dialect, a factor which would inhibit the authors from using certain non-standard forms. Nevertheless some non-standard language is found and it tends to be associated increasingly with the comic elements which were introduced to provide some relief from the more serious matter of the cycles.

If we consider the Chester Mystery Cycle we may note at once the absence of any dialect forms and of the corruption of any English word except the occasional formula. There is indeed throughout this cycle very little non-standard language. What there is consists largely of abuse. For the most part this is put into the mouths of the wicked characters such as Herod, but it can be uttered by almost anyone when the situation warrants. Thus when Herod's soldiers massacre the innocents, one of the mothers reviles them in the most plain terms. The non-standard forms include the corruption of *God's* to *cockes* in such formulae as *By cockes sowle* (p. 172) and *By cockes bones* (p. 282), and the frequent pejorative words in *-ard* like *maugard, populard, dotard, villard, sluggard* and *scalward*. These latter may well be literary in their origins. The abuse is often scatological and frequently reinforced by alliteration. A typical example of general abuse is:

> Garcius   Fye on your loynes and your liverye,
> your liverastes, livers, and longes,
> your sose, your sowse, your saverraye,
> your sittinge withowt any songes! (134/202-5)

Rather more pungent abuse is uttered by Herod when he calls Mary 'that mysebegotten maremasett' (185/15) and when he orders the massacre of the innocents by saying 'Dryve downe the dyrtie-arses all bydeene' (190/143). Once again the abuse is more literary than colloquial, though the occasional word may have been taken directly from speech. If there is malapropism or corruption of language, it is of Latin rather than of English formulae since these, as part of the religious background, were sufficiently stable and foreign to be tampered with successfully. A notable example occurs in *The Paynters Playe* about the shepherds after the angels had sung 'Gloria in excelsis Deo et in terra pax hominibus bonae voluntatis'. The Latin words are corrupted by the shepherds and Garcius in many ways, though only a few lines may be quoted here.

Tertius Pastor
for I am eldest of degree
and alsoe best, as seemes mee,
hit was 'grorus glorus' with a 'glee'.
Hit was neyther more nor lasse.

Garcius
Nay, yt was 'glorus glarus glorius'. (142/380-4)

The Wakefield plays of the Towneley Cycle share many of the features found in the Chester Cycle. These plays are written in a North Midland dialect and this can present problems of interpretation of the vocabulary and syntax. It is not easy to say how far some of the words were intended to be colloquial by the playwright since insufficient material survives against which to judge the forms. Thus expressions like *walk in the wenyand* 'confound you' (4.405) and words like *maroo* 'mate' (4.436, of uncertain origin) may have been intended to suggest a different register from the rest of the language. Certainly the author is a master of abuse which he puts into the mouths of the wicked and the low, and this shows he had some appreciation for different levels of language. Thus Herod is shown as a man of raging passions, great boasting and torrential abuse. Much of the last is, however, fairly traditional. These plays are best known for the *Second Shepherds Play (Secunda Pastorum)* in which one of the shepherds, Mak, pretends to be a southerner. When he joins the other shepherds out in the fields he has his cloak over him and uses southern forms to conceal his identity, because of his reputation as a sheep-stealer. The southernisms Mak uses are concentrated within a brief passage, for the others are not taken in by it, and they are not consistently used by Mak. The passage just gives a southern flavour and is not so convincing as Chaucer's representation of the northern dialect in *The Reeve's Tale*. The features the author uses are *ich* for *I*, *be* for *am*, and -*th* for -*s* in the third person singular of the present indicative of verbs. The form *sond* may be intended as a southern variant of *sand*, though *sond* is found elsewhere in the plays. Similarly *sich* for *swylk* may be meant as a southernism, but it, too, is found elsewhere in the text. The spelling *some* for *same* may be the result of assuming that northern *a* should be replaced by southern *o*, even though this was not the case with this word. But these examples hardly amount to a very thorough representation of a different dialect, and many forms remain northern. The verb *goyth* has the southern inflexion, but a northern diphthong; and *thwang* has northern *a* for southern *o*. Nevertheless the other shepherds take Mak's language to be southern, for one of them says:

65

Now take outt that Sothren tothe,
And sett in a torde! (4.215-16)

This underlining of the dialect form may indicate that the author was not certain that all his audience would recognize the language. The southern dialect may have suggested a higher social status, for Mak claims to be a yeoman and thus presumably far superior to mere shepherds. The reason for the inclusion of the dialect can only be humour; different language forms are still comic and need carry no further implications. Nevertheless, this example is of interest in that as writings in dialects outside London gradually ceased, naturally the use of southern forms as a non-standard variety came to an end.

The cycle plays could develop comic situations only by inventing scenes and characters not in the original biblical stories or by developing the wicked characters in a grotesque way. Such comic scenes and characters were then suitable vehicles for non-standard language. Nevertheless the opportunities remained limited. The morality plays and interludes were not inhibited in the same way for, if their stories were traditional, the playwrights felt free to develop them as they saw fit. These plays often involve the confrontation of good and evil usually through allegorical personifications, as in *Everyman*. As a result the character of Vice develops in a traditional manner in which non-standard language plays an important part. These plays, though moral in intention, are more secular and popular than the cycle plays; they include many popular elements linked with folk plays. Some indeed witness to the union of the new humanism with the popular theatre of mirth and comedy. There is frequently a polarity in them between the two so that a scatological scene can follow one devoted to the niceties of elevated courtship. Not unnaturally the scenes of propriety are given to the more elevated characters socially whereas the comedy is the preserve of the servants and lower classes. The vices are linked linguistically with these classes so that their language is of the same character as that of the servants. In a framework like this, non-standard language could develop an important dramatic role.

Mankind, probably written 1465-70, is one of the three *Macro Plays*. Written in an East Midlands dialect, it may originate from the Norfolk or Cambridgeshire areas to which there are many local references. The play was performed by six travelling actors who used impromptu stages in village inns and market places, the actors needing to appeal to their public in order to survive. In this play Mankind finds himself under siege from Mischief, Nought, New

Guise, Nowadays and Titivillus, but he is aided by Mercy. These characters divide up readily enough into good and bad. A good example of the dialogue in which the bad characters participate is the following:

> *Mercy.*　The corn xall be sauyde, þe chaffe xall be brente.
> 　　　I besech yow hertyly, haue þis premedytacyon.
> *Myscheffe.*　I beseche yow hertyly, leue yowr calcacyon.
> 　　　Leue yowr chaffe, leue yowr corn, leue yowr dalyacyon.
> 　　　Yowr wytt is lytyll, yowr hede ys mekyll, ȝe are full of predycacyon.
> 　　　But, ser, I prey þis questyon to to claryfye:
> 　　　Mysse-masche, dryff-draff,
> 　　　Sume was corn and sume was chaffe,
> 　　　My dame seyde my name was Raffe;
> 　　　Onschett yowr lokke and take an halpenye.
>
> *Mercy.*　Why com ȝe hethyr, broþer? 3e were not dysyryde.
>
> *Myscheff.*　For a wynter corn-threscher, ser, I haue hyryde,
> 　　　Ande ȝe sayde þe corn xulde be sauyde and þe chaff xulde be feryde,
> 　　　Ande he prouyth nay, as yt schewth be þis werse:
> 　　　'Corn seruit bredibus, chaffe horsibus, straw fyrybusque.'
> 　　　Thys ys as moche to say, to yowr leude wndyrstondynge,
> 　　　As þe corn xall serue to brede at þe nexte bakynge.
> 　　　'Chaff horsybus et reliqua',
> 　　　The chaff to horse xall be goode prouente,
> 　　　When a man ys forcolde þe straw may be brent,
> 　　　And so forth, et cetera.
>
> *Mercy.*　Avoyde, goode broþer! 3e ben culpable
> 　　　To interrupte thus my talkyng delectable. (43-65)

Mischief interrupts Mercy and her 'talkyng delectable'. It is not surprising that Mischief should wish to respond by using a language which is quite the opposite of the elevated rhetoric used by Mercy. The following points may be noted. Mercy uses a language which is high-flown and includes many abstract Latinisms. She also relies on traditional proverbial wisdom. Mischief parodies this type of language by using some words of Latin origin and by uttering short pithy clauses which give the appearance of being proverbial and sometimes are. The phrase 'Mickle head, little wit' is often cited in other writings of this period. Mischief also makes use of puns, as in the name Raffe, which suggests a pun on the noun *raff* 'refuse'. He also employs a nonsense language, asking Mercy to provide the solution to a question which has more the nature of a nonsensical riddle. Within this nonsense verse the pairs *mysse-masche* and *dryff-draff* are worthy of note, for their occurrence here underlines the character which such pairs had at this time. Finally he relies on corrupt Latin to increase the humour of the passage. He takes the English words *bread, horse* and *fire* and gives them a Latin dative plural ending in *-ibus* (with *-que* 'and' added to the last item) to create hybrid words which actually make sense in the passage; the author evidently knew his Latin. For the audience the echo of liturgical Latin may have been sufficient to create amusement, whether they understood the Latin endings or not. These features, with others, are found at other points in the play. Inevitably obscene language is used, as when Nought says

> Lo, master, lo, here ys a pardon bely-mett.
> Yt ys grawntyde of Pope Pokett,
> Yf ʒe wyll putt yowr nose in hys wyffys sokett,
> ʒe xall haue forty days of pardon. (143-6)

There is also the usual amount of swearing and other forms of asseveration. A few idiomatic usages occur as in *Hay, doog, hay! whoppe whoo! Go yowr wey lyghtly!* (720) and *Stow, statt, stow* (729). The former is used also by Skelton and was probably colloquial; the latter may have been constructed for the alliteration which occurs frequently enough as a feature of the speech of the vices. We have in the author of *Mankind* a man who was learned and drew his humour from traditional literary forms rather than from colloquial or regional varieties of speech. The humour comes from the incongruity of the different linguistic levels and to some extent from the vulgarisms present.

In some respects Skelton is not dissimilar in his play *Magnificence*. He does, however, seem to have relied on more non-standard lexical items, for many words which became part of the stock-in-trade of Elizabethan comedies appear first in his play; they include *coistrel* and *hodipeke*, both used as terms of abuse. Other words he used include *knuckleboneyard* and *prong* which are otherwise unrecorded in the senses used in Skelton. He also used words which are found at earlier periods in northern texts and which may have had a more colloquial status further south. A word like *skelp*, which occurs for the first time in the York cycle plays, is used for its alliterative effectiveness by Skelton; it never became common in southern literary works. In addition his play appears more racy because he includes allusions and idioms which are topical, folklorist or proverbial. Furthermore his nonsense language is far more vigorous. An example occurs at Stage 2, scene 12:

Courtly Abusion   Huffa, huffa, tanderum, tanderum, tain, huffa, huffa!
Cloaked Collusion This was properly prated, sirs! what said a?
Courtly Abusion   Rutty bully, jolly rutterkin, heyda!
Cloaked Collusion *De que pays êtes vous?*
Courtly Abusion   Deck your hofte and cover a louse.

The absence of Latin corruptions gives this nonsense talk greater vigour and a more colloquial nature, even though it is likely to be as literarily composed as that in *Mankind*. The French is used to indicate affectation and indicates that foreign languages had acquired definite connotations which could be exploited for humorous effect.

The use of a foreign language is something we meet in Henry Medwall's *Fulgens and Lucres* published by John Rastell in 1515, a play which has many points of interest. At one stage in this play there is a reference to Spain and Flanders. One character refers to 'a bace daunce after the gyse of Spayne' (II 380-1) and another imitates the language of the Flemings when he says of the minstrels:

Mary, as for one of them his lippe is sore,
I trow he may not pype, he is so syke.
Spele vp tamboryne, ik bide owe frelike. (II 387-9)

Here words like *spele* and spellings like *ik* and *frelike* indicate that Flemish is being imitated or spoken. The problem is to decide how to take this particular piece of linguistic bravado. Henry Medwall was chaplain to Cardinal Morton, Archbishop of Canterbury, and he seems to have been reasonably well known at court. In 1497 the court of Henry VII entertained ambassadors from Spain and Flanders, and the occasion was one of considerable diplomatic importance. Morton may have been a party to the negotiations and the play may have been written as part of the festivities he arranged to entertain the visitors. If this is so, the Flemish language adopted by one of the English characters would have to be regarded as straight rather than humorous; it would be a compliment to the ambassadors. This indeed seems the most likely explanation and it means that the adoption of a foreign language by a character does not have to be interpreted as comic at this time. This is an interesting conclusion for the character in question is B, one of the comic servingmen of the two contenders for the hand of Lucres. The conclusion may be supported by other linguistic features in the play, as Medwall employs a surprising number of archaic words and forms, northernisms, and unique words and spellings. Archaisms include *yede* 'went' (I 584), *garce* 'gash' (I 1262) and *chise* 'choose' (II 852); northernisms include *warand* 'warrant' (I 192), *what* 'wot' (I 301) and *wull* 'will', (I 825); and unique forms and spellings occur in *reall* 'realm' (I 630), *what calt* 'whatever you may call it' (I 24), *fewster*, a variant of *fester* (I 1267) and *mouset* 'little mouse' (I 841). These words appear to have no significance in the play and cannot be interpreted as non-standard. They show once more how difficult it is to use variant forms in any meaningful way before language became standardized. The words and forms may be considered the idiosyncracies of the author (or even the compositor) which bear no connotations within the play. There is, nevertheless, some verbal humour in the play. For instance, B is asked by Cornelius to deliver a message about the hollow ash in the garden to Lucres. B gets confused and perverts the hollow ash into *the noke of the ars*, though he goes on to explain that he cannot remember whether it was *the noke or the hole* (II 283-7). In addition both A and B use a number of vulgarisms which have now become traditionally non-standard such as *Cockis body* (I 859) as well as more general vulgarisms.

The southern, or more particularly south-western, dialect continues to be the principal non-standard dialect found in plays and is increasingly evident as the sixteenth century progresses. Its first appearance in a comedy as distinct from a morality occurs in Nicholas Udall's *Ralph Roister Doister* from about 1550. Here it is given to Dame Custance's nurse Madge Mumblecrust, though she makes use of the dialect only sporadically. She is however given such speeches as

> God 'ield you, sir; chad not so much, i-chotte not when;
> Ne'er since chwas born, chwine, of such a gay gentleman. (I.13)

She is responding to a kiss given her by Roister. The forms will be discussed shortly when we consider lengthier treatments of the dialect. Madge does not have a large part and much of her language is standard. Her dialect forms are introduced without reference to her origins or her present status and the reason for the inclusion of the dialect remains uncertain. We may assume that it indicates an inferior status, though nothing is made of this situation in the scenes where it is used. It is only when we come to *Respublica*, a morality written about

1553 and attributed by some to Nicholas Udall also, that we find a character using the south-western dialect consistently. Here the character in question is People, a kind of allegorical clown who represents the suffering peasant community. A typical example of People's language is:

> Marie chill tell yowe: as soone as ye were agoe
> hither cam a zorte of courtnalls, harde men and zore
> Thei shaked me vp, chwas ner zo rattled avore.
> Theye vell all vppon me catche awoorde that might catche,
> well was hym that at me people geat a snatche.
> Choulde have been at home rather then anewe grote.
> Iche maie zedge to yowe, Isfearde pulling owte my throte.
> they bade me pieke me home, and come att yowe no more.
> An iche did, thei zware Isshoulde bee corrupt therefore.
> Zo thieke prowte howrecop, what call ye hym? (1584-93)

Features in this dialect representation which are worthy of note are the voicing of initial consonants *f* and *s*, and the *ich* forms of the pronoun. The former can be seen above in *vell* 'fell', *avore* 'before', *zo* 'so', *zorte* 'sort' and *zore* 'sore', i.e. 'fierce'. As the form *zorte* shows, this voicing can affect words of romance origin as much as those from Old English. The *ich* forms occur predominantly before vowels or before *h* or *w*. The forms include *chill* 'I will' and *chwas* 'I was' above, as well as *cham* 'I am', *cha* 'I have' and *ichwin* 'I ween'. The *ich* forms may also occur before consonants as in *iche maie* and *iche did*, though there is a tendency for *ich* to become *is* in that environment as in *is fearde* 'I was afraid' and *is shoulde* 'I should'. Some unusual elisions which occur include *erche* 'ere I', *shalche* 'shal I' and *anche* 'if I' (from *an iche*). These two dialect features may be said to be the classic ones used to represent the south-western dialect in drama of this period, though other elements were added. These include the prefix *i-* with past participles, the ending *-th* for the 3rd person plural of the present indicative, the forms *ha* for 'have', and *a* for 'he', as well as certain occasional spellings such as *whare* 'where' and *mustress* 'mistress', which may naturally in this manuscript be copying mistakes. In addition there is often a lack of concord between subject and verb as in *youe liest* (638). Some words may also be intended to represent the south-western dialect such as *kyxe* 'a dry stalk', *perke* 'to thrust oneself forward' and *sqwatte* 'squash'. In addition to these elements there are many features which can be described as vulgar rather than dialectal. Among these are the many malapropisms found in People's language. Thus we have *Rice*

71

puddingcake (for *Respublica*), *permounted* (for *promoted*), *perzente* (for *represent*), *besiraunce* (for *desirous*) and *bezeivers* (for *deceivers*). These malapropisms include forms corrupted into another word as well as those corrupted into a meaningless form as when *de-* forms are replaced by *be-* forms. Additionally there are certain elisions like *ninnat* 'will not' and syncopated forms like *ientman* 'gentleman', *mace* 'master' and *warte* 'warrant'. *Jesus* is once perverted to *Jisse*, which may be a euphemism. Finally there is another group of words which are neither south-western nor vulgar; presumably they were included to add to the non-standard feel of the language. They include *cobbes* 'lords' and *smoult* 'smooth'.

The features found in the speech of People in *Respublica* consist of a mixture of traditional south-western dialect elements as well as vulgar and other dialect usages. This mixture is common enough at the time for the dramatists were not intent on giving an accurate representation of a particular dialect. They were more interested in drawing a particular character in a certain light, and for this purpose a variety of non-standard features was quite acceptable. Indeed there is no regularity in the use of these features by People, who occasionally relapses into more standard forms. It was enough for the author to give a general delineation of language.

The elements we find in *Respublica* are also found in other plays of this time to a varying degree. Thus in *The London Prodigal*, an anonymous comedy from 1605, Oliver is given a rustic-type speech. The two standard features, voicing of initial *f* and *s*, and the *ich* forms of the pronoun, are well represented. To them are added others such as *-s* as the inflexional ending of the 1st person present indicative; *y-* added to the past participle; *ha* and *a* for 'have'; *a* for 'he'; and *a* instead of *e* before *r* in forms like *ysarved*, though the status of this remains debatable. There are also some words designed to give a non-standard flavour such as *lerripoop* and *whisterpoop*, both meaning 'a blow', *thick* 'such' and *vang* 'to take'. There is not much to note here except that the additional features are not necessarily those used by previous writers. In the representation of this dialect some features were standard and others merely added at the whim of the author.

Other writers of Shakespeare's time and immediately afterwards use this stage dialect in their plays occasionally. Its last important manifestation before the closing of the theatres occurs in Ben Jonson's *A Tale of a Tub*. In this play the dialect is used not by an individual but by a whole group of characters, those of the lower echelons of society. Its use is significant, for although the play is set in Finsbury Hundred, London, the local inhabitants of that area are made to speak in a kind of south-western speech. Clearly the dialect had become so closely identified with the lower classes by this time, that its supposed connection with a region of England was no longer regarded as important. Even so, the dialect is not used consistently throughout the play. It occurs most commonly at the beginning and then gradually becomes less marked. No doubt Jonson had made his point about the status of the characters, and it may be that he also became tired of using this particular form of English. Once more the two regular features of this dialect are found, linked to others. The latter include shortened forms like *amost* 'almost', *gi* 'give', *ha* 'have', *stan* 'stand' and *wu'not* 'would not'; initial *y-* in the past participle; the forms *hun* or *'un* for either 'him' or 'them'; and certain words like *kyrsin* 'Christian' and *thik* 'this'. In addition there are some malapropisms, particularly perversions of prefixes as in *parzent* 'present', *perportions* 'proportions', *praformed* 'performed' and *purcept* 'precept'. Besides these items which include general non-standard forms rather than simply south-western dialect ones, there are regional forms which do not belong such as *I is* 'I am' which is more characteristic of the North.

As we saw in the last chapter, the origins of this form of non-standard language in literature are to be sought in the changes in the incipient London standard in the fifteenth century, which left the Kentish dialect as the one which was both closest to London and yet most different from the speech there. It became a language which acquired connotations of folly and country behaviour. The features in it are not specifically Kentish, and references in the sixteenth and seventeenth century indicate that writers considered the basis of this dialect to be south-western rather than south-eastern. However, as the dialect was characterized only by two major points, there is little to show whether this was so for all writers. Indeed most of them clearly never listened to dialect speakers in order to obtain the forms they introduced into their plays. For the most part they took over what others had written and added to it their own ideas of what constituted low-class speech. Although this non-standard variety is theoretically a rustic form of English, writers used it for a variety of purposes. In the moralities it tended to be used for the wicked characters who were often portrayed as grotesque and hence as comic. In other plays it was used more for low-class characters, who generally purvey the more knock-about types of humour. It was also used to indicate rusticity with the implications of simplicity or stupidity. Even before the theatres were closed, this type of non-standard language was dying out, perhaps because the comedies turned to portray city vices and attitudes, for which a country or low-class dialect was of no value. It may indeed be the associations of this type of language which made it unusable in other situations, particularly those where slick comedy was needed. Similarly its associations with rusticity prevented it from being used to portray evil characters who became far more sophisticated at the end of the sixteenth century. An Iago who spoke this countrified dialect is unthinkable.

Because the south-western dialect was closely associated with comedy, those who spoke it were also given other forms of non-standard language. These were, in particular, a variety of vulgar words like *arse*, different forms of word corruption or malapropism like *ingrant* 'ignorant', and by deviations from the norm which was being recognized in London, as in lack of congruence between subject and verb or the addition of initial *h* in forms like *hable* 'able'. These were part of the comic language which was added to that ground swell of the south-western dialect which was the recognition symbol for this type of language. Naturally many items from other regional varieties were included in the language of the comic characters, for the authors were not intent upon giving an accurate representation of a dialect; they were simply giving the audience a clue as to how to respond to a given character. Hence we sometimes find that this type of language is clustered either at the beginning or at important parts of the play when it is essential that the audience is not misled about the nature of the characters.

The south-western dialect was the regular non-standard language in the plays of this period. It is the one used most frequently by the dramatists, because a tradition had grown up about its meaning so that any audience would know how to react to its presence. There are, however, examples of northern dialect to be found in plays from this time, and by northern I include either north English or Scots. The earliest example is found in a morality by Nathaniel Woodes, *The Conflict of Conscience*, which was printed in 1581. The play is an attack on Catholicism and is concerned with the conversion of one character to Protestantism. The principal Catholic in the play is a priest called Caconos, even though he plays only a small part. He reveals the shortcomings of the Catholic church in his attitude to life and people. No mention is made of where Caconos comes from, but he speaks in a language that has marked northern characteristics. It may be that his language is intended to represent Scots as part of an implied attack on the Catholicism of Mary Queen of Scots who was in prison in England. The following is an example of his language:

> In gude feth, sir, this newis de gar me lope,
> Ay is as light as ay me wend, gif that yo wol me troth,
> Far new ayen within awer lond installed is the Pope,
> Whese legat with authoritie tharawawt awr cuntry goth,
> And charge befare him far te com us priests end lemen bath,
> Far te spay awt, gif that he mea, these new-sprang arataykes,
> Whilk de disturb awr hally Kirk, laik a sart of saysmataykes,
> Awr gilden Gods ar brought ayen intea awr kirks ilkwhare,
> That unte tham awr parishioner ma affer thar gude-will. (III.4)

Woodes has constructed his dialect for the most part by substituting what he considers Scottish spellings for those more customary in London, though this is not carried out consistently. The major spelling alterations consist of replacing *o* by *a* in *mare* 'more', *ol* by *aw* in *awd* 'old', *ai* or *ay* by *ea* in *mea* 'may', *i* or *y* by *ai* in *may* 'my', *oo* by *u* in *gude* 'good', *sh* by *s* in *sal* 'shall' and *ch* by *k* in *kirk* 'church'. This is done quite automatically whether the resulting word is Scots or not, as in *befare* 'before' or *tharawawt* 'throughout'. In addition there are some Scottish forms like *ken* 'know' and *mun* 'must', though there are very few Scottish words as such. More importantly, perhaps, Woodes also gives Caconos some malapropisms and vulgarisms such as *arataykes* 'heretics', *saysmataykes* 'schismatics', *distructed* 'instructed' and *may narse* 'my arse'.

The speech of Caconos is northern, though not specifically Scottish, for it includes some spelling conventions that indicate northern pronunciations such as *hwick* for *quick*. It is clear, nevertheless, that he knew the conventions that governed the writing of Scots and that he could give a fair representation of those conventions. But he wanted to portray his character as a prejudiced fool and so he gave him improper and corrupt language as well, thus turning his Scots into a matter for scorn. His use of that dialect is therefore not unlike other writers' use of the south-western dialect. The difference lies not only in the acquaintance he shows with the conventions, but also in his use of this dialect at all, which at that time had few comic associations.

In *Sir John Oldcastle*, a work by Munday and others published in 1600, but no doubt written somewhat earlier, the northern dialect is also used. In this play a carrier and his niece stay at the same inn at which Lord and Lady Cobham (i.e. the Oldcastles) had put up on their flight. The home of the carrier is implied to be Lancashire and this seems to be confirmed by some of his linguistic usages. In particular he uses *I'se* 'I am', *thou's* 'you are' and *cawd* 'cold'. The part of the carrier is a small one and the forms are not used frequently. Since there are also Irish and Welsh speakers in this play, as we shall see, we may assume that these features were introduced for local colour and to portray the lower echelons of society. It is of interest simply to note that dialect forms can be introduced so incidentally in a play like this even though there was no tradition of northern speech in London drama at this time.

A play written about the same time as *Sir John Oldcastle*, but printed two years earlier, is Robert Greene's *The Scottish History of James VI*. This contains an Induction in which Oberon, King of the Fairies, talks with a misanthropic Scot called Bohan about the play. They reappear between acts to comment on the progress of the play as though they perform the function of a chorus. In the Induction, Bohan uses many Scottish forms similar to those found in *The Conflict of Conscience*. The spelling changes here include *ui* for *oo* in *guid* 'good', *ai* for *i* in *fain* 'fine', *au* for *ol* in *haud* 'hold', *s* for *sh* in *sal* 'shall', *k* for *ch* in *whilke* 'which' and *wh* for *qu* in *whayet* 'quiet'. In addition there are many words and idioms of Scottish origin such as *git thee ganging* 'be on your way', *bonny* 'pretty', *gar* 'make', *mirk* 'dark' and *whiniard* 'dagger'. These forms are found in Bohan's language in the Induction and occasionally in his language or the speech of the Scottish noblemen within the play. But mostly the other characters and Bohan himself use standard English throughout. The use of Scots must here be regarded as part of the scene-setting, and once the point has been made in the Induction Greene obviously felt that there was no need for anything else than an occasional reminder. Although Bohan is misanthropic, his use of Scots is not to be regarded as comic or in any way indicating vulgarity or a low-class nature.

Subsequent plays continue to use northern or Scottish forms occasionally. The two most successful are perhaps Richard Brome's *The Northern Lass* printed in 1632 and a play called *The Late Lancashire Witches* printed in 1634 which, it has been claimed, was revised by Brome. These use northern forms more for local colour than for comedy, for it is the heroine of the former play who is the dialect speaker. Nevertheless the northern dialect is used for comedy in other plays, mostly from the early seventeenth century. This dialect seems to have gained in popularity as the south-western variety fell into disuse. Perhaps the rustic associations of the latter had become so pronounced as to limit its usefulness. On the other hand, the accession of James VI of Scotland as James I of England led to an increase in familiarity with the Scottish dialect in London and, no doubt, to the availability of books printed in a Scottish orthography. It may be from these that the playwrights were able to deduce the spelling changes necessary to turn a particular character into a northerner. Even so, when one considers how many plays were produced in this period, the most surprising feature is that so few of them attempted to portray English regional speech. A tradition to do so existed, but it was not much exploited because of its limitations. What one cannot tell, of course, is whether in the actual dramatic productions some characters were made to speak with a regional accent as is done in modern productions, even though there is no indication of any accent in the text.

In addition to English regional speakers there are also in plays from this period speakers from Wales, Scotland and Ireland as well as those from abroad. Since Shakespeare contains many examples of these I will defer their consideration until the next chapter – except for Dutch, which Shakespeare never represents. By Dutch I understand people from either Holland or Flanders. England had had close dealings with the Low Countries for many years, and at the end of the Middle Ages the trade in wool and the cultural importance of the Dukes of Burgundy who lived increasingly in Flanders led to even closer contacts. Religious links between the Protestant Dutch and English were developed in the sixteenth century, and these together with political reasons led to the English involvement in the Low Countries in the fight against Catholic Spain. Many Dutch and Flemings emigrated to England to find better working conditions or to escape persecution. Hence the Dutch language was probably quite familiar in London and other major trading centres. However, it is interesting that the Dutch were not given a good press in the drama of the period. They were pilloried for their drunkenness and gluttony, often associated with their love for butter and herrings. As Dutch and English were closely related dialects of West Germanic it was relatively easy to represent Dutch attempts to speak English. Two tell-tale signs are the treatment of *w* and *th*. Orthographically *v* was often introduced for *w* or even *wh*: *vas* 'was', *vell* 'well', *vat* 'what' and *van* 'when'. Instead of *th* it was common to write *t* or, less often, *d*: *ting* 'thing', *tousant* 'thousand' and *dirty* 'thirty'.

One major attempt to represent how Dutch speakers tackled English can be found in Dekker's *The Shoemaker's Holiday*, probably completed in 1599. In this play Richard Lacy, who is in love with Simon Eyre's daughter, disguises himself as a Dutch shoemaker called Hans Meulter, for Hans was the traditional name in drama for a Dutchman. Later in the play a real Dutch skipper makes his appearance. Both speak in a language which is half Dutch and half English, though naturally Lacy is more at fault here. He can say things like

> Vere ben your edle fro, vare been your mistress? (IV. ii.56)

Here there are two spellings of 'where', there are attempts at Dutch words like *edle fro* and there are pure English words like *your mistress*. It is difficult to know what the audience made of this, for Lacy is one of the heroes of the piece. The language as such is partly comic, though as a disguise that does not affect the man himself. In the play the language spoken by the two Dutch speakers could just be comic in itself but it promotes comedy because Firk, one of Eyre's journeymen, mimics a great deal of what they say, and in mimicking it he turns it into nonsense. Thus when the skipper says:

> Your meester Simon Eyre sal hae good copen: wat seggen yow, Hans?

Firk immediately retorts

> Wat seggen de reggen de copen, slopen? Laugh, Hodge, laugh!
> (II. iii.5-8)

This is gibberish which imitates the sounds made by the Dutchman and then puts them into nonsense rhyming pairs 'reggen ... seggen, copen ... slopen'. Attempts to speak English by Dutchmen are naturally funny because they cannot pronounce the sounds accurately. But this is a humour that springs from circumstance and does not necessarily imply foolishness or low-class status on the part of the speaker, but rather good-natured fun.

Other plays could be more critical of Dutchmen or Flemings depending on the role they had to play in them. In both *Englishmen for my Money* (1597) and *The Weakest goeth to the Wall* (1600) the foreigner is made into a repellent character whose language is mocked by one of the English characters. In these plays a certain xenophobia is present which leads to harsh treatment of the Dutch and Flemish speakers. Rather different is Marston's *The Dutch Courtesan* (1605) in which the courtesan Fraceschina tries to revenge herself on her lover when he gives her up to marry someone else. Her language is a mixture of a little Dutch with a lot of English. Not untypical is this utterance:

> O mine seet, dear'st, kindest, mine loving, O mine tousand, ten tou-
> sand, delicated, petty seetart! Ah, mine aderlievest affection!
> (I. ii.48-50)

Her language is neither one thing nor the other, and certainly it lacks the consistency of Dekker's Dutch speakers. It is made up of a variety of elements, few of which are Dutch. Thus the forms *seetart* 'sweetheart' and *delicated* have nothing to do with Dutch; they are merely introduced to make her language seem different. There is no particular reason for the courtesan to be Dutch and her language hardly gets any comment in the play. The language differentiates a character, but is otherwise unnecessary, and it is not clear whether the audience would find it amusing. After Marston other playwrights do continue to introduce occasional Dutch forms, but there are no comprehensive attempts to portray Dutch speakers of English.

Chapter 4

SHAKESPEARE

🙚🙚🙚🙚🙚🙚

IN ORDER TO DIVIDE the available material up into manageable units the Renaissance period has been split over three chapters – this and the two preceding ones. This division is quite arbitrary though I have tried to avoid some of the dangers, such as repetition, inherent in that scheme. It does, however, also have the advantage that with the first two chapters outlining the general developments, this third one can be devoted to a single author and to more general considerations which can be discussed in detail in relation to his work.

One interesting point concerns Shakespeare's use of regional varieties of English and of attempts by foreigners to speak the language. It is unusual to find regional varieties casually inserted into his plays; for the most part they are grouped together, as in *Henry V* and *The Merry Wives of Windsor*. The exception to this is the language which Edgar adopts as a disguise near Dover in *King Lear*. He has pretended to allow his father to throw himself over the cliff, when suddenly Oswald meets them and claims Gloucester as his prize. Edgar prevents him from killing the old man and addresses Oswald in the standard south-western dialect, of which this passage is representative.

> Good gentleman, go your gait, and let poor volk pass. And 'chud ha' bin zwagger'd out of my life, 'twould not ha' bin zo long as 'tis by a vortnight. Nay, come not near th'old man; keep out, che vor' ye, or ise try whither your costard or my ballow be the harder. Chill be plain with you. (IV.vi)

This contains the features typical of the dialect: the voicing of initial voiceless *f* and *s* in *volk, zo*; and *Ich* for *I* in a variety of shortened forms in *'chud* 'I could', *chill* 'I will'. In addition there are some idiomatic expressions like *che vor' ye* 'I warrant you' and numerous shortened forms like *ha'* 'have'. There are also forms which are not appropriate to the dialect like *ise* 'I shall' and *ballow* 'cudgel', both of which are from more northerly dialects. This is therefore not a representation of a true dialect, but the use of a stage dialect consisting of certain regular features with the haphazard addition of other non-standard items which had no place in the South-West. Oswald refers to Edgar as a 'base peasant' before the latter speaks in the dialect, so that his speech reinforces rather than announces his class. Presumably Edgar used it to lure Oswald to his death, for as a coward he was prepared to attack only those he thought he could easily get the better of, as is suggested by his contemptuous 'Out, dunghill' to Edgar.

In this example Shakespeare shows himself familiar with the stage conventions of his time whereby this dialect could be used to represent a peasant language without particular local associations. The way it is inserted into the play without any preamble or comment underlines how well established this type of speech was by the end of the sixteenth century in drama, and in this instance it is introduced without any comic overtones.

What is important is that Shakespeare did not use this dialect elsewhere even though he had opportunity to do so. Thus in *As You Like It* the country wench Audrey and the other country people make no use of it; similarly the clowns in all plays and the characters like Dogberry who mangle the language are not given this dialect. The reasons for this omission are speculative. In part it may be that many of the plays concern court or city people for whom a peasant dialect was inappropriate whatever their class; and in part it may be that Shakespeare found its use too restrictive. The dialect was too well used to allow much scope for the characters who spoke it, for the audience would react to them in a predictable way and Shakespeare was too adventurous in his comedy to use something which was so stereotyped. It was all very well for a character in disguise to adopt it momentarily, but it would have been quite different for a character to use it as his 'real' language throughout a play.

This is the only English, as distinct from British, variety employed by Shakespeare. It is unlikely that ignorance of other dialects is responsible for this position; it is more likely to be partly tradition and partly dramatic suitability. Dialects were still not sufficiently distinguished from the standard language to have made a gulf between the two. Shakespeare used many words from his own Warwickshire dialect in his plays without any implication that they suggested rusticity or lack of sophistication. The fact that many regional pronunciations were heard daily in London may have made it difficult to isolate one for particular use in a dramatic situation. As we have seen, some dramatists did use the northern variety, but this use again may have led to Shakespeare's unwillingness to employ it because it carried with it certain attitudes. It is also important to note that

Shakespeare used no city dialect. Cockney and thieves' cant were no doubt as well known to him as to many of his contemporaries, but he did not employ them in his plays. This is not for want of occasion, for the two *Henry IV* plays depict the seamier side of London life and its characters, but Shakespeare was not intent on drawing realistic character portrayals. When he wrote comedy his humour sprang from a witty use of language rather than from regional variety.

He is quick to satirize certain types of language, but this satire does not extend to regional pronunciation, since it is not reasonable to pillory a man for the accent he was born to. Shakespeare's satire falls upon linguistic affectations, upon those uses of language one is not born to but which one adopts to cut a figure in the world. It is for this reason that he pokes fun at Osric in *Hamlet* who uses the court language of hyperbole. Hamlet mimicks this affectation mercilessly:

> Sir, his definement suffers no perdition in you, though I know to divide him inventorially would dizzy th'arithmetic of memory, and yet but yaw neither in respect of his quick sail, but in the verity of extolment, I take him to be a soul of great article, and his infusion of such dearth and rareness, as to make true diction of him, his semblable is his mirror, and who else would trace him, his umbrage nothing more. (V.ii)

In *Love's Labour's Lost* it is the pedant as well as the braggart who are satirized in their linguistic outpourings. The influence of Latin had led some teachers to apply it too rigorously to English with the result that English pronunciation was quite altered. Holofernes is made to say:

> I abhor such fanatical phantasims, such insociable and point device companions, such rackers of orthography, as to speak dout fine, when he should say doubt; det, when he should pronounce debt; d e b t, not det. ... (V.i)

But these forms of language are hardly non-standard, though they deviate from what Shakespeare considered the norm and hence from what was acceptable. In their deviation they may be said to be above rather than below that norm.

A typical feature of his representation of low-class people is malapropism, which he is the first dramatist to use in an extended and meaningful way. The reason for this may be partly his interest in words, but partly because malapropism did not carry with it the overtones of linguistic prejudice of some regional varieties. Generally the malapropism is associated with particular characters like Dogberry and

Mistress Quickly; it is not used indiscriminately as a marker of low class. In many ways this use of malapropism is not very different from the inappropriate use of Latinate words, for the one involves a misplaced morpheme and the other a misplaced context highlighting the characters's unfamiliarity with their use. The humour springs from the inappropriateness in both types. It is therefore not surprising that Mistress Quickly who uses malapropism should also refer in *Henry V* to a 'burning quotidian tertian' (II.i). This seems to refer to a fever which comes both every day and every third day, and exhibits an unfamiliarity with learned medical language. For the most part her malapropisms involve the substitution of one word by another rather than the variation in a simple morpheme. In *Henry V* she mistakes *incarnate* for *carnation* (II.iii), and in *The Merry Wives of Windsor* she uses *speciously* for *specially* (III.iv) and *canary* for *quandary* (II.ii). It is only once that her malapropism involves a regional pronunciation, and by that token it is not certain that malapropism is the right word for the usage. Instead of *vertuous* she uses *fartuous* with *ar* for *er*, which is found today in the pronunciation of *Derby*, and *f* for *v*, which is the reverse of the normal voicing of voiceless initial consonants. As such the latter could be interpreted as a low-class mistake involving unnecessary correction, for the usual low-class *v* for *f* could lead to *f* being substituted erroneously for *v*. The intention of the form is to suggest a pun on *fart*, and the pun is more important than the reasons which may have led Shakespeare to create the form. The example does illustrate how one type of linguistic comedy shades so easily into another.

Dogberry, in *Much Ado About Nothing*, produces malapropisms frequently though they are also interwoven with other kinds of linguistic aberration. His malapropisms take the form of the substitution of one morpheme for another, and this is particularly frequent with prefixes. Thus he uses *suspect* for *respect* and *opinion'd* for *pinion'd*. He can also produce meaningless words like *aspicious* for *suspicious*, though these are not frequent. His malapropisms often involve a meaning completely contrary to what he intended, as when he uses *senseless* for *sensible* and *tolerable* for *intolerable*. He also mixes an occasional individual sound, as in *vigitant* for *vigilant* and *suffigant* for *suffisant*. Another characteristic mistake is to use an utterance in an inappropriate context, almost as a kind of syntactic malapropism. Thus when taking his leave he mistakenly says 'I humbly give you leave to depart' instead of something like 'humbly take my leave'. Although these forms can be classified as malapropism, they exhibit a particular lack of familiarity with Latin words and thus suggest an attempt to elevate his speech. In Dogberry's case these corruptions are comic rather than satirical.

Rather than examine all Shakespeare's plays together I have thought it more sensible to consider a few plays in greater detail. I shall start with *Henry V*. In this play we meet a variety of characters from different parts of the country who talk with regional dialects. One of these is the Welsh captain, Fluellen. Although Welshmen appeared in English plays before Fluellen they were not given a distinctive language. Thus Rice ap Howel in Marlowe's *Edward II* is identified as Welsh by his name and by his companions, not by his language. Even Owen Glendower in *1 Henry IV* is given standard English to speak. Although Hotspur says of him 'I think there's no man speaks better Welsh' (III.i), he is satirizing his belief in astrology and magic rather than his pronunciation. Fluellen's only equal in Shakespeare's plays is Parson Evans in *The Merry Wives of Windsor*. Although Fluellen's use of regional forms is no doubt meant to be funny, as when he refers to *Alexander the Pig* (for 'big', i.e. 'great'), it is not satirical. One respects Fluellen more than Evans, for he is a true soldier even though he prefers to conduct warfare by classical precept. Everyone admires his professional qualities, and Gower says of him to Pistol:

> You thought, because he could not speak English in the native garb, he could not therefore handle an English cudgel: you find it otherwise; and henceforth let a Welsh correction teach you a good English condition. (V.i)

He thus illustrates the difference between appearance and reality, a common enough theme in Shakespeare.

The most characteristic feature of Fluellen's pronunciation is the substitution of *p* for *b* initially; *pridge, prave, prains, porn*. Others include the substitution of *f* for *v* both initially, *falorous* 'valorous', and medially, *aggriefed* and *prerogatife*. In addition he once uses *orld* for *world*, *sall* for *shall*, *asse* for *as* and *voutsafe* for *vouchsave*; and he occasionally has *Cheshu* for *Jesu*, *aunchiant* for *ancient* and *athversary* for *adversary*. The form *doo's* may be meant to indicate a regional variety, but *Godden* is colloquial rather than dialectal. Syntactically he uses *you* after imperative forms. The most frequent is *look you*, but *tell you*, *mark you* and *see you* also appear. Nouns usually appear in the plural form whether they have a singular or plural meaning. This results in apparent faulty concord, for a plural noun (in a singular meaning) takes a singular verb, as in *the mines is*. This extends to *there is* even when a true plural complement follows. Fluellen also has a number of unusual verb forms: *is pear* 'will bear', *is give* 'has given', *was have possession* 'had gained possession' and *intoxicates* for 'intoxicated' may also be part of this usage. Some unusual idioms are doubtless intended as Welsh usages. He says 'speak fewer' which means 'speak lower', for this is the form Gower uses in reply. He also says 'he is not any hurt' for 'he is not at all hurt'. Of these forms the ones that occur most regularly are *p* for *b*; the addition of *you* to imperatives; and the plural for the singular in nouns. The others occur only incidentally and were used to increase the flavour of a regional variety, though some are genuinely Welsh.

One of the other captains is the Irishman Macmorris. He is the only example of an Irish speaker in Shakespeare's works and, indeed, Irishmen do not appear frequently in the drama of the period. The contemporary attitude towards them was fairly contemptuous, though it was recognized, as in *Macbeth*, that they could be fierce soldiers. Macmorris appears only in the scene of the siege of Harfleur and so plays no significant role in the play. Like Captain Jamy, he is introduced to underline the national composition of Henry's army. Even so, the attitude towards him is more ambiguous than that towards the other dialect speakers. Even before he makes his appearance Fluellen describes him as an 'ass' who 'has no more directions in the true disciplines of the wars, look you, of the Roman disciplines, than is a puppy dog' (III.ii). But as Gower has just referred to him as 'a very valiant gentleman', Fluellen's opinion of Macmorris may be designed to tell us more about him than about Macmorris. The two prominent features of his language are the occurrence of *sh* for final *s* or *st* in *tish* 'tis', *ish* 'is' and *Chrish* 'Christ', and the frequent use of the interjection *law*. Other phonological features include *beseeched* 'besieged', *be* 'by' and *sa* 'save'. Syntactically there occurs lack of congruence in *there is throats* and in *the trumpet call us* 'the trumpet calls us'. In *the trumpet sound retreat*, the verb has a past significance for the meaning is 'has sounded'. The latter features are found usually only once and even the two prominent features are by no means regular. They are commoner when Macmorris is first introduced and tend to be replaced by standard forms as the scene progresses.

While Fluellen's opinion of Macmorris is low, his praise of Jamy the Scot is unbounded. But Jamy's part in the play is even smaller than

Macmorris's. His speeches are full of spellings designed to give a Scottish flavour to them, though in many cases it is difficult to know precisely what Shakespeare intended by them. Consider the following

> By the mess, ere theise eyes of mine take themselves to slomber, ay'll de gud service, or I'll lig i'th'grund for it; ay, or go to death: and I'll pay't as valorously as I may, that sall I suerly do that is the breff and the long: Marry, I wad full fain hear some question 'tween you tway. (III.ii)

In this speech these spellings are presumably meant to be dialectal: *Mess* 'mass', *theise* 'these', *ay* 'I', *de* 'do', *gud* 'good', *lig* 'lie', *grund* 'ground', *ay* 'yes, indeed', *sall* 'shall', *suerly* 'surely' *breff* 'brief', *wad* 'would', *tway* 'two'. Some of these forms, like *tway* and *gud*, are certainly northern and are found in other plays of the time; even *wad* is an acceptable variant for *wald*, the more usual spelling in Scotland at the time. But some words are not given a northern spelling like *go*, where one would expect *ga* or *gang*. There are also spellings which are problematical, like *de* and *theise*, for they hardly represent distinctively Scottish pronunciations. In addition Jamy's speech, like that of other regional speakers, contains many elisions like *i'th'grund* and *'tween*. Presumably Shakespeare felt that dialect had to be made colloquial as well as regional.

For the most part Shakespeare is familiar with the standard representations of the dialects he portrays in *Henry V*. He uses features commonly found in plays of his time and rarely introduces anything which suggests a particular familiarity with any dialect. His main method of dialect representation is through spellings to imply a regional accent and to a lesser extent through syntactic patterns, whereas vocabulary is not employed as a dialect device here. The other captain who makes up the quartet in *Henry V* is the Englishman Gower. It is interesting that he is not given a regional variety of speech. Clearly he could not use the peasant dialect of the southwestern type for he is socially too elevated for that; and no other dialect was suitable or sufficiently distinctive. Or possibly the use of any English regional dialect may have had the effect of making Gower look ridiculous. As it is, his standard English makes him appear the straight man among a crowd of comic regional speakers. To see him this way would be wrong, for the regional accents here are not meant to be comic, though an element of comedy cannot be excluded. The intention was probably to show Henry's glory in that his appeal could unite such a seemingly disparate army. A secondary motive was also to underline that a man's outer appearance, of which speech is a part, is no guide to his true worth. However, in Shakespeare's time, the use of dialect in productions must have dissipated these desired effects to some extent just as it does in modern productions.

French is the only foreign language found in *Henry V* and it is the only one to be corrupted in Shakespeare's plays. The general attitude towards the French in contemporary English writings was relatively unfavourable. The French were mincing dancing masters who were noted for their lascivious propensities, though they had good tailors, excellent chefs, well-bred horses and elegant ladies. All these attributes were out of place in *Henry V* where France is first the enemy and then the ally through marriage with England. Within the play the King and Queen of France use standard English, but their daughter, who becomes betrothed to Henry V, speaks only a broken English. This underlines an important aspect of non-standard language in Shakespeare and other writers. The broken English is not used naturally or to create an illusion of verisimilitude. Nothing could be more unlikely than the idea that the daughter of a king and queen who spoke excellent English and who lived in a court where others also spoke standard English should herself be almost entirely ignorant of the language. Katharine's broken English is thus designed to reveal her defencelessness, her youth and her charm, though it is hardly realistic. It is naturally not without its humour, but it has no touch of vulgarity or trait of a low-class marker.

Katharine appears in two scenes. In the first she starts to learn English from her lady-in-waiting. Here she mispronounces several of the words she tries to master. In the second scene she is wooed by Henry who conducts his courtship in English. Katharine tries to reply in her newly acquired English, though she makes many mistakes. Characteristic features include the substitution of initial *th* by *d* in *dat*, *de*; of *wh* by *w* in *wat*; and of *sh* by *s* in *sall*. Initial *h* is lost in *ave*. She uses English words incorrectly as when she says 'I cannot speak your England', with *England* used for *English*. She also uses *me* incorrectly as the subject in 'me understand well'. There is interference from French when she exclaims 'Dat is as it shall please de roi mon pere'. All these features occur only sporadically, as the occurrence of *shall* rather than *sall* in the last example shows. Alice, her lady-in-waiting, also speaks broken English. Although she is supposed to be Katharine's teacher and acts as the interpreter for Henry and Katharine, her command of English is in some respects worse than her mistress's. She uses *vat*, not *wat*, for 'what', and *Anglish* for *English*. Some of her constructions are distinctly idiosyncratic as when she says, 'Dat it is not be de fashion pour les Ladies of France; I cannot tell vat is baiser en Anglish.' It may be that Shakespeare intended a distinction between the two ladies with Alice's somewhat grosser mistakes indicating a lower social position, but since her part is relatively minor, one must be cautious about drawing such a conclusion from so few examples. It is unlikely that the average Elizabethan theatregoer would notice any difference between the two.

The lower orders in *Henry V* are represented principally by Pistol, Mistress Quickly, Nym and Bardolph, though there are also three ordinary soldiers in John Bates, Alexander Court and Michael Williams. The soldiers use standard English as do Nym and Bardolph. Indeed the language of these characters is as correct as that found in the mouths of socially more elevated people because Shakespeare was not interested in giving them a colloquial language. It is noticeable that they use very few oaths or other asseverations, often a sign of colloquial usage. Indeed Fluellen and Macmorris use far more oaths than any of these more ordinary people. Mistress Quickly also uses a relatively unmarked form of language though she does, as we have seen, indulge in malapropism. In addition she occasionally uses *a'* for 'he' and elided forms like *o'th'tide*. These latter were probably intended to indicate a colloquial level of language though they can be paralleled in poetic speeches which are in a more elevated vein. The problem is to decide how such elisions are to be understood. The position is complicated because we have no holograph by Shakespeare and so have no yardstick by which to judge how far the early seventeenth-century quartos and folios represent his spelling intentions. Even if we could be certain that they did represent his intentions accurately there is the question of interpreting what he meant by such forms. In general it seems best to accept that they were meant to indicate a less formal language only if they occur frequently in the speech of an individual character and if they occur in association with other features of non-standard language. Thus the Hostess's malapropisms and Fluellen's dialect support an interpretation that the contractions in their language are significant.

Pistol's language is very far from what we might call colloquial, though it is quite individual. Although, like most lower-class characters he mostly uses prose, he occasionally relapses into verse:

> O braggard vile and damned furious wight!
> The grave doth gape, and doting death is near;
> Therefore exhale. (II.i)

What is of interest in this passage is the use of half-line units with either two or three stresses. Frequently the stresses are linked by alliteration. The language is quite elevated, with many adjectives and the placing of some adjectives after their nouns in a poetic fashion. Although the above passage is frequently printed as verse, Pistol's next speech is printed as either prose or verse in modern editions though it has exactly the same rhythmical pattern:

> An oath of mickle might; and fury shall abate.
> Give me thy fist, thy fore-foot to me give;
> Thy spirits are most tall.

In this and other examples Shakespeare reverts to the traditional alliterative style which hovers on the brink between prose and verse. But since alliteration had gone down in the world since the fifteenth century, its use by Pistol is indicative of his status. As such it undermines his attempts to cut a figure through his language. This he attempts through his measured, if somewhat staccato, prose, his parallelisms, his classical allusions, his somewhat archaic syntax and his Latin and French forms. As part of the archaic syntax we may note the position of the object in 'I thee defy again' and 'thy fore-foot to me give'. His Latin and French are not perfect. Thus he uses the expression *couple a gorge* for *couper la gorge*. He sometimes overreaches himself in his use of English and produces absurdities as in 'his heart is fracted and corroborate' (II.i). As a corrupter of language he comes into his own in Act IV, scene iv, where he captures Monsieur le Fer. He puts various questions to his captive who does not understand his English and replies to him in French. Pistol misunderstands what is said in French by seizing on certain words and taking them to be English. Thus *moi* is taken to be a 'moy', a unit of money, and *bras* 'arm' is interpreted as 'brass'. This is the more usual comic approach to language. But for the most part Pistol is not a corrupter of language; he inflates it in a way that can hardly be described as colloquial. This is an important point to emphasize since so many critics claim that the language of the low-class characters in Shakespeare is based on the rhythms of everyday language.

Henry V is an unusual play in its non-standard language. Although Shakespeare uses many of the stock dialect features found in contemporary representations of provincial speech, he does so with discretion, and he does not use the language primarily for comedy or satire, but for wider purposes. The representatives of the outlying regions of

Great Britain, like their counterparts in the Old English *The Battle of Maldon*, signify the unification of the country under a particular leader and their regional speech merely reminds the audience of the diversity of cultural backgrounds found in these islands – a diversity which needs a strong central power to fuse into one. Similarly the mistakes made by the French princess underline her innocence and so help to suggest that it is love rather than political expedience which welds the marriage of England and France. This is one play in which linguistic diversity is used almost straight; one must say 'almost' for, however much one might wish that deviation in language was not comic, it is not possible to avoid comedy entirely and Shakespeare does not try to do so. In its use of regional dialects *Henry V* may be compared with *The Merry Wives of Windsor* because many of the same characters and the speech forms occur in both.

In *The Merry Wives of Windsor* the Welsh speaker is Sir Hugh Evans, a parson, and the Frenchman is Doctor Caius, a physician, two professions which were frequently pilloried by satirists. Evans has many of the same linguistic characteristics as Fluellen. He uses *p* for *b* and *f* for *v;* he uses plurals for singular forms in the nouns; and he employs an abstract noun when a count noun would be more appropriate. In addition he uses a variety of forms which mark out his speech as being very different from Fluellen's. Thus he says *per-lady* 'by our Lady', *possitable* 'possibly', *the three party* 'the third party', *vizaments* 'advisements' and *her father will make her* 'her father will leave her'. He replaces final *d* by *t* in *goot, Got* 'good, God' and he omits initial *w* commonly in *'ork*, and *j* occasionally in *Got 'udge* 'God judge'. A typical example of Evans's language with its frequent non-standard forms is:

> It is a fery discretion answer; save the fall is in the 'ord 'dissolutely': the 'ort is, according to our meaning, 'resolutely'. (I.i)

The language is different from Fluellen's, for the latter uses one or two prominent features to give his speech the flavour of Welsh, though without creating a feeling of vulgarity or excess. But with Evans, Shakespeare is prepared to exploit the low comedy of a Welsh voice as much as he can. It is part of the grotesque portrait that Evans plays a part which leads him to dress up as a *jack-an-apes* or monkey in the final scene where his language comes in for some unfavourable comment from Falstaff. For when Evans tries to pronounce 'cheese' and 'butter', Falstaff retorts:

'Seese' and 'putter'? Have I lived to stand at the taunt of one that makes fritters of English? This is enough to be the decay of lust and late-walking through the realm. (V.v)

Doctor Caius does not have such a large part as Evans and his language is more difficult to interpret. Katharine made mistakes in her English in a quite predictable and hence understandable way. Caius uses an Anglo-French which is often unintelligible as it stands in the First Folio. The problem is to decide whether Shakespeare intended some of this to be gibberish or whether what he wrote has been corrupted by compositors. His very first speech is:

Vat is you sing? I do not like des-toyes: pray you go and vetch me in my closet, unboyteen verd: a box, a green-a box: do intend vat I speak? a green-a box. (I.iv)

Here we may assume that *des-toyes* is a Frenchman's way of saying 'these toys', but an interpretation of *unboyteen verd* is less easy. The Arden editor accepts Craig's emendation *une boitine verde* 'a small green box', though *boitine* is an otherwise unrecorded form. Other editors keep the Folio reading and accept that this is gibberish. Some features of Caius's speech like initial *v* for *wh* are found in Alice's, but not in Katharine's, language; but neither lady uses the suffix *a* as in *green-a*. This reminds one of Skelton's non-standard forms. Caius also has here the malapropism *intend* for *attend* with the common substitution of one morpheme by another. In view of these many mistakes, which are not necessarily characteristic of French speakers of English, and in view of Caius's general portrayal and role in the play, we must conclude that these features were intended to be humorous, even grotesque. Caius is made the butt of cruel laughter and his language is made very different from Katharine's in *Henry V*.

Throughout the rest of Shakespeare's output there is little non-standard English. There are some dialectal words here and there and there may well be puns based on a non-standard pronunciation, but these forms were meant to be built on allowable variants rather than as examples of a deviant language. The occasional use of a dialectal form or pronunciation is not significant; it is only the consistent use of non-standard language by a character which can be regarded as evidence of a desire to exploit variation. Consequently, one is forced to admit that in view of Shakespeare's output it is the paucity of non-standard language which is the most telling element about its use.

Shakespeare's interest in language was largely confined to wit and satire, with the former being built round puns and the latter round affected language. When it does occur, non-standard language is indicated principally through simple pronunciation variants or through idioms typical of a region. The vocabulary and syntax are rarely significant in their deviance. The reason for this must be that the vocabulary was still being enlarged on all sides to such an extent that it was impossible to decide what was standard and what not. As for syntax, grammar was yet insufficiently codified and taught for standard forms to have been accepted. Nevertheless, it has been suggested that in the storm scene of *King Lear* the king's rage and uncertain temper are reflected in his language which, it is claimed, contains grammatical solecisms. Thus in 'Nor rain, wind, thunder, fire, are my daughters' (III.ii.15) the *are* is said to be a solecisim for *is* which is grammatically correct.[1] This is, however, quite unlikely, for many examples of a similar lack of congruence occur frequently in Shakespeare and his contemporaries. No audience would think twice about usages such as this one as the language had not yet developed in a way that would let them do so. In any case Shakespeare for his part was more interested in elevating the language than in non-standard or colloquial forms. These he used only occasionally when a particular reason demanded.

1. A.C. Partridge, *The Language of Renaissance Poetry* (London: Deutsch, 1971), p.205.

Chapter 5

THE SEVENTEENTH CENTURY

☙☙☙☙☙☙

THE EXUBERANCE of Elizabethan literature brought an inevitable reaction. The feeling current in the Elizabethan period that the language needed enriching through extensive borrowing from foreign languages gave way to the view that those gains now required to be ordered and systematized. Bombastic rhetoric yielded place to a more restrained use of language. Dictionaries were compiled to explain hard words in English, and grammars explained the principles of English usage. The question of what spelling was suitable for English was much debated. The standard language, which now had a literature to give it more body and tradition, thus became increasingly subject to codification, though the main impetus in this respect came only in the eighteenth century. English was increasingly a source of pride, and this made people more conscious of the need to preserve the merits of the language; self-appointed guardians of the genius of the language appeared. Another important element in the gradual change in linguistic attitudes was the puritan movement, which encouraged the use of a simpler style so that the word of God could easily be understood by all and which frowned on the grosser comedy of the preceding age. The cultivation of a plainer style was also fostered by the growth of science, which was interested in truth rather than fancy. Thomas Sprat in his *History of the Royal Society* (1667) shows how the Royal Society was foremost in propagating a new style suitable for scientists.

If, on the one hand, a plainer language was increasingly in vogue, on the other hand, knowledge of the varieties of English was becoming more common. Among the more important writers on language from the early seventeenth century was Alexander Gil, who was born in Lincolnshire in 1564/5 and whose *Logonomia Anglica* appeared in 1619 and again in 1621. In this work he attempted to provide a systematic survey of the English dialects, though how far he had actually studied them is a matter for speculation. He may have repeated the common dialectisms of his age and certainly his attitude towards dialects reflects

93

contemporary opinions. Thus he dismissed the Somerset dialect as particularly barbarous. Since the south-western dialect was the peasant language in Elizabethan drama, Gil's dismissal surely reflects that situation. The features he selects are those typically found in the stage dialects too. Of the southern dialect he notes the following characteristics: *v* for *f* in *vil* (for *fil*) and occasionally *f* for *v* in *fineger* (for *vineger*); and *z* for *s* in *zing* (for *sing*). He also notes the forms *ich* (for *I*), *cham* (for *I am*), *chil* (for *I wil*), and *chi vor yi* (for *I warant you*). All these types are found in *King Lear* as we saw in the last chapter and may have been taken by Gil from such a source. Even so he records more about the various dialects than could be found in the drama, though the dialectisms he notes may have been common knowledge in the London of his time. An interesting feature of Gil's book is his description of the language of those he calls the *Mopsae*. They are the London speakers who affect certain pronunciations in order to be modish. These pronunciations derive for the most part from Essex and exhibit early forms of what was to become the accepted pronunciation in London. They were abhorred by the more traditional speakers such as Gil thus indicating that people were becoming more conscious of such differences and concerned about affected pronunciations. The *Mopsae*, according to Gil, pronounce their vowels in a thin way; as examples he gives *deans* for *dans* (dance) and *kiver* for *kuver* (cover). Although the exact sounds intended by these spellings are disputed, it is clear that the vowels used by the *Mopsae* were higher than those approved by Gil. Whereas up till now all variation had been regional and usually, by implication, vulgar, in the seventeenth and eighteenth centuries focus was directed towards genteel speech and its peculiarities.

It is for this reason that the traditional south-western dialect of low-class or peasant speech disappears in the early seventeenth century. Although it may have become so stereotyped to have lost its usefulness, that cannot be a sufficient answer since most other regional dialects disappear from the drama as well. An interesting example of what could happen as a result is presented by *A Jovial Crew* by Richard Brome, probably written in 1640. In this play not only are there beggars, but also some of the gentry dress up as beggars in order to escape from undesirable matches. Their language is intended to be distinctive and various characters point to the differences. Randall, a servant of Oldrents, says of the beggars' language 'I understand their canting' (II.ii.287); and Oldrents himself says to a friend who has temporarily adopted some of the features of the beggars' language 'Pray forbear that language' (II.ii.303). Some of the respectable characters may occasionally adopt some of the phrases from the beggars' cant when they refer to aspects of the beggars' life for which they had no adequate expressions. The beggars, for their part, usually make use of this cant, though by no means invariably so. In set pieces, such as songs, it occurs regularly, but in ordinary conversation it tends to disappear. A typical example of the beggars' cant is provided by the song in II.ii.

> Here, safe in our skipper, let's cly off our peck,
> And bowse in defiance o'th'harman-beck.
> Here's pannum and lap, and good poplars of yarrum,
> To fill up the crib, and to comfort the quarron.
> Now bowse a round health to the go-well and come-well
> Of Cisley Bumtrinket that lies in the strummel.
> Now bowse a round health to the go-well and come-well
> Of Cisley Bumtrinket that lies in the strummel.

The song is notable because there is no attempt to indicate variant or low-class pronunciation or even syntax. The burden of indicating the level of language falls upon the vocabulary alone. But this vocabulary is essentially a literary one which has been taken from various books. Among them are Thomas Harman's *A Caveat or Warning for Common Cursitors* (1573), Thomas Dekker's *English Villainies* (1638) and *The Bellman of London* (1608). All of these were available in Brome's time. In the song quoted, Harman provided *cly* 'seize, take', *pannum* 'bread', *lap* 'buttermilk' and *quarron* 'body'; Dekker provided *skipper* 'barn', *peck* 'meat', *bowse* 'swill, drink', *harman-beck* 'constable' and *poplars of yarrom* 'milk pottage'; and *strummel* is a general canting word for 'straw'. This song represents a literary exercise in creating a new language from the evidence available in other books about low-class society. No one can have spoken like this; and Brome has not bothered to listen to low-class speakers himself. Because of this he was forced to rely upon vocabulary which was the aspect of language most commented upon in descriptions of various cants. However, this reliance upon vocabulary is a new and significant development which reflects the growing consciousness of words and their connotations. Increasingly words will be divided into categories that are appropriate for certain levels of language, and the use of the appropriate diction is an important element in Augustan propriety. It is the absence of this propriety in Elizabethans like Shakespeare which so offended Augustan critics like Johnson.

The gentry who adopt the disguise of beggars in *A Jovial Crew* also try to adopt some of the features of their cant. Their adopted language rarely reaches the same depth as that of the real beggars. So much so indeed that one of the characters who hears it is forced to say:

> They beg as high as the man-beggar I met withal! Sure the beggars are all mad today, or bewitched into a language they understand not. The spirits of some decay'd gentry talk in 'em sure. (III.i.319-22)

The audience was evidently supposed to see the difference between true and false beggars' cant.

As for colloquialisms, there are the occasional *Psew, Pseugh* and *Fagh*. Otherwise a character like Randall the servant can say 'Do'ee hear 'em in the barn?' (II.ii.121). The *'em* is common enough from now onwards in plays and novels and was used by characters of all ranks. The *do'ee* is less common, though Tallboy who is in love with the Justice's niece can use the variant *d'ee*. Oliver, the Justice's son, can also use less formal language, as in

> What the devil ails the fellow, trow? Why! Why, Master Tallboy, my cousin Tallboy that should'st ha' been, art not asham'd to cry at this growth? And for a thing that's better lost than found, a wench? (IV.i.3-6)

The elided forms represented through apostrophes are doubtless meant to represent an informal speaking manner appropriate to all levels of society; they imply no reflection on a speaker's level of education or breeding. They indicate rather the growing stabilization of the orthography which allowed writers to make significant use of written forms such as these.

With the prevailing tendency towards propriety and appropriateness in language it is not surprising that there is not much exploitation of non-standard language in poetry or prose at this time. After the experiments in prose narrative found in such works as Thomas Nashe's *The Unfortunate Traveller*, the novel remained relatively undeveloped during the seventeenth century. Writers like Bunyan were too deeply immersed in the language of the Bible to experiment with language of a more colloquial kind. Poets, for their part, restricted themselves to particular genres such as the epic, heroic and satire. For the first two varieties the dictates of the genre demanded a lofty style, as for example in *Paradise Lost*, which naturally militated against the use of non-standard language. The participants were too noble and even those who were evil were still noble in spirit. Their portrayal could not be undermined by an inappropriate diction in their own speech. It is true that Milton does occasionally use a dialect word like *scrannel* (*Lycidas* 123) which is still found in Lincolnshire, and because he imitated Spenser he could also make use of archaisms like *frore*. But these, like the dialect words, are rarely employed in a consistent manner. They are merely means of extending the vocabulary in a colourful way and not an attempt to exploit non-standard forms as such. More important in many ways are Milton's experiments with spelling to indicate the particular sound or emphasis he required. His differentiation between *hee* and *he*, and *their* and *thir*, are well known and point to an awareness of stressed and unstressed forms in the language and to the ability to indicate that difference satisfactorily in writing. Writing was now sufficiently regularized for such variations to be significant and for others to regard them as marked. Milton's insistence on spelling like *walkt*, *wrauth* and *haralds* indicates how particular he was that a certain sound was used in recitations of his work, for he was the last great English poet who paid particular attention to the oral performance of his poems. From now on subtle variations in spelling become more important in the representation of deviant forms of language.

In the last variety of poetry, satire, there might seem to be much greater scope for non-standard language, but in practice this rarely comes about. Although the poets of this time were quite clear of the difference between high and low styles and frequently used these styles in particular types of poem, the language they used for the low style was rarely drawn from non-standard varieties. The high style appropriate to epic and heroic poems had become so restricted that the language available for the low style was much wider than one might have expected. Even so, the type that was exploited was grotesque or incongruous rather than specifically non-standard. The most famous satire of the period is Samuel Butler's *Hudibras*, the first part of which appeared in 1663. Butler uses cant idioms and unseemly diction as well as doggerel and deformed rhyme. He also makes use of traditional proverbial lore and folk wisdom. There is no attempt to reproduce a living language. Butler is intent on creating a particular style which will serve the intentions of his poem, for he wanted to point to the gap between reality and pretention; and his poem is a comment on the hypocrisy of the age. In this the grotesque forms of language help to highlight the difference between what is said and what is meant. Hence he perverts language and places incongruous elements in proximity with each other. In many ways he resembles Skelton in this, though he rarely uses the same range of language. A typical passage from *Hudibras* is:

> A *Persian* Emp'rour whip'd his Grannum
> The Sea, his Mother *Venus* came on;
> And hence some Rev'rend men approve
> Of *Rosemary* in making *Love*.
> As skilful *Coopers* hoop their Tubs
> With *Lydian* and with *Phrygian* Dubs. (II.i.845-50)

Here there are two words worth comment. *Grannum* is a colloquial variant of *Grandam* and is occasionally found elsewhere in literature. It is used because it seems out of place when set beside a Persian emperor. The other is *dubs*, a word used in the sense of 'a blow struck as in drumming' only by Butler: it is likely to be a nonce word. The association with drumming again fits ill with the classical reference to *Lydian* and *Phrygian*. There are many words of a colloquial nature in the poem. Words for a stupid person or simpleton include *buzzard, owl, calf* and *goose*; long, curled locks of hair are *heart-breakers;* the cleft in the buttocks is the *nock*; and food is *belly-timber*. Many of the words used have literary and political rather than colloquial associations. It is partly for this reason that the non-standard forms in this poem are lexical; there is no attempt to indicate variant pronunciation or syntactic usages. Butler also uses many apostrophes as in *Emp'rour* and *Rev'rend*, and these give a colloquial feel to his poem. Such forms are met with in other poems of the time, though they are more frequent in *Hudibras* than elsewhere. Since shortened forms were beginning to be frowned on, we may assume that Butler introduced the elisions here as a mark of the low style.

With the linguistic attitudes that prevailed in the seventeenth century, it is hardly surprising that most examples of non-standard language are to be found in the drama. With the restoration of the monarchy in 1660 the theatre flourished once again, and a stream of plays were written and performed. Many of these were in the French manner, partly because of Charles II's exile in France and partly because of the development of classicism. Many plays were written in a heroic style about classical subjects, and in these there was little room for non-standard language. Even the comedies which were largely built round the sexual intrigues of the courtly gallants contained less non-standard language than one might expect. Thus the servants of these gallants rarely use a non-standard form since such language would hardly re-dound to the credit of their masters. Occasionally there is a contrast in the plays between the sophisticated life of the town and the deprived culture of the country, and this can promote some non-standard language. The gallants themselves affect a certain style of speech, and this also needs to be considered here. Because of the French character of late seventeenth-century London life, it is natural that French speakers should appear in some plays; and from time to time regional speakers appear as well. Hence in the rest of this chapter we shall have to deal with four types of language: that of unsophisticated country folk; the affectations of the nobility; the language of foreign speakers; and the language of regional speakers.

The contrast between the fashionable town and the unsophisticated country can be represented by Wycherley's *The Country Wife*, first performed in 1675. The country wife is Margery Pinchwife, who is recently married to a jealous middle-aged man who fondly believes that he can keep his wife ignorant of town ways. Not unnaturally the wife wishes to savour the delights of the town to the full. She apparently comes from Hampshire and has never been to London before, but she does not use any dialect. Indeed there is little in her language to mark her out as different from the other characters in the play. She addresses her husband as *bud*, *dear* and *love* which are forms of ad-dress not employed by the fashionable. Her exclamations like *pish* and *Jeminy* are also unique to her in the play. She is given rather more elliptical forms like *ha'n't* 'have not' than the other characters and she uses forms like *beholding* for *beholden*. She also uses the prefix *a-* in such words as *a-walking* and *a-weary*. Her vocabulary occasionally ex-hibits a colloquial flavour as in *toused* and *moused*, both words imply-ing rude handling of a woman, *froppish* 'peevish' and *nangered* 'angered'. None of these words can be claimed to be only colloquial, for they are used in other works in contexts which suggest that they had only slight connotations of colloquiality. But a word like *hugeously*, which she also uses, is often put into the mouth of un-fashionable people. There is then a slight attempt to discriminate the language of the country wife from that of the other characters, but it is little more than a token. Most examples are lexical, and there are few words which indicate a different pronunciation and few syntactic corruptions. In this respect Wycherley is quite typical of his time.

In Congreve's *Love for Love* there are two characters who have been brought up outside the town environment and who are to be regarded as rough diamonds in the fashionable world. These are Ben, the younger son of Sir Sampson, and Miss Prue. The latter uses words which offend the town ladies. She addresses her mother as *mother* instead of *madam*, and she uses the word *smocks* whereas true ladies refer only to *linnen*. These alternatives are commented on in the play (II.10). Miss Prue also uses the form *an't* 'am not', though otherwise her language is unexceptional. Congreve merely notes her lack of education in the first scene in which she appears with fashionable ladies and then lets her speak an acceptable variety. Ben, however, has rather more examples of non-standard language in his speech. He has been brought up partly at sea and partly in the country. He uses familiar forms of names, items of vocabulary not found in the speech of the other characters like *an* 'if', *thof* 'though', *may-hap* 'perhaps', *dirty dowdy* 'stupid girl' and *woundy* 'excessively', and archaic forms of some verbs. Thus he says 'You ben't marry'd again, Father, be you?' (III.6) with *be* for 'are'. Words like *say* have a present plural in *-n* instead of an endingless form, so that Ben says *we sayn*. He also uses the form *an't*. Elision of *him* to *'n* is common as in *let'n* and *giv'n*, and elision of *his* to *'s* appears in *tell'n so to's Face*. He uses idioms like *a stern a* for 'behind' and *a going* for 'going'. Otherwise he, like Miss Prue, does not have a large element of non-standard language. With Ben we may assume that Congreve intended the audience to think of this language as being provincial and nautical rather than low-class. Even so, it is doubtful whether he had a particular region in mind as the home of Ben's language. The audience was not expected to localize the language; they were merely nudged into noticing that Ben's language had some distinctive features.

The plays of this period are mainly about fashionable people, and their language inevitably reflects this, particularly in the use of expletives. Although the language used by such people is generally unremarkable, occasionally a feature is included to remind us of the social situation or pretensions of the people. Expressions like *i'gad*, *demm*, *udswoons*, *'sdeath*, *'slife* and *oons* recur frequently. They are the mark of the fashionable man about town. Occasionally a character is given a fashionable pronunciation to make him ridiculous or to suggest his social vanity. This applies to Lord Foppington in Vanbrugh's *The Relapse*, first produced in 1696. Amanda says of him

> Now it moves my pity more than my mirth, to see a man whom nature has made a fool, be so very industrious to pass for an ass. (II.1)

Here she no doubt referred to his language as much as to the rest of his behaviour. The principal feature of his foppish pronunciation is the substitution of *a* for *o* in words like *stap* 'stop', *packet* 'pocket', *praper* 'proper', *naw* 'now', *pawnd* 'pound', *lard* 'lord' and *tartures* 'tortures'. *God* also appears as *Gad* even outside expletives. This feature is introduced regularly and although it may have had some truth to life, it seems exaggerated in the examples found in the play. Once Lord Foppington uses *jedge* for 'judge'. He is fond of exclamations like *stap my vitals and rat me*, and these are probably to be regarded as fashionable colloquialisms of the time. He uses the form *a'n't* 'are not' as well as the odd French expression. His vocabulary includes a few words like *pad-nag* 'horse' which may have been slang at the time. Lord Foppington carries to excess a tendency which is inherent in many fashionable characters of the time, but there are few who can match his extremes of pronunciation. That his language is non-standard may be accepted from the way the other characters react to him and the way he speaks.

Lord Foppington's language could be regarded as fashionable cant. A different variety of cant is found in Thomas Shadwell's *The Squire of Alsatia* of 1688. This is thieves' cant which an ignorant country gentleman, Belfond senior, is persuaded to accept as the fashionable language of the town. The problem with this cant was the difficulty of understanding it. So Shadwell included 'An Explanation of the Cant' at the beginning of the printed edition. This consists of a glossary of some of the difficult words, among which are

> *Prig, Prigster.* Pert Coxcombs.
> *A Put.* One who is easily wheadled and cheated.
> *Megs.* Guineas.
> *A Tattmonger.* A Cheat at Dice.

Naturally the audience did not have this vocabulary with them at the play, so Shadwell often gives an explanation within the play for the terms have to be taught to Belfond senior. Exchanges like the following occur:

> *Cheatly* My noble Heir I salute thee: The Cole is coming, and shall be brought in this Morning.
> *Belfond sen. Cole?* Why 'tis Summer, I need no firing now. Besides I intend to burn Billets.
> *Cheatly* My lusty Rustick, learn and be instructed. *Cole* is in the language of the Witty, Money. The *Ready*, the *Rhino*; thou shalt be *Rhinocerical*, my Lad thou shalt.

Naturally this cant consists simply of vocabulary items and was, no doubt, culled by Shadwell from one of the glossaries of cant available at this time. It reminds one of Brome's use of cant, but it was not an experiment that was repeated, probably because of the difficulties of intelligibility and the general hostility of the time towards cant.

Because of the fashion for French culture it is not surprising that the only foreigners who appear at this time are Frenchmen. They are usually the servants or teachers of those who want to cut a social figure and consequently they are often given a broken English, for in this way the affectation of the master or mistress seems to be accentuated by the comic speech of the servant. Those with social pretensions naturally have French valets or maids. It is thus quite natural that Lord Foppington should have a French valet, La Varole. His role is not very large and so he has little to say. What he does say is uttered in broken English, the most characteristic feature of which is the substitution of *d* for initial *th* as in *de* 'the'. Lady Fancyfull's maid, just called madamoiselle, in Vanbrugh's *The Provok'd Wife*, has a larger part. Vanbrugh has altered certain aspects of her pronunciation, though the rest of her language is left relatively untouched. Her speech is thus a mixture of predominantly standard language with the occasional unusual pronunciation. Some of the changes in pronunciation are, however, not even regarded as characteristic of French speakers of English. Thus madamoiselle replaces initial *b* with *p* and medial *d* with *t*. The result is

> My opinion pe, matam, dat your latyship naver look so well in your life. (I.2)

where the language is mostly standard, though there are some markers of a foreign speaker which are not specifically those of French. Other features of her speech are *d* for initial and medial *th* in *den* 'than', but *t* for final *th* in *trute* 'truth'; *s* for *ch* in *Frense* 'French; *v* for *wh* in *ven* 'when'; *e* for *a* in *den* 'than'; and *ee* for *i* in *leetel* 'little'. The latter two occur once each. She uses several French words like *eclat, justement comme ca*, and occasionally breaks out into whole sentences in French. Syntactically she uses *me* as a subject, *no* as the negative marker in *I no eat, be* for the first person singular of the present indicative of 'to be', and the present for the preterite in *look* in the quotation above. Idioms like 'set de fire in de house' may also be intended to give a French flavour to her speech.

Dufoy, the servant of Sir Frederick Frollick in Etherege's *The Comical Revenge or Love in a Tub* (1664), has a different form of broken English. His language is distorted more than that of most French people in English plays. He has a rather bigger role than is usual, for he is the descendant of the pert servants in Roman plays. He is more than a pale reflection of his master's social snobbery and very much a character in his own right who adds considerably to the comedy of the play. A typical example of his speech is this:

> Good-mor', good-mor' to you vorshippé; me am alvay ready to attendé your vorshippé, and your vorshippé alvay ready to beaté and to abusé me; you vare drunké de lasté nighté, and my head aké today morningé. See you here, if my brainé have no ver good raison to counsel you, and to mindé your bus'nessé. (I.2)

From this it can be seen that Etherege gives Dufoy the habit of adding a final sounded *e*, presumably [i:], on many words, particularly nouns and verbs. This is a personal idiosyncrasy which has little basis in French speakers' attempts to speak English, though it reminds one of some modern varieties of pidgin. However, he omits final *y* in *ver* 'very' (but not in *ready*) and the final syllable in *Good-mor'* 'good morrow'. He replaces *w* with *v* initially and medially: *vare* 'ware' and *alvay* 'always'. He uses *me* as the subject instead of *I*, omits the unstressed medial syllable in *bus'nesse*, and uses the French spelling, and presumably hence the French pronunciation, in *raison* 'reason'. What pronunciation is implied by the spelling *vare* 'were' is far from clear. These examples are typical of his speech and are repeated elsewhere, though naturally other features also occur.

From these characters it will be appreciated that French speakers of English were given a language that was grossly distorted in some particulars, but not in others. There was no regularity in the features employed, though some, like *d* for *th* and *v* for *w(h)*, are fairly standard. Characters of this type are used either for comedy or for social satire, and hence their speech is made a little grotesque. It was not intended to be naturalistic.

Whereas the French are often portrayed as cunning and experienced in intrigue, to the Irish is given the role of the honest servant who tries to help his master in a way which always adds to his problems. The prototype of this Irish comic character is Teague in Sir Robert Howard's comedy *The Committee* (1665). According to a family tradition Sir Robert was in Ireland when he had occasion to send a servant, an Irishman, to England with important papers needed to free his son who had been imprisoned by Parliament. When the messenger returned to Dublin, he did not go straight to his master to inform him of the happy release of his son. Instead he spent the time telling everyone else the news and getting drunk to celebrate. It was only after he had been back a few days that Sir Robert caught up with him. He was so amused by the behaviour of his servant that he used him as a model for Teague in his play. This part appealed to some of the best actors of the time, and it is clear from Pepys's *Diary* and other contemporary records that the public was charmed with Teague's antics. Other dramatists decided that an Irishman was a must in a play, and usually they borrowed the name as well. In *The Committee* Teague does not have an Irish accent, but he does have Irish turns of phrase. He adds tags like *that there are* or *that I cannot* at the end of clauses as in 'I cannot tell what to do else, by my soul, that I cannot'. He uses *be* for 'are' as the plural of the present indicative of the verb 'to be'. He says 'I have went and gone' which was doubtless considered incorrect at the time, though not necessarily Irish. Other expressions and expletives like 'forty cows, and the devil a bull amongst them' probably fall into the same category.

Sir Robert's example was followed by Shadwell in *The Lancashire Witches* (1681). This play contains an Irish priest appropriately named Teague O Divelly. Unlike his namesake in *The Committee* this Teague is given an Irish pronunciation, though the language he speaks is not a very accurate representation of an Irish speaker. His opening speech is:

> Arrah, and please ty Oorship, I am come here to dis plaash to maake a visitt unto thee; Dosht dou not know me, Joy? (Act III)

He omits initial *w* before a long vowel in *Oorship*, though elsewhere before short vowels it appears as *v*, as in *vid* 'with'. Initial *th* appears as *d* in *dis* and *dou*, but as *t* in *ty* 'thy'. Whether spelt *s* or *c(e)* in standard English [s] is usually written *sh* as in *plaash*, but not in *dis* 'this'. It is not clear whether *tt* in *visitt* is meant to be significant. Vowels are frequently doubled, presumably to indicate a long sound as in *Oorship*, *plaash* and *maake*. This representation is rather erratic and never affects digraphs such as *please*. The vowel most consistently doubled is *a*, though it is not in *Arrah*. This expletive and the use of *Joy* as a term of endearment are no doubt meant as Irishisms. The priest is a buffoon and his use of dialect is intended both as a help to the comedy and as a thrust against Catholicism.

Although the portrayal of an Irish speaker is unsatisfactory, the play exhibits a good example of the Lancashire dialect. This is particularly noteworthy because this play is modelled on Richard Brome and Thomas Heywood's *The Late Lancashire Witches* which combines northern and north-west Midland features in a dialect which is substantially different from Shadwell's and also further away from the modern dialect. Presumably Shadwell used his local knowledge to improve the representation of the dialect, and as he is known to have had strong links with Chadderton he was probably familiar with the East Lancashire dialect. The dialect is used principally by Clod, whose name reveals his country origins. It is also used by Thomas o Georges, another rustic, and by Young Hartford, the heir of the hospitable and gentlemanly Sir Edward Hartfoot. His son, however, is described as 'a clownish, sordid country fool that loves nothing but drinking ale and country sports'. The same dialect is used in *The Squire of Alsatia* where is it spoken by Lolpoop, whose accent is contrasted with the cant of Whitefriars. From all these speakers we can see that Shadwell used dialect as part of his social comment. It is used by those who have not been exposed to refined society and who put country pursuits before intellectual and moral improvements. As such it is found in the sons of gentlemen as much as among country people. It is not, however, used by the witches or even by the chambermaid. How far the average audience understood the language is uncertain, for they may have echoed Doubty's comment on Clod's language: 'The fellow's mad, I neither understand his words, nor his Sence' (Act I).

Lexical forms of interest include *buggarts* 'evil spirits', *clemd* 'very cold', *lone* 'lane', *plec* 'place', *powts* 'young birds', *threped* 'argued' and *wons* 'dwells', which can all be attested from the modern dialect. Also of interest are the forms *mun* 'must', *sin* 'since' and *an* 'if', though these are not confined to Lancashire. The present plural of verbs usually has an *-(e)n*, as in *yeow shoulden* and *yeow seen*. 'Have' appears as *ha* in the first person singular present indicative and as *a* when an auxiliary. The future can be expressed by *'st* as in *yeou'st be welcome* and *ay'st talk*. The plural *-n* of nouns is preserved in *eyne*. As for sounds, ME [i:] is written *ai* or *ei*, as in *mail* 'mile', though how that sound was supposed to differ from the sound heard in London at the end of the seventeenth century is not clear. Short vowels are to be understood in *tack* 'take' and *brocken* 'broken'. When *a* is followed by a nasal, it appears as *o* in *mon* 'man', *con* 'can' and incorrectly in *strongers* 'strangers'. Forms with *a* like *can* also appear. The use of *aw* for *ow* in *dawn* 'down' and similar words is inappropriate for this dialect and it echoes the fashionable pronunciation of those like Lord Foppington. ME *i* before palatal *h* appears as *ee*, representing [i:], in *theegh* 'thigh' and *neeght* 'night', though Shadwell has forgotten to drop the *gh*. The pronoun 'you' appears as *yeow* or *yeou*, and initial *e* sometimes appears as *ye* as in *Yedward* 'Edward'. Among the consonants *l* is dropped frequently. In *aw* 'all' and *caw'd* 'called' the *w* probably signifies the lengthening of *a* caused by the fall of *l*; but it is not dropped in *talk*. Finally *l* is lost in *fow* 'foul', *steepo* 'steeple' and *angee* 'angel'. Assimilation of *lv* to *ll* is found in *yoursells* 'yourselves'. Final *d* is unvoiced to *t* in *hont* 'hand' and similar words. Initial *qu* appears as *wh* in *wheint, whaint* 'quaint' and *whean* 'quean, woman'. A few syncopated forms like *dee'l* 'devil' also occur. Although the representation of the dialect is far from perfect, it remains one of the best to be found by this period. Shadwell has gone much further than the average dramatist in his use of dialect and we can only assume that his knowledge of the area encouraged him to show his expertise. But, as already noted, from the audience's point of view he may have gone too far.

One final play from this period should be mentioned. This is *A Journey to London*, a fragment of a play by Vanbrugh, which, after his death, was completed by Cibber and renamed *The Provok'd Husband*. The play deals with the arrival in London of a country knight and his entourage, some of whom speak with a north country accent which in most respects appears to be modelled on that in Shadwell's *The Lancashire Witches*. The daughter of the knight, Miss Betty, gives some idea of the dialect when she says:

> What a difference there is, between your way, and our country companions; one of them would have said, What, you are aw gooing to the playhouse then? Yes, says we, won't you come and lead us out? No, by

good feggings, says he, ye ma' e'en ta' care o' your sells, y'are aw awd
enough. (III.1)

Here we see the doubling of a vowel, in *gooing*, to indicate length and
perhaps a different height; the representation of *al* by *aw*, probably to
indicate a long vowel; the assimilation of *lv* to *ll*; and the frequent indication of elision. The word *feggings* is probably a northern form.
Other characters speak the dialect more naturally. Most features in
Shadwell's plays recur, though there are some differences. 'Half' is
represented as *hafe*, not *hawf*. All words written with *a*, whatever its
sound, are written with an *ea*, so we find *measter* 'master', *bearn* 'barn'
and *feace* 'face'. 'Gone' and 'wont' appear as *gwon* and *woant*, the latter of which will appear again in the next century, though the sound
intended is difficult to identify. Preterites often take a weak form as in
catcht 'caught'. The use of *ye* for initial *e-* is more extensively used, as
in *yeasily, yeaten*. There are few lexical items of note, and one may
conclude that the dialect given by Vanbrugh is a much more muddled
thing than that in *The Lancashire Witches*, and that the additional
features do not contribute to a more accurate representation.

In the seventeenth century most examples of non-standard language
are thus found in the drama. Poetry contains some archaisms and in its
burlesque tradition some cant; neither feature was introduced in any
comprehensive way. Even in the drama the amount of non-standard
language is limited and is usually present on account of exceptional
circumstances. Thus Sir Robert Howard's experiences in Ireland and
the notoriety of the trials of the witches in Lancashire generated most
examples of dialect material. The age was in general antipathetic to
what rural life represented, and so when dialect occurs it is a sign of
the wrong kind of breeding.

Chapter 6

THE EIGHTEENTH CENTURY

𝔚𝔚𝔚𝔚𝔚𝔚

THE EIGHTEENTH CENTURY inherited and perpetuated the attitudes towards dialect and other non-standard language from the preceding century. The cultivation of a standard English became the mark of a gentleman as outlined in his letters by Lord Chesterfield, who was regarded by many at the time as an authority on such matters. The clamour for an academy to regulate the language was stilled only by the publication of Johnson's *Dictionary* in 1755, which to many made an academy superfluous. Towards the end of the century grammars became increasingly prescriptive in relation to syntax and increasingly popular. Those by Bishop Lowth and Lindley Murray ran into many editions. Writers of literary works were not exempt from the attention of the grammarians who frequently found fault with what had been written by the most admired authors. Everywhere people were looking for models to imitate and rules for guidance in their search for correctness. The language of the lower classes and of the regions was automatically branded as base. The best language was thought to be that of educated men of 'good company', as Lord Chesterfield put it. Bad pronunciation in an age much given to conversation was particularly criticized by Chesterfield and we may assume he was followed in this opinion by his contemporaries. He comments in his letter of 1761 on the vulgar pronunciation of *yearth* for 'earth' and *obleige* for 'oblige', and these examples illustrate that some variant pronunciations were quite widely known. Correct spelling was also made much of by Lord Chesterfield and deviation from the accepted norm was now a marker of non-standard language.

Another eighteenth-century figure who commented frequently on language matters was Jonathan Swift. Not only did he devote individual tracts to the subject, he returned to it frequently in many of his literary works. Although he did not apparently object to the introduction of French words, he did object to the indiscriminate extension of the vocabulary, for new words would mean that the language was in a constant state of flux. He was very critical of provincialisms and fashionable slang from whichever level of society it emanated. He

108

singled out Scots and Irish as particularly low dialects, for he even went so far as to create a short parody called *A Dialogue in the Hibernian Style* in which Irish words and pronunciations came in for satirical exposure. He also disapproved of the use of vulgar language; his criticism of Bishop Burnet's *History of his Own Times* was motivated in part by what Swift considered the bishop's use of low words and phrases. He also objected to the use of clipped forms like *mob*. Nevertheless, although Swift was always ready to attack the inappropriate language found in the works of others, he did not refrain from using slang and cant words himself. How are we to explain this apparent double standard? The reason may be that different levels of language were considered appropriate for different styles, and that the low style was now extended to include slang and cant so that a colloquial feel could be given to it. Formal style was to be kept as pure, regulated and stable as possible, but more ephemeral works like a *Journal to Stella* could employ more ephemeral forms. However, it was the need for propriety and correctness which was emphasized by all writers of the age. Low or vulgar language was generally criticized, though it might be tolerated in some works. However, this tolerance was never given explicit expression at the time and can be detected only from the writings that survive. The façade that everyone was supposed to write correct English all the time was maintained.

If the dialects were getting lower in general esteem, they were increasingly used as vehicles for literature in their own right. *Yorkshire Dialogues* in verse had appeared in 1673 and 1684, the *Exmoor Courtship* in 1746, and the Lancashire writings of John Collier published over the name of Tim Bobbin from 1746. Such English dialect writings probably made little impact outside the area in which they were written, and we are here not concerned with dialect writing of that type. In Scotland, however, the work of Allan Ramsay and later of Robert Burns made the Scots variety of English well known to all educated people. Many collections of cant terms were also published in the eighteenth century. Knowledge of non-standard varieties probably increased considerably between 1700 and 1800, but the prevailing linguistic attitudes prevented it from being exploited except in specific dialect writing.

The poetry of the eighteenth century may be discounted as far as dialect is concerned. Even the drama is not very rich in new developments except for the rise of Cockney. Occasional use of what one may take to be dialect is found, though the items are often so few in any one play that they cannot be localized, and were in any case probably intended to signify low-class speech rather than a regional dialect. In Goldsmith's *She Stoops to Conquer* (1773), Diggory and the other servants of Hardcastle are given a few spellings which are low rather than regional, even though several can be paralleled from dialect representations in the previous century. Diggory says *yeating* 'eating', *ould* 'old' but *bauld* 'bold', *canna* 'cannot' and *wauns* 'wounds' (used as an expletive); and the other servants say *pleace* 'place', *sartain* 'certain' and *I'se* 'I shall'. Diggory also uses *unpossible*, a form that had ceased to be acceptable for some time. Some of these spellings have northern affiliations and may have been taken from different representations of northern dialects and then mixed with other low forms. They are used only in one scene and then abandoned by the servants. Sheridan, in *The Scheming Lieutenant* (1775), introduced two countrymen who also use an occasional dialect form. They have *be* as the plural and first person singular of the present indicative of 'to be'; *main* as an intensifier in 'main clever'; and spellings such as *measter* 'master', *feyther* 'father' and *noa* 'no'.

Cockney appears again in literature in the eighteenth century, though there is little attempt to localize the dialect socially or regionally, for at first it is used for comic purposes. In *The Mayor of Garratt* (1764), Jerry Sneak has some features of language which were later to become distinguishing features of Cockney. Jerry is the son-in-law of Sir Jacob Jollup and is the only character in the play to speak with these features. The most prominent are the replacement of initial *w* by *v* and of initial *v* by *w*. Thus we have *vere* 'were' and 'where', *vife*, *vhat*, *vhy*, *vould*, *vit* and *viskey* on the one hand, and *woice*, *wirgin*, *wisit* and *wittles* 'victuals' on the other. Other pronunciations include *furder* 'further', *hos* 'horse' and *purfarment* 'preferment'. Syntactically he uses *-(e)s* as the verbal ending of the first person singular present indicative as in *I never does, I never contradicts*. He also says *we ben't*. Lexically he uses *mayhap*, a form which seems to have been low at this time. Isaac Bickerstaffe's *The Hypocrite* (1768), based on Colley Cibber's *The Non-Juror* (1718), satirizes the zeal of the nonconformists, among whom there is the pious shopkeeper Mawworm. He has no deviant pronunciations, and his non-standard language is largely indicated through syntax. He uses *-(e)s* in all persons of the present indicative, as in *I rebukes* and *we lets*. He has such turns of phrase as *I'm but deadly poorish, you never know'd as how I was instigated*, and *as last Thursday was sen'night*. He uses *a* with *-ing* nouns, *a preaching, a breaking* and *a roving*. He uses the forms *axing* 'asking' and *mayhap*. And he also makes use of malapropisms as *clandecently* 'clandestinely', *contagious* 'contiguous' and *mislest* 'molest'. Both plays are set in London, though neither Sneak nor Mawworm is low class. The variants they use, which occur only intermittently, are used to illustrate their characters, which are cowardly and mean; and have little regional or social significance.

Although Sheridan's use of dialect is unadventurous, he created two interesting developments. The first is a nonsense language which passes as a foreign language to fool a jealous father in *The Scheming Lieutenant*. This provides a different approach to linguistic comedy which is now available to replace non-standard language in comedies. The second, in *The Rivals* (1775), is the creation of Mrs Malaprop, who has since given the term malapropism to the language. Sheridan was not the first to use malapropisms, but he brought the corruption of language to a fine art. Mrs Malaprop corrupts words by using the wrong affix or by using a word of a similar make-up in the wrong context as in *a nice derangement of epitaphs* for 'a nice arrangement of epithets'. Her mannerism is used for comedy rather than for social comment. She is by no means low class, though she does pretend to a degree of learning which she does not possess. This trick is her only linguistic fault, though it was so all-pervading and so successful that it effectively prevented later writers from imitating it.

Swift's *Polite Conversation* (1738) can hardly be called a play, but it is cast in dialogue form. In it Swift accumulates all the catch phrases, proverbial utterances and vogue words he knows of to create a *potpourri* of the fashionable language of the day. There can be no doubt that Swift disapproved of this language, though whether it should be called non-standard is less easy to decide. In his introduction Swift notes:

> Nor, have I been less diligent in refining the Orthography, by spelling the Words in the very same Manner that they are pronounced. ... Of these Spellings, the Publick will meet with many Examples, in the following Book: For Instance, can't, hav'n't, sha'n't, didn't, coodn't, woodn't, isn't, e'n't; with many more. Besides several Words, which Scholars pretend, are derived from *Greek* and *Latin*; but now pared into a polite Sound, by Ladies, Officers of the Army, Courtiers and Templers; such as Jommetry for Geometry, Verdi for Verdict, Lard for Lord, Larnin for Learning; together with some Abbreviations exquisitely refined: As, Pozz for Positively, Mobb for Mobile, Phizz for Physiognomy, Rep for Reputation, Plenipo for Plenipotentiary, Incog for Incognito, Hipps, or Hippo for Hypocondriacks, Bam for Bamboozle, and Bamboozle for God knows what. (p.33)

The polite pronunciations and the fashionable abbreviations here come in for his particular scorn. As for the former we may note that spelling is now so regularized that these spellings are marked; and as far as Swift is concerned they are a corruption of language. Later he goes on to refer to the language of one of the characters, Sir John Linger:

> If you compare the Discourses of my Gentlemen and Ladies with those of Sir *John*; you will hardly conceive him to have been bred in the same Climate, or under the same Laws, Language, Religion, or Government: And, accordingly I have introduced him speaking in his own rude Dialect, for no other Reason than to teach my Scholars how to avoid it. (p.36)

Sir John's language differs hardly, if at all, from that of the other characters, though the subjects of his conversation may be grosser. The only dialect expression he uses is 'Well, I'm weily brosten', as they sayn in *Lancashire'* (p.150). Whether this is meant to be just another proverb, for the work is full of them, or an example of Sir John's dialect, is uncertain. The former seems more likely since there is no reason for a Derbyshire man to speak in the Lancashire dialect, though the expression *weily brosten* 'well nigh burst' is not confined to that dialect alone by any means. Even allowing for Swift's particular brand of satire, we can see that the attitude to dialects and to those who had the misfortune to grow up away from London was very condescending.

A typical example of the language used in the dialogues is:

Neverout	Pray, my Lord, don't make a Bridge of my Nose.
Sparkish	Well, a Glass of this Wine is as comfortable, as Matrimony to an old Maid.
Col. Atwit	Sir *John*, I design one of these Days, to come and beat up your Quarters in *Derbyshire*.
Sir John	Faith, Colonel, come and welcome; and stay away, and heartily welcome. But you were born within the Sound of *Bow* Bell, and don't Care to stir so far from *London*. (pp. 131-2)

Each speech contains some vogue expression or proverbial utterance, and Sir John is no different in this respect. This dialogue reveals the interest there was in polite language and how many felt that the fashionable talk was as bad as the corruptions of country or trade language. The language used in such circles was over-refined and so might be described as non-standard. It did not match up to educated and elegant use of a correct language.

Nevertheless, the most comprehensive use of non-standard language in this period comes from the novelists. Unlike the poets and the dramatists they abandoned the assumption that the poor and the oppressed were not worth writing about. In their descriptions of the poor they also abandoned the generalized language of the poets for a much more 'realistic' portrayal of the prevailing social conditions. This may be seen already in the work of Defoe, who combined a vivid imagination with an eye for detail. In *Robinson Crusoe* (1719) Defoe was faced with the problem of Friday's language. Friday was a Carib who was taught to speak English by Crusoe. Generally Defoe is content to report what passed between the two in indirect speech, but occasionally he uses dialogue. When Friday speaks he indicates his faulty command of English through syntax rather than through vocabulary; there is no interference from his own mother tongue. Elision is a frequent feature as is his failure to use the correct grammatical marker of case. This resulting simplification has certain points of similarity with some varieties of pidgin, as does Friday's use of the ending *-ee* in such words as *teachee*. It is possible that Defoe had some acquaintance with some Caribbean pidgin. Examples of Friday's language are:

> Why, you angry mad with Friday, what me done?... Why send Friday home away to my Nation? ... Yes, yes, wish be both there, no wish Friday there, no Master there ... You do great deal much good, says he, you teach wild Mans be good sober tame Mans; you tell them know God, pray God, and live new Life.

The omission of a verb or auxiliary is common. The use of *me* for *I* is regular; in *wish be both* 'I wish that both of us were' many items are omitted; and the use of *Mans* for *men* is a typical analogical extension. Within its limits Friday's language is made convincing. He appears as a noble savage who is not familiar with the superficial proprieties of European civilization, but who has absorbed the essential moral meaning of life.

The novelists of the eighteenth century exhibited a great interest in language and none more so than Tobias Smollett whom I shall consider first, though he was writing later than Richardson and Fielding. His linguistic virtuosity begins with the names of his characters, and extends through puns to the meaningful distortion of language. He indulges in philological diversions, for example, by allowing Dr Wagtail in *Roderick Random* to comment on the etymology of the verb *drink* and related words in the classical languages. We may note first that Roderick, the hero of the novel, and some of his friends like Hugh Strap, are Scotsmen, but they are not represented as talking with a Scots accent or lexis. Even so, when these two arrive in London (ch. 13) they meet up with some wits in a tavern. One of them, realizing that Roderick and Strap come from Scotland because of their 'dialect', begins to insult them. During the ensuing altercation the English wag asks Strap what he has in his knapsack: 'Is it oatmeal, or brimstone, Sawney?' The name *Sawney* is a variant of Sandy, which was used as a derogatory appellation for Scotsmen, so it is clear that the English were quite aware of the origins of Roderick and his friend. At other places in the novel Smollett refers to the differences between Roderick's language and that of other characters. But his language as given in the novel is always in standard orthography. It would have been too inconvenient for Smollett to give his principal character a variant language, for Roderick was both the narrator and the hero. The question of what language to use in the narration, if the hero spoke Scots, would be a perpetual problem. Furthermore, it could be that English readers would have reacted against a Scots speaker and so withheld their approval for the hero in his various exploits. With the attitude towards dialect being so condescending at the time, because of the need to preserve propriety and correctness, it was difficult for a hero to use anything other than standard English on paper, whatever he was supposed to say in practice.

The non-standard language found in the novel falls into three categories: provincial dialects, the language of foreigners and professional language. The last is the most interesting type, for it forms a new departure in English, though it could be said that Holofernes in *Love's Labour's Lost* employs the pedantic language of the schoolmaster. In *Love's Labour's Lost* this type of language is used for satire, as it can be in *Roderick Random*, but Smollett also employs it to give a greater realism and colloquial feel to the dialogue. It becomes an important aspect of the portrayal of individual characters, and although by its nature it may be humorous, it is a humour which is affectionate rather than satirical. The best example of this type of language is put into the mouth of Lieutenant Bowling, Roderick's uncle, who is in the navy. This is how he speaks:

> Your servant – your servant. What cheer, father? – what cheer? – I suppose you don't know me – mayhap you don't. My name is Tom Bowling; and this here boy – you look as if you did not know him neither; 'tis like you mayn't. He's new rigg'd, i'faith; his cloth don't shake in the wind so much

as it wont to do. 'Tis my nephew, d'ye see, Roderick Random – your own
flesh and blood, old gentleman. Don't lag astern, you dog. (ch. 3)

Bowling uses elided forms like *don't, mayn't* and *d'ye* and some syntactic constructions which might be regarded as low or colloquial as
this here boy and the double negative in *not know him neither*. The
latter type was still acceptable in the eighteenth century. The speech is
also punctuated by many dashes. These features may be regarded as
signs of a bluntness and straightforwardness in speech. Although the
uncle has no accent or unusual pronunciations, his language is full of
nautical expressions like *rigg'd, shake in the wind, lag astern* and the
use of *you dog* as a mark of affection. Since these were professional or
trade terms, they would be regarded as impolite by Augustan standards of language, and some characters in the novel react to the uncle
as though he was uncouth. Thus one accuses him of being 'a scoundrel
of a seaman … who has deserted, and turned thief'. But Smollett is intent to show that a man's language is no guide to his character. The
use of nautical idioms adds a depth and honesty to Bowling's
language, and all who speak in this way in the novel are to be regarded
as honest, straightforward and blunt people.

A quite different aspect of professional language is found in Concordance, Strap's friend and relation, a schoolmaster and elocutionist
who has emigrated from Scotland to work in London. He has dropped
his native speech in order to acquire the fashionable language of the
time and in so doing he has in effect overcompensated for his provincial origins so as to become comic. This is an example of how he
speaks:

> Dress, you may caal it fat you please in your country, but I vaw to Gad, 'tis
> a masquerade here. No Christian will admit such a figure into his hawse.
> Upon my conscience! I wonder the dogs did not hunt you. Did you pass
> through St James's market? God bless my eye-saight! you look like a cousin-
> german of Ouran Outang. (ch. 14)

Although Concordance is not consistent in his usage, characteristic
features include the use of *f* for *w* or *wh* as *fat* 'what', *aw* for *ow* in *vaw,
hawse, a* for *o* in *Gad, aa* for *al* in *caal*, and *ai* for *i* in *saight*. Of these
Gad is, as we have seen, fashionable in the eighteenth century and *fat*
may be a continental affectation since he also teaches French and
Italian. But *vaw, caal* and *saight* are more difficult to interpret, since
they may be taken to represent the sounds of these words in the eight-

eenth century more accurately than the standard orthography. Thus ME [i:] had been diphthongized by the fifteenth century though the spelling had not been modified, and although it is not easy to decide what stage this diphthongization had reached in fashionable London speech at this time, any spelling which suggests a diphthong is more accurate than the monophthongal spelling. Nevertheless *saight* is not an accurate representation since the *gh* is retained, although the sound that had given rise to that spelling had long since disappeared. Two interpretations of these spellings seem likely. The one is that they imply a speaker who is right up to the minute in his pronunciation. The other is that they imply deviants from the standard which tell us something about the speaker rather than anything specific about his pronunciation. In either case we have to assume a level of affectation in a man who is teaching English and who therefore ought to stick as close as he can to the standard.

Provincial varieties of English are well represented in *Roderick Random*. The first person to be given a dialect is Joey, the waggon driver who takes Roderick and Strap from Newcastle to London. It is not stated where he came from, but one makes the assumption that he lives in the vicinity of Newcastle since the waggon starts from there. He certainly has no traces of vulgar London English. Some of the features of his language are dialectal without being characteristic of any region. He uses *afear'd* for 'afraid' and *I'se* for 'I will, I am'; 'he' is reduced to *a*; and the spellings *ow, ou* appear as *aw, au* in *waunds* 'wounds', *yaw* 'you' and *knaw* 'know'. This latter may represent the simple substitution of *a* for *o* which had almost become a northern stereotype. But many readers may have found it difficult to decide how these spellings differed from the presumably refined forms *hawse* and *vaw* found in Concordance's language. Diggory in *She Stoops to Conquer* had used the form *wauns* 'wounds', and he is unlikely to have been considered a northerner. Joey also has *whay* for 'why', which might be equated with Concordance's *saight* for 'sight', but has *moind* for 'mind' rather than *maind*. However, the spelling *moind* can hardly be accepted as northern, for Smollett himself, in *Peregrine Pickle*, gives to the Cockney Deborah Hornbeck the spelling *coind* for 'kind'. Joey's dialect is something of a mixture. The spelling *satisfie* for 'satisfy' may be taken to imply that the final vowel was pronounced as [i:] rather than as a diphthong, though that can hardly be dialectal. The spellings *meake* 'make' and *neame* 'name' remind one of Sheridan's *measter* 'master' and, as we shall see, have a close parallel in the language of the Suffolk peasants in this same novel. Most of these spellings, therefore, probably represent a dialect speaker rather than indicating precisely where that speaker came from. However, there are some spellings which do suggest a northern pronunciation, even if not a specifically Newcastle one. Where Standard English has *u*, Smollett gives Joey *oo*, probably to indicate [u] as against [ʌ] or something similar: *oop* 'up', *sooffer* 'suffer' and *coom* 'come'. He also uses this spelling in *atoonement* 'atonement'. The spelling *oa* in *woan't* is found in Shadwell's *The Lancashire Witches* and may have been regarded as a northernism, though *doan't* is found in the language of the Suffolk peasants. The variants *coptain* 'captain' and *mon* 'man' can hardly be regarded as regionally significant. There are no syntactic features in Joey's language worth noting.

In general, then, Smollett used some features which are probably northern in a wide sense, as well as many that are dialectal rather than characteristic of a region. Some of the spellings may have been borrowed from other literary writers, and the result is a very mixed language. An example is:

> 'Odds bodikins! sure, coptain, yaw would not commit moorder! Here's a poor lad that is willing to make atoonement for his offence; and an that woan't satisfie yaw, offers to fight yaw fairly. An yaw woan't box, I dare say, he will coodgel with yaw, – woan't yaw, my lad? (ch. 12)

Joey does not have a large part and so Smollett is able to keep the dialect writing going without too much difficulty, though there are words like *would*, *not* and *he will* which one might have expected to be given a different spelling. Joey's oaths also seem somewhat literary.

The next dialect is usually regarded as Cockney, though the lady in question never appears as a character. Clarinda's language is manifest only in a letter she addressed to Mr Jackson:

> DEER KREETER, – As you are the animable hopjack of my con-templayshins, your aydear is infernally skimiing before my keymerycal fansee, when Murfy sends his puppies to the heys of slipping mortals; and when Febus shines from his merrydying throne. Whereupon I shall canseeif old whorie time has lost his pinners, as also Cupid his harrows, until thou enjoy sweet propose in the loafseek harms of thy faithfool to commend, CLAYRENDER
> Wingar-yeard, Droory-Lane
> January 12th

This is probably meant as a caricature of Cockney writing which is to be equated with Deborah Hornbeck's letter to Peregrine and with Jonathan Wild's letter to Miss Tishy in Fielding's novel. All indicate a growing interest in the Cockney dialect, though that interest takes rather a grotesque form. Almost overnight Cockney became the principal vulgar language of novels. In many ways this is not surprising, since it contrasts readily with the standard and since it was probably better known to the average author and reader than any regional dialect simply because London was the largest city in the country and so many novels were produced there. Furthermore, in the second half of the eighteenth century, comments on vulgar London pronunciations begin to appear with increasing frequency in grammars and other works on language. The effect of these grammatical works was to make Cockney better known and hence to be accepted as the epitome of bad usage. Indeed James Elphinstone (1720-1809), a Scottish schoolmaster settled in London and the author of many books on language, even went so far as to produce one of his renderings of Martial's epigrams in Cockney.

However with Clarinda's letter Smollett is indulging in linguistic play rather than accurate dialect representation. Thus he perverts many words to suggest a pun as in *faithfool* and *puppies* 'poppies'. Other forms indicate a faulty command of the written language, such as *Febus* 'Phoebus', and are low class rather than dialectal. The same probably applies to *wh* for *h* in *whorie* 'hoary', though again this suggests a pun rather than a low-class spelling. Nevertheless, the introduction of inorganic *h* in such words as *heys, harrows* and *harms* was to become one of the hallmarks of Cockney. Yet the variation between final *ng* and *n* in *merrydying* 'meridian' was found among the most socially elevated speakers up to this time and indeed after. Hence, although it is usual to refer to Clarinda's letter as an example of Cockney, there is little in it that is unambiguously so. Most of the forms have been introduced as part of Smollett's linguistic play.

On board the Thunder, Roderick meets the first mate Mr Morgan who is a Welshman. He speaks a variety of Welsh which is represented mainly through changes in some of the consonants. As Morgan plays quite a large role in the novel, these changes are by no means introduced consistently. In general the voiced consonants represented by *b, d, g* and *v* are represented as voiceless ones through the spellings *p, t, c* and *f*. Thus Morgan says *pelly, roppery, tog, Got* or *Cot,* and *salfation*. In many instances the necessary changes are not made, or they are made in some, but not all, examples of a word; *dead* and *tead* interchange in his speech. The affricates, represented in the standard language as *g* or *j* and *ch*, appear in Morgan's language as *sh*, since these sounds do not occur in Welsh. Thus he says *shentleman* and *sheese*. He also uses the expression *look you* frequently. Morgan also employs some forms which by this time would be regarded as solecisms. Principal among them is the double comparative as in *more elder* and *more petter*. Such forms are not to be regarded as Welsh; Smollett may have intended them to be archaic. It is possible that Smollett may have borrowed some of these Welsh forms from Fluellen in *Henry V* since there are occasional expressions which seem to echo Fluellen's choice of vocabulary.

The only other regional speakers in *Roderick Random* are some Suffolk peasants among whom Roderick falls when he has been abandoned in a sorry state by his shipmates. These peasants are said to speak in a 'broken accent'. They use *a* for 'he' and *en* for 'him'; 'christian' appears as *christom*. Like Joey they have *oa* for *o* in *doan't* and *o* for *a* in *mon*; they also use *eaa* rather than just *ea* for *a* as in *leaad* 'lad', though it is difficult to read through this last form. They do have certain forms which are more specifically southern, particularly the voicing of *f* and *s* to *v* and *z* in *vather* and *zea* as well as *be* for *are* forms in the verb 'to be'. The use of *thou* for *you* is dialectal and archaic, though not particularly southern; it was also used by Clarinda. However, these peasants also use the *-(e)st* form of the verb to go with *thou*, whereas Clarinda did not. Once again one may note that the language spoken by the dialect speakers consists of some forms which might be described as non-specific, as well as some which are characteristic of the area the speakers are supposed to come from.

The two foreign speakers of English are both Frenchmen, for in this respect the eighteenth-century novel differed little from the seventeenth-century play. One is Mr Lavenant, the apothecary, with whom Roderick takes employment. He uses a great many French words and expressions such as *bierre* and *ma foi*. He has features which were traditional in French speakers of English in literature: 'very' appears as *ver*, initial *th* as *d* in *de* 'the' and initial *w* or *wh* as *v* in *vil* 'will' and *vat* 'what'; he also employs *me* for 'I'. Rather less to be expected are his *tomarrow* for 'tomorrow' which could be fashionable, and *by gar* 'by God', though the latter could be borrowed from earlier playwrights. He also uses *mine* where 'my' would be more appropriate. The second Frenchman is the valet, Vergette, of Chaptain Whiffle. All he says is:

Pon my vord, I do tink dat dere be great occasion for your honour losing one small quantity of blodt; and the young man ave quelque chose of de bonne mien. (ch. 35)

Here initial *th* is represented as *t* in *tink*, but as *d* in *dat* and *dere*. *Pon* is a colloquialism, and it is difficult to imagine that *dt* in *blodt* represents any French sound. Initial *h* is dropped in *ave* and many French words appear. In both instances there is an attempt to indicate some French features, but they are mixed with others of a colloquial or incomprehensible nature.

In *Humphry Clinker* (1771), his last novel, Smollett was able to indulge his penchant for linguistic exhibitionism, because the novel records the travels of Squire Bramble and his entourage around England in the epistolary form. Many of the correspondents lack a perfect command of English; and they also meet with several dialect speakers. One of these is a Scot, Captain Lismahago. He is given only a few dialect forms before his language returns to the standard. He has *leddies* for 'ladies', which indicates a short vowel, and the *ee* spelling in *scandaleezed* and *heed* presumably indicates [i:]. These are suitable enough representations of Scots, as is the use of *ye* for 'you'. But more important in some ways are Lismahago's comments on language since these may enshrine Smollett's own views.

He observed, that a North-Briton is seen to a disadvantage in an English company, because he speaks in a dialect that they can't relish, and in a phraseology which they don't understand. – He therefore finds himself under a restraint, which is a great enemy to wit and humour. (p. 199)

This difficulty of the Scots dialect may be a reason why Smollett was not able to use it at any length in his novels, which were meant mainly for English readers. Lismahago went on to applaud the advantages of the Scots dialect as compared with London English, for the former had preserved the original language in its true vigour and purity, whereas London English had become weakened and corrupted. It is interesting to see that an attempt is being made here to upgrade one dialect so that it was not looked upon as unsophisticated or ineloquent.

However, Smollett himself, later in the novel, allows another Scot to speak in the dialect, and as this Scot is a cawdie, an errand boy, who is also a veteran pimp, readers may well have come away thinking that the Scots dialect was suitable only for less reputable people in Scotland. This cawdie, Fraser, makes only a brief appearance at the banquet in Leith which he had organized. As well as speaking a noticeably Scots dialect, he also uses many vulgar, cant words. A typical example of his language is: 'Lang life to the wylie loon that gangs a-field with a toom poke at his lunzie, and comes hame with a sackful of siller.' (p. 227) This Scot uses both Scottish words and pronunciations. *Loon* 'worthless fellow' and *lunzie* 'side' (a variant of *loin*) were Scots words, and *toom* 'empty' had disappeared from standard English during the sixteenth century. *Gangs* is a northern form of 'goes' used also in *The Lancashire Witches*; and the use of *a* in *a-field* is more colloquial than Scottish. The representation of 'long' and 'home' as *lang* and *hame* suggests a low back vowel rather than the fronted one which is more typical of Scots. Smollett himself represents 'own' as *ain*. The assimilation of *lf* to *ll* in *siller* is both Scots and North England. There are other forms used by Fraser in his few speeches and they are generally an accurate enough representation of Scots. It may be that Smollett invented them from his own knowledge of his native dialect, but as he refers in one of the letters in the book to the works of Allan Ramsay, it is more likely that he drew upon the Scottish orthographic tradition which was developing a literary respectability in the eighteenth century.

The Irishman, Sir Ulic Mackilligut, who is said to have 'a true Hibernian accent', is given some forms to make this claim good. He uses the exclamation *gar*, the Irish equivalent of 'my dear', an expression he also uses. He also employs the typical Irish construction *if you are after coming* for 'if you come'. He pronounces 'civilly' *shivilly*. All these Smollett could have picked up from late seventeenth-century drama. The other spellings are less Irish: *callum* 'call him' is colloquial, and *sea* 'see' is probably merely a different spelling to suggest an unusual pronunciation. The spelling *prepasterous* could indicate a pronunciation which was fashionable rather than Irish. Other words which are changed are *saoul* 'soul' and *becaase* 'because', both of which may imply a lengthened diphthong or vowel, though its quality is not clear. However, Mackilligut soon stops talking in this Irish way and reverts to standard English.

Miss Tabitha Bramble, the Squire's sister, writes in a manner which may indicate the language of Monmouthshire where Brambleton Hall was evidently located. But Smollett is probably more intent on poking fun at Tabitha and using her linguistic corruptions to suggest puns or even obscenities:

I desire you'll clap a pad-luck on the wind-seller, and let none of the men have excess to the strong bear – don't forget to have the gate shit every evening before dark. – The gardnir and the hind may lie below in the landry, to partake the house, with the blunderbuss and the great dog; and I hope you'll have a watchfull eye over the maids. I know that hussy, Mary Jones, loves to be rumping with the men. Let me know if Alderney's calf be sould yet, and what he fought – if the ould goose be sitting; and if the cobler has cut Dicky, and how the pore anemil bore the operation. (p. 6)

Most of the mistakes can be attributed to a faulty command of written English rather than to a dialect, though it is possible that spellings like *ould* and *sould* indicate a West Midlands variety. Essentially Tabitha is a purveyor of malapropisms rather than a dialect speaker.

The same applies to Win Jenkins, perhaps the best-known figure in the novel. As with Tabitha, it might be possible to claim that some of the features in her language were intended to reflect that spoken in Monmouthshire, but this seems quite unlikely. Her speech is idiosyncratic, with puns and corruptions being very frequent; for the rest the variations from standard spelling indicate a want of education rather than a regional origin. Many of her corruptions certainly have no basis in the way Welsh people speak English, though a few could be understood in that way. As regards the latter she frequently fails to pronounce [tʃ] and [dʒ] correctly, for these sounds are not found in Welsh; for 'chin' she writes *sin* and for 'jakes' *geaks*. But she also corrupts words to produce these sounds so that 'joined' becomes *chined* and 'journied' *churned*. As an example of her language consider the following:

She has tould me all her inward thoughts, and disclosed her passion for Mr Wilson; and that's not his name neither; and thof he acted among the player-men, he is meat for their masters; and she has gi'en me her yallow trollopea; which Mrs Drab, the manty-maker, says will look very well when it is scowred and smoaked with silfur – You knows as how, yallow fitts my fizzogmony. God he knows what havock I shall make among the mail sex, when I make my first appearance in this killing collar, with a full soot of gaze, as good as new, that I bought last Friday of madam Friponeau, the French mullaner. (p. 42)

In this passage *manty-maker* is Scots for 'mantuamaker, one who makes gowns for ladies', and *trollopea* is an eighteenth-century word for 'gown'. Some words are Win's own corruptions like *fitts*, *fizzogmony* and *mullaner*, while others are probably corrupted to set up a pun like *meat, collar, soot* and *gaze* 'gauze'. Other forms may be described as dialectal in the eighteenth century, without being characteristic of a particular region. This goes for *thof* 'though', *yallow* and *silfur*. The syntactic errors probably indicate an incomplete command of standard English, such as *You knows as how*. The double negative in *not his name neither* was becoming unacceptable, but had not perhaps reached that stage yet. The elided forms, of which there are comparatively few, give the whole a more colloquial air. In Win Jenkins's language we find Smollett at his most inventive; he is not trying to describe a dialect.

Though Henry Fielding comes just before Smollett in time, he has not been treated before, because he is not so inventive in his use of language. This is surprising, considering his experience as a playwright. His forays into non-standard language follow traditional patterns. In *Jonathan Wild* (1743), his first novel, he experimented with cant. Jonathan says in the novel 'If we have no name to express it by in our Cant Dictionary, it were well to be wished we had' (ch. 13). It is not clear which dictionary Fielding had in mind, though only two had appeared by the time he wrote these words: *A New Dictionary of the Terms Ancient and Modern of the Canting Crew* (1699) and *A New Canting Dictionary* (1725). The latter is based on the former and was the one that Fielding probably knew. He used it for words which he could introduce into the novel. When he used a cant term, he italicized it and often glossed it as well. Thus when *prig* is first mentioned Jonathan explains 'for so we call what the vulgar name a *Thief*' (ch. 5). Other terms employed include *Mill-ken* 'housebreaker', *Bridle-cull* 'highwayman' and *file* 'shoplifter'. These words are relatively few in comparison with the length of the novel and they hardly add a great deal to it or to the characterization of Jonathan.

In *Tom Jones* (1749) he introduced a regional dialect. This is the traditional southern rustic variety which is here put into the mouth of Squire Western. It may be intended to reinforce the down-to-earth character of the squire, though the dialect is not carried through consistently. The squire has too large a part for that, and Fielding was content to remind his readers from time to time of his regional links. The characteristic feature of this language is the use of initial *v* and *z* for *f* and *s* in *vind* 'find' and *zee* 'see'. He also often uses *un* for 'him' or 'them'; the *-st* ending of the second singular form of verbs as in *dost*, sometimes with *thee* as a subject form; and the *-th* form of the third person singular present indicative as in *hath*. He also varies some standard spellings to suggest a regional accent: *a* becomes *ea* in *veather* 'father' and *feace* 'face'; *o* becomes *uo* in *huome* 'home' and *c* becomes *qu* in *quoat* 'coat'. The first of these was common enough in dialect representations, and the second is an acceptable attempt at rendering the sound found in some southern and western dialects. But Fielding does not put many dialect words or phrases into the squire's mouth, though he does use such expressions as *gee a brass varden*, i.e. 'give a damn'. Fielding may well have realized from *Jonathan Wild* what the problems were with using strange words. Finally, the squire's language is full of elided forms which continue to represent a colloquial level of language. Forms like *o't* 'of it' and *many's* 'many is' are typical of his usage. The southern dialect was used from time to time elsewhere by Fielding, but never to the same extent. In *Joseph Andrews* the Trullibers use it occasionally. Mr Trulliber uses expressions like *caale vurst* 'call first' and his wife says *ifacks* 'in faith', which was now considered rather provincial and which may be why Mrs Slipslop uses the related form *ifakins*.

The final type of non-standard language employed by Fielding is malapropism. This is found particularly in Mrs Slipslop's language in *Joseph Andrews*. For example, she corrupts 'detect' into *reflect*, 'commendation' into *commensuration*, 'violence' into *virulence* and 'characteristic' into *currycuristic* (II.12). Whether the captain who later in the same novel pronounces 'humanity' as *imanity* (III.7) is creating a malapropism or simply uttering a low pronunciation is not clear. Certainly these two could be mixed up, as in the legal disposition compiled by James Scout and Thomas Trotter which Fielding reproduces, as he says, *verbatim et litteratim*. Trotter is a yeoman and in his part of the deposition there are dialect forms, faulty spellings and malapropisms for punning effect, which is why Fielding claims to have reproduced the text accurately. Spelling was now an important marker of educational attainments:

> betwin the ours of 2 and 4 in the afternoon, he zeed Joseph Andrews and Francis Goodwill walk akross a certaine felde belunging to layer Scout, and out of the path which ledes thru the said feld, and there he zece Joseph Andrews with a nife cut one hassel twig ... and the said Francis Goodwill ... did receive and karry in her hand the said twig, and so was cumfarting, eading, and abatting to the said Joseph therein. (IV.5)

Fielding was also influenced by the plays of the time to portray some upper-class speakers with particular characteristics in their speech. Thus Bellarmine in the same novel uses many fashionable oaths and lards his language with French words.

At the end of the eighteenth century an interesting change arises in
the novelists' use of non-standard language – a change which is occa-
sioned by the move from satire to sentiment. Where Smollett and
Fielding had used language as part of their general exposure of the
follies of man and were therefore prepared to deploy it in a grotesque
way, to Fanny Burney a novel was a 'picture of supposed, but natural
and probable human experience'. Language can be used in the portrayal of character, but it must not depart too far from what is probable
or else the naturalism aimed at will be destroyed. The novel in her
hands is just as moral, but the means used are different. The characters
may be criticized for their behaviour, but they must not develop into
caricatures. Hence some of the standard practices of the earlier
novelists fall into disuse. Malapropisms and the traditional peasant
dialect are neglected and the development of a more rigid attitude to
correctness in usage allows for more subtle distinctions in language.
The characters of whom the authors disapprove may now use grammatical solecisms or slang expressions to reveal their lack of true
breeding. In *Evelina* (1778) this can be seen in Madame Duval and the
Branghtons.

When she is first introduced into the novel, Madame Duval says *'Ma
foi, Monsieur*, I have lost my company, and in this place I don't know
nobody' (I.xiii). The French words are italicized as are many of the
slang expressions in the novel – and in this way they are shown to be
different from standard English. They are not so much wrong as inappropriate in the circumstances. Although the double negative used by
Madame Duval might still be used by some at the end of the eighteenth century, it had been criticized severely by the grammarians and
is never used by the 'good' people in the novel. Among her other
solecisms are *I would not live among none of you, you're the ill-
bredest person ever I see, I don't believe no such a thing* and *you han't
no eyes*. There are no lexical distortions or outrageous syntactic disloca-
tions in Madame's language. Her speech is clearly non-standard, but
not obtrusively so. The Branghtons for their part are characterized as a
'low-bred and vulgar' family (I.xxi). In their talk they use colloquialisms, slang and the occasional solecism. They therefore talk in an
English way as compared with Madame Duval, though their English is
evidently not the polite standard. The son says 'If aunt pleases, we'll
talk o' somewhat else, for Miss looks very uneasy-like' (I.xvii). Here the
elision of 'of' to *o'*, and the use of *somewhat, Miss* and *uneasy-like*
mark out the language as colloquial. They use slang terms like
crinkum-crankum 'a winding passage', but here used more in the sense

'something worthless'. Other colloquialisms include *grumpy, take-in* and *a pin's point*. Their solecisms include the omission of the ending *-ly* in adverbial intensifiers. The expression *monstrous dear* is italicized in the text to point out its unacceptable nature. The use of such endingless intensifiers was common enough till the end of the seventeenth century, but the onslaught of the grammarians against them had resulted in their gradual demise in the eighteenth century. They also say *catched* for 'caught', *have fell* for 'have fallen', *I puts* for 'I put', and *father don't scold* for 'father doesn't scold'. In such subtle ways like this the Branghtons reveal their lack of true feeling, even though they give themselves such airs.

Captain Mirvan, who is portrayed as a blunt and somewhat irascible person, can also employ non-standard items. He uses slang and even some words which might be considered dialectal. Thus he says *I ben't* for 'I am not'. The Branghtons would use *an't*. He uses many elided forms like *'fore* 'before', *d'ye see* and *'em* 'them'. He also has many slang expressions such as *to play the old Dowager off* 'to finish her off' and *you'll find yourself in a hobble* 'you'll end up in an awkward situation'. The captain's slang is rather more vigorous than the Branghtons'.

It should be remembered that the end of the eighteenth century witnessed a great proliferation in the number of novels published. Many of these imitated Smollett's or Fielding's works and so some non-standard language is found in them. Most frequent is the south-western dialect variety which imitates the language of Squire Western. Novels with a regional setting also became popular immediately before 1800 with Scotland being a particularly favourite locale for many writers, and the growth of regional stories went hand in hand with the burgeoning interest in history and romance. All of these developments were to bear fruit in the romantic period, which forms the subject of the following chapter.

Chapter 7

THE ROMANTICS

🗗🗗🗗🗗🗗🗗

THE ROMANTIC PERIOD opens in 1798 with the publication of the *Lyrical Ballads*, and Wordsworth's preface to the second edition of 1800 provided the writers of the time with some of their *obiter dicta*. Among the most important of these is that poetry should contain 'a selection of the real language of men in a state of vivid sensation'. For the poems in the collection were drawn chiefly from incidents and situations from common life, for which the 'language really used by men' was considered the most appropriate. This claim by Wordsworth was part of his attack on the poetic diction of the late Augustans and his appeal to return to the more natural language found in Chaucer and the Elizabethans. The poetic diction of the eighteenth century was something artificial. By 'real language', however, Wordsworth did not mean the spoken language or dialects of the country, but the standard language shorn of poetic diction. Although he wrote about many poor people who would not have spoken the standard language, he never uses dialect or colloquialism in his poetry as part of their speech patterns. When, for example, he wrote *Michael* about a shepherd's family in the Lake District, he did not give Michael any dialect words or expressions. In fact Michael speaks a slightly archaic language, which reminds one of biblical style:

> But, lay one stone –
> Here lay it for me, Luke, with thine own hands,
> Nay, Boy, be of good hope; – we both may live
> To see a better day. At eighty-four
> I still am strong and hale; – do thou thy part;
> I will do mine.

The *thou, thee, thine* and *nay* are characteristic of his speech. He also has a larger vocabulary than one would expect a shepherd to be master of. Coleridge, for his part, is no different from Wordsworth in this matter, though he did experiment a little more with language. He wrote *Lines in the Manner of Spenser* which includes a few archaic features like initial *y-* with past participles, and he was influenced by the language of the ballads and Sir Walter Scott particularly in the *Ancient Mariner* and *Christabel*.

Although Wordsworth and Coleridge did not themselves make use of non-standard language, the attack they launched on poetic diction was of great importance for the future. The idea that there was a special language for poetry was compromised, and later writers were thus able to draw upon different varieties. At first this freedom was extended only to archaic language. Archaisms had always been tolerated to some extent because of the influence of the Bible. A few had also been used in late eighteenth-century plays. But the move to look beyond the Augustans to poets like Chaucer and Spenser naturally encouraged more archaisms. This movement was further encouraged by the publication of Bishop Percy's *Reliques* and the 'Rowley poems' which had appeared in 1777. These forgeries by Thomas Chatterton were attempts to write in a late medieval style. Generally, as the following example from *Englysh Metamorphosis* reveals, this amounted to no more than tampering with the spelling and using archaic or unusual words and constructions.

> Whanne Scythyannes, salvage as the wolves theie chacde,
> Peyncted in horrowe formes bie nature dyghte,
> Heckled yn beastskyns, slepte uponne the waste,
> And wyth the morneynge rouzed the wolfe to fyghte, ... (1-14)

In these lines *horrowe* was glossed as 'disagreeable' and *heckled* as 'wrapped'. These poems were important in forcing writers to think more about the language they should use and in undermining the notion that poems had to be in a correct language. Even Wordsworth's use of archaisms in Michael's speech is significant in that it encouraged the view that speech should be represented by a different variety of language from that used in the narrative.

Of the other Romantic poets only Byron, Moore and Scott are of importance here; and Scott's contribution to the use of non-standard language is perhaps best approached through his novels. In some respects Byron may be considered an eighteenth-century poet and this applies particularly to his satirical works. In them he mixed high and low styles in the way Butler had done in *Hudibras*. But Byron's style is more colloquial and it rarely rises to the same heights of the grotesque. In *Beppo* he draws on a wide range of vocabulary: Italian words jostle with English slang, and poetic diction lies side by side with colloquialism.

> But to my story. – 'Twas some years ago,
>   It may be thirty, forty, more or less,
> The Carnival was at its height, and so
>   Were all kinds of buffoonery and dress;
> A certain lady went to see the show,
>   Her real name I know not, if you please,
> And so we'll call her Laura, if you please,
> Because it slips into my verse with ease. (stanza 21)

In this stanza the poeticism *'Twas* follows immediately after the colloquial *But to my story*, which at this period of correctness in grammar
might well have been attacked as an incomplete, and hence incorrect,
sentence. The *more or less* of the second line makes the number in-
consequential and thus creates the effect of someone talking. There
are the colloquialisms *we'll* and *if you please*. Nevertheless, the
language is more traditional in *Her real name I know not*, in which the
object is advanced to the front of the clause and auxiliary *do*, which in
negative constructions was by then fairly regular, is omitted.

In *Beppo* Byron may be intent on creating a mixed style, but *Don
Juan* is written in a colloquial manner though even here he does not
neglect the eighteenth-century ways of heightening style. His
vocabulary contains colloquial items like *hen-peck'd, go-between, us
youth, never mind* and *blunder*, as well as abbreviated forms like *what
d'ye mean* and *who've*. There are many dashes and incompletely formed sentences. Often the rhyme falls on a pronoun or preposition, and
this produces an unusual stress pattern for English which helps to
destroy the formality of the utterance. But these features are used by
Byron as the means of creating a particular style; they were not
employed as part of an attempt to record the colloquial language of his
day. Poetry was thus extending its range of vocabulary, but at first it
was more in the direction of archaism and more elaborate language.
Byron used a more colloquial style, but he was more in the mould of
the eighteenth-century satirists than an innovator in linguistic usage.

Thomas Moore was a friend of Byron's and had the same affection
for the eighteenth century and its writers. His poetry is generally written in the late Augustan mode. Occasionally in his more satirical works
he relies upon slang, colloquial idioms and other varieties of low
English; and in this he follows his eighteenth-century models. Thus in
his Epistle from *Tom Crib to Big Ben* (the latter being a nickname for
the Prince Regent) he uses slang expressions like *Blue ruin* for 'gin' and
words associated with the boxing ring, since that is the analogy he pro-
poses for the contest between England and France. A typical example
of the poem is:

Hence it comes, – BOXIANA, disgrace to thy page!–
Having floor'd, by good luck, the first *swell* of the age,
Having conquer'd the *prime one*, that *mill'd* us all round,
You kick'd him, old BEN, as he gasp'd on the ground!
Ay, just at the time to show spunk, if you' got any –
Kick'd him, and jaw'd him, and *lag'd* him to Botany! (22-7)

The slang word *lag'd* means 'transported', for the poem was written to protest at the exile of Napoleon to St Helena. The slang gives the impression of being pitchforked into the poem, but it lacks some of the force and vigour of much earlier satire, perhaps because it is too much of a literary device.

The Romantic period was not a great age of drama, though many plays continued to be written and performed. Many of these were both lighter and more ephemeral than the plays we have considered so far. It is evident that at this time there was a stage version of Cockney which many actors adopted if they wanted to portray any less educated character. In a book published over the name 'Anthony Pasquin' (which may have been an alias for one John Williams) called *The Eccentricities of John Edwin, Comedian* (1791) there are many anecdotes about actors in the latter half of the eighteenth century. Apparently they often imitated the Cockney dialect both on stage and in their private banter off stage. Although the compiler of the anecdotes disapproved of the language, he nevertheless gave examples of it, of which the following is one:

I *wow* its the *wery* best of *whittles*, isn't it, eh? and for a man to say as how that *weal vas* betterer then *wenson* is certainly *wery* monstrous and *woid* of all reason; isn't it, eh? He might as well say that *wice* ought to be *walued* above *wirtue*, or that *vawnuts* can be pickled *vithout winegar*; mightn't he, eh? – I *axt* him, says I d'ye think now, neighbour *Spriggings*, that *cowcumbers* are good without *ingons*, and so he gave *sich* an out o'th'way arnswer, that I told him, says, says I, Mr *Spriggings*, you *werily* deserve to be pelted *vith brick bracks*, and rolled in the *kindle* says I, till you are as black in the face as a *chimbly sweeper*.

In this example, not all of which can be quoted, the principal feature is the interchange of *v* and *w*. The loss of consonants is found in *vawnut* 'walnut' and *summat* 'somewhat', the *v* of 'give me' is assimilated to *m* in *gimme*, and a *b* is inserted in *chimbly* 'chimney'.

Many of these were not specifically Cockney pronunciations, for even the interchange of *w* and *v* was found fairly widely in the south-eastern dialects. Most of these features may be regarded more as vulgar than as Cockney, though as Cockney was becoming the primary non-standard dialect it attracted to itself many non-standard features. The same general rule applies to the vowel representations, among which may be noted *sich* 'such', *ingons* 'onions', *vonted* 'wanted', *apinion* 'opinion' and *vitsen* 'Whitsun'. It is difficult to decide in many instances what precise pronunciation is intended, and the variation in the given forms suggests that frequently the written forms were introduced as variants of the standard rather than as representations of the Cockney dialect. The form *cowcumber* is interesting as it had until recently been regarded as the more correct form, but it had been replaced at the end of the eighteenth century by the modern pronunciation which is based on the Latin form. Syntactically there are several colloquial features, particularly the use of double negatives and non-standard comparatives as in *I don't vant no more conwersation* and *betterer* or even *more betterer*. While the latter forms were now definitely non-standard, the former had not been entirely abandoned by the polite as the novels of Jane Austen show. It is only the company they keep which brands these examples as non-standard.

One of the best known representations of the Cockney dialect occurs in the play *Tom and Jerry* by W. T. Moncrieff which made its debut at the Adelphi Theatre on 26 November 1821. This was only four months after the appearance of Pierce Egan's prose work *Life In London*, from which *Tom and Jerry* was adapted, though even then Moncrieff's version was the third dramatic adaptation. The original prose describes how Tom, a Londoner, visits Jerry in the country and persuades him to come to London to see the sights. During this visit the two share in many escapades together. On one occasion they are arrested by the watchman, Barney O'Bother, who is evidently an Irishman. When he charges the two of them before the magistrate he constantly represents the sound [i:] by *a* as in *plase* 'please', *ase* 'ease', *pace* 'peace'; and he uses the form *jontlemen* for 'gentlemen' (ch. 9). Most of the locals, however, are naturally represented as Cockneys. The dog-fancier is one of the first to make his appearance and speaks in this way:

> Mayhap, as how, Sir, you *vou'd* like to see a bit of *fun* to night *vith* this here little *phenonmy* Monkey. He has *spoilt* all the dogs that has fought him. *Jacco Maccacco* is nothing else but a *hout-and-houter*, Sir; and is *vell vorth* your notice (ch. 10).

He exhibits what was to become one of the most characteristic features of Cockney, the inclusion of an initial *h* as in *hout-and-houter*. He also indulges in what may be intended as malapropism, *phenonmy* 'phenomenon'. Most of the other features of his language have already been encountered. Further examples of Cockney are provided by the inhabitants of Tothill Fields and by the 'costardmonger' and his 'voman' who had an altercation when their donkey slipped his foot into a hole. In addition to the features which we have already met, the denizens of Tothill Fields use a lot of slang both for money and for localities in London. Twopence is a *duce* and a penny is a *win*; and the Elephant and Castle is referred to as the *Pig and Tinder-Box*. Other slang words like *goggles* for 'eyes' appear. In fact the whole book contains many slang and cant words from the more fashionable elements of society as well as from the Cockney speakers. But this slang is introduced only sporadically, just as the Cockney features occur together with more standard items of language. The forms were introduced to give a racy and colourful nature to the book; not to portray a dialect faithfully.

In Moncrieff's stage version the non-standard varieties are much enlarged, though they are also made more ludicrous. Egan's Cockney passages are few; but Cockney forms are spread by Moncrieff throughout his play and they are mixed in with other linguistic oddities. The result is a play which ceases to have any genuine pretensions to accurate linguistic representation; for dialect and slang have been harnessed to comedy and the grotesque. Malapropism reappears as a strong feature. Although Teddy McLush is described as an Irish watchman, his language has little that could be described as Irish in it. Instead he reminds one of Dogberry in his malapropisms. Not untypical is:

> Plaise your honour, I have brought before your worship a most notorious substitute and common street talker, who for her foul doings, has been cooped up in the Poultry Compter, as often as there are years in a week. – I caught her charging these honest gentlemen in a most impositious manner. (II.iv)

Apart from *plaise*, which is introduced as an Irish version of *please*, there is little that is Irish here.

There are, however, plenty of Cockney speakers such as Jemmy Green and Mr Jenkins. These appear throughout the play and give it part of its linguistic colouring. They speak in this way:

Mr J.	Halloa, my little un?
Green.	Eh! come you a done now; you a done vith you.
Mr J.	Sluice your dominos – vill you? –
Green.	Vot! I never plays at dominos – It's too wulgar!
Mr J.	Wy, then vash your ivories?
Green.	I've got no hivories to vash.
Mr J.	Drink vill you? don't you understand Hinglish? (II.vi)

Here we can see that many of the phonetic features of the dialect are more muted so that attention can be focused on the vulgar slang. Even so, characteristic features like inorganic initial *h-* and the interchange of *w* and *v* continue to appear. But the author was more intent on giving the feel of London through its specialized vocabularies. Even Tom cannot avoid exposing Jerry's ignorance of current fashionable slang. After all he and Logic are intent on instructing Jerry into the niceties of city life. They can therefore come forward with a whole range of slang, as when Logic says:

> Blunt, my dear boy, is – in short what is it not? It's every thing now o'days – to be able to flash the screens – sport the rhino – shew the needful – post the pony – nap the rent – stump the pewter – tip the brads – and down with the dust, is to be at once good, great, handsome, accomplished, and every thing that's desirable – money, money is your universal good. (I.iv).

On another occasion the two say:

> *Logic.* Aye, aye, give him a rap over the mazzard, Tom.
> *Tom.* I've nobb'd him on the canister; he napp'd it under the lug, too. (II.iv)

Jerry naturally indicates his progress in London by uttering certain fashionable words constantly. For once vocabulary has become as important as, if not more important than, pronunciation. It is hardly surprising that this musical comedy ran for so long. It is a great linguistic hodgepodge which acted as a comic strain to the songs, for there was little plot to the drama itself. It, with Egan's prose, helped to establish Cockney as the primary vulgar dialect; but it helped to encourage the use of slang and colloquialisms rather than pronunciation as a characteristic of that style.

Somewhat earlier than this Maria Edgeworth, who is rather better known for her novels, included a Cockney in her play *Love and Law*, which was published in 1817. This is Miss Bloomsbury, described in the Dramatis Personae as 'A fine London Waiting-maid'. She is given many of the characteristics of a Cockney though they occur only sporadically. She is, however, contrasted with Honor McBride, the heroine of the play who seeks employment with Mrs Carver with whom Bloomsbury is already employed. This gives Bloomsbury the chance to lord it over a simple Irish girl and thus to reveal her own brand of tyrannical kindness. Her speech contains the usual interchange of *v* and *w* in *vindor* 'windows' and the use of inorganic initial *h* in *Hirish* 'Irish' and *hears* 'ears'. She also uses the form *vice* 'voice', a pronunciation which had been acceptable in polite society in London until well into the eighteenth century and so its branding as vulgar was relatively recent. 'Learn' is written as *larn*, which exhibits a pronunciation which was increasingly considered vulgar and so attributed to Cockney and other dialect speakers. There is assimilation of *d* in *Lon'on* 'London', assimilation and syncope in *petticlar* 'particular' and syncope alone in *dic'snary* 'dictionary'. Several of these words contain a different spelling from the standard in unstressed syllables, though these may be more in the nature of sight variants than pronunciation differences. Syntactically one may note *seed* 'seen', *i'n't* 'is not' and *you'se* 'you are'. There are some unusual lexical items like *shuts* 'shutters' and *bettermost* 'excellent'. Constructions like *this here* also occur. Since Maria Edgeworth was writing in Ireland, though she maintained contacts with English literary life, it is clear that the standard representation of Cockney was now well established. Nevertheless, in the published form of the play many of the variant spelling forms are italicized as if to draw attention to their special character. The dialect was not so familiar that it could stand on its own without this pointing.

Miss Edgeworth is well known as a creator of the Irish dialect, and since her play is set in Ireland it has several Irish characters. They all speak in the Irish dialect to some degree. As with her representation of Cockney she does not produce a comprehensive dialect; she introduces enough features to remind her listeners or readers that the people are Irish. The three features which occur with the greatest regularity include the substitution of [i:], however written in standard English, by *a*, *aa* or *ay*, which probably represent [ei]. Hence we find *rason* 'reason', *clane* 'clean', *raal* 'real', *flay* 'flea', *sacrets* 'secrets' and *convanient* 'convenient'. However, 'beard' appears as *bird*, which may indicate that this word had a short vowel sound. The second feature is that *s* is written *sh* in such words as *counshillor, shister, proposhals* and *shuting* 'suiting'. The third feature is the representation of short *e*, whether before a nasal or not, as *i* as in *contint* 'content', *sind* 'sent', *plinty* 'plenty' as well as *cliverly* 'cleverly' (not *clivirly* or *clivarly*), *niver* 'never', *expict* 'expect', *wilcome* 'welcome' and *pritty* 'pretty'. Other features include the representation of *o* before *l* + consonant as *ou* in *ould* and *boulted* 'bolted', and of *er* as *ar* in *sartified* 'certified' and *prefar* 'prefer'. 'Paid' has a short vowel *ped*; and other words with variant spellings include *jantleman* (not *jintleman*), *beyant* 'beyond', *ax* 'ask' and *apotecary* 'apothecary'. The most noteworthy lexical item is the occurrence of *sure*; though occasionally a speaker will add 'at-all-at-all' at the end of an utterance. One character draws attention to the difference in the local vocabulary by saying 'Why, by a spoonful of the univarsal panacea, *flattery* – in the vulgar tongue *flummery*' (I.ii). In general, few specifically Irish words are used, though naturally the odd word like *shillelah* crops up. Syntactically one may note that the continuous forms of the verb are found where the standard uses the simple tenses. This occurs, for example in 'Mrs Carver is wanting a girl' and 'No man dare be letting the whiskey into his head'.

Miss Edgeworth's representation of the Irish dialect in her novel *Castle Rackrent* (1800) is better known and certainly more influential; it was the first regional novel in English and possibly in Europe too. Spellings indicating an Irish pronunciation are found, but they are rare; usually no more than two or three examples of each variant are found throughout the novel. Thus [i:] is spelt as *a* only in *Jasus, sacret, plase* 'please' and *cratur* 'creature', and even then this spelling is not regularly used. The spelling *sh* for *s* is found only in *shister*. The group *er* occurs as *ar* once each in *larning* and *prefarred* 'preferred'. The word *pen* is spelt *pin* on a single occasion, though there is a note to the effect that it should read *pen* which 'formerly was vulgarly pronounced *pin* in Ireland'. However, there is no indication as to what is meant by either 'formerly' or 'vulgarly'. Certainly no other examples of the group *en* spelt *in* are found in the novel. Other spellings which may have been designed to give an Irish flavour to the work are *tings* 'things', *chuse* 'choose' and *fader* 'father'. As for vocabulary there are some Irish words and usages. Some of these are commented on in a glossary added by the author for the benefit of the English reader while the novel was being set up for its first edition. She noted that people had suggested 'that many of the terms and idiomatic phrases with which it abounds could not be intelligible to the English reader without farther explanation'. Among the words glossed are *whillaluh* 'a lamentation for the dead', *barrack-room* 'a bedroom fitted with many beds used by the occasional visitor', *mad* 'angry' and *kilt* 'badly hurt'. Some Irish expressions like *power* in 'a power of company' are not glossed. Similarly *sure* which is used to introduce a question as in 'Sure can't you sell though at a loss?' and the reduplication of *at all* for emphasis receive no comment. In general the author has made no attempt to look out the unusual word, and only those words are included which arise from the different society and culture prevailing in Ireland.

The bulk of the Irish forms are found in the syntax. Unusual plurals are found in *chiler* and *womens*, and *ye* is still used as a subject pronoun, though there is nothing specifically Irish about these forms. The verb phrase has many Irish features. The use of *be* with the present participle instead of the simple verb occurs in 'Don't be talking' and 'to be telling'. Irish extensions of the verb occur in such verb groups as *talking on* 'talking about', *I'm after speaking of* 'I'm talking about' and *dressing of her* 'dressing her'. Other striking idioms which occur include: *how should it but be as dry as a bone, after all the fires we have kept in it day and night* (p. 26); *My heart was all as one as in my mouth* (p. 45); and *but they all were the same sorry* (p. 78). The most significant feature of the novel is the playing down of pronunciation and lexical differences in favour of syntactic and idiomatic usage. This was an important development. Although Thady, the main Irish speaker, has his humorous side, he is in no way a comic or ludicrous figure. The restrained reliance on syntactic and idiomatic usage prevents the reader from misunderstanding Thady. He is not like the grotesque Irish stage figures who were merely brought on for comic relief. He is a provincial who speaks in a provincial way, but who is nevertheless allowed his own dignity and sensibility. In this respect the novel represents a breakthrough in challenging the stranglehold of the standard language as the only polite language and in suggesting that dialect speakers need not be mere caricatures. Naturally this novel showed other writers how they could exploit non-standard varieties not only for regional, but also for historical, novels. The greatest beneficiary was Sir Walter Scott, who emulated Miss Edgeworth's examples. He was to accomplish for Scotland what she had achieved for Ireland. His success, however, eclipsed Maria Edgeworth's work so that her contribution to the regional novel and its speech has not been fully appreciated. It should nevertheless be stated that Scott himself was never in any doubt about the importance of his predecessor.

The situation facing Scott was very different from the one which Maria Edgeworth encountered. Irish had been a comic dialect in

English writing since Shakespeare's *Henry V* and from the end of the seventeenth century an Irish comic character had appeared in many plays. There were no serious works in Irish English known to the average English reader, and the attitude towards the Irish hardly encouraged Englishmen to regard them as civilized or sophisticated. Scots had fared much better. There was still a vigorous poetry in the early sixteenth century written in that variety of English. Scotland was an independent kingdom which had been united to, rather than subjugated by, England. It was less usual in plays or novels to find comic characters speaking with a Scots accent. The arrival of Burns and the growing interest in older poetry such as the Border ballads created a respect for the Scots dialect which made it acceptable as a vehicle for serious literature. Scott himself could not match the light touch of Maria Edgeworth in his characters, but conversely his creations had a soberness and solidity which hers never achieved. His popularity and output made Scots well known.

Even so it was Miss Edgeworth who gave Scott the confidence to make a provincial novel with non-standard speakers; she also set him a model for dealing with ordinary people. The language he used had become familiar enough to him both through everyday speech and through his reading. In 1802 his edition of *Ballads from the Border Minstrelsy* appeared. These ballads were written in a form of Scots, but they also appeared in an archaic spelling. Thus the opening of *The Sang of the Outlaw Murray* reads:

> Ettricke Foreste is a feir foreste,
>   In it grows manie a semelie trie;
> There's hart and hynd, and dae and rae,
>   And of a' wilde bestis grete plentie.

Spellings in this stanza like *foreste, manie, hynd, bestis* and *grete* have no significance for the pronunciation of the language; they are simply archaic. Scott was to draw more extensively on this source of language for his historical works. But other spellings like *feir* and *rae* are significant dialectally. In his own poems Scott drew on subjects from the past which had a romance flavour; in these dialogue was given an archaic, rather than a dialectal, colouring. This was principally achieved through the use of archaic spellings, the 2nd person singular forms of the personal pronouns, archaic words and localized words which were often archaic at that time. In the *Lay of the Last Minstrel* a herald can speak in this way:

And ill beseems your rank and birth
To make your towers a flemens-firth.
We claim from thee William of Deloraine,
That he may suffer march-treason pain.
It was but last St Cuthbert's even
He prick'd to Stapleton on Leven,
Harried the lands of Richard Musgrave,
And slew his brother by dint of glaive. (IV. xxiv)

There are no archaic spellings in this example, but *lady* is spelt *ladye* in
the following stanza. General archaisms include *beseems, prick'd* and
glaive. More localized words include *flemens-firth* and *march-treason*.
The first of these is used by Scott in the sense 'an asylum for outlaws',
which is not a sense it had earlier. Its older meaning was 'the offence of
harbouring a banished person'. The second may well be a compound
invented by Scott to give an archaic flavour. The second person
singular of the personal pronoun is used in *thee*, but not in *your*.
Other syntactic archaisms are employed, such as *spoke* as the past participle 'spoken'. Without Maria Edgeworth's example Scott might never
have gone beyond this type of language.

In Scott's novels non-standard language may be considered under
three categories: the Scottish novels which deal with events in the present or recent past, novels set in medieval England, and those set in
medieval or reformation Scotland. I will consider *The Heart of
Midlothian, Ivanhoe* and *The Monastery* as examples of these groups
respectively.

In *The Heart of Midlothian*, as indeed in his other works, Scott
shows how sensitive he was to variations in pronunciation and spelling,
for he makes incidental comments upon these matters during the
novel's course. A typical example follows Jeanie Dean's letter to
Reuben Butler:

The orthography of these epistles may seem to the southron to require a
better apology than the letter expresses, though a bad pen was the excuse of
a certain Galwegian laird for bad spelling; but, on behalf of the heroine, I
would have them to know, that, thanks to the care of Butler, Jeanie Deans
wrote and spelled fifty times better than half the women of rank in
Scotland at that period, whose strange orthography and singular diction
form the strangest contrast to the good sense which their correspondence
usually intimates. (ch. 28)

Jeanie had concluded her letter by writing 'Excuse bad spelling and writing, as I have ane ill pen'. Scott does not elaborate on what spelling she was aiming at, though he seems to have viewed Scottish speech and writing as permissible, though not as acceptable as standard English. His upper-class characters like the Duke of Argylle speak and write English rather than Scots, and Scott himself could not escape the trend to correctness in spelling and grammar which we shall see even more cogently expressed in the writings of Jane Austen.

In this same chapter Scott alerts the reader to Mrs Bickerton's language. This lady was the hostess of the Seven Stars inn at York, but she had been born and bred in Scotland. Her residence in the North of England meant that 'her acquired English' mingled 'with her natural or original dialect'. This is a chance remark thrown off by Scott, and it is difficult to detect the precise amount of mingling because all the Scottish characters who are given a form of Scots have it mingled with many English forms. Another example of his concern for dialect comes at the end of the novel where the Duke is telling the Butlers about Jeanie's sister, though he is ignorant of their relationship. He says:

> She is a Scotchwoman, and speaks with a Scotch accent, and now and then a provincial word drops so prettily, that it is quite Doric. (ch. 48)

'Doric' is used at this time of a dialect which is rude and provincial, though it is here evidently meant in a more complimentary way. The odd dialect word adds an extra spice and interest to the language of the lady, though it is implied that as a lady she naturally speaks standard English otherwise. His tone is defensive, as it is when he writes of Jeanie's reading of the Bible that she 'read it, notwithstanding her northern accent and tone, with a devout propriety' (ch. 33). Scott is trying to fight against the tide of the time which rejected provincial pronunciation and spelling as lacking refinement. It is not surprising, therefore, that he rarely introduces a comic Scots speaker, since this would undermine the respect he tries to acquire for the dialect. The nearest he comes to a comic speaker in this novel is Mr Saddletree who is tiresome and pedantic and falls into the occasional malapropism as when he used *Substitutes* for *Institutes*.

As the novel is set principally in and around Edinburgh, it is Lowlands Scots which provides most examples of dialect speech. The majority of the characters are from the middle or lower classes, and so they all speak Scots to a greater or lesser extent. While he is intent on indicating their Scottishness, he does not try to introduce a thoroughgoing Scots language for the dialogue. He is satisfied simply to remind his readers of the Scottish nature of the characters, and he is anxious not to make the story too difficult to read. Some subjects are therefore presented more in standard English than Scots. David Deans speaks to Mr Saddletree in this way:

> And as to murmur again them, it's what a' the folk that loses their pleas, and nine-tenths o' them that win them, will be gay sure to be guilty in. Sae I wad hae ye ken that I haud a' your gleg-tongued advocates, that sell their knowledge for pieces of silver, and your worldly-wise judges, that will gie three days of hearing in presence to a debate about the peeling of an ingan, and no ae half-hour to the gospel testimony, as legalists and formalists, countenancing, by sentences, and quirks, and cunning terms of law, the late begun courses of national defections – union, toleration, patronages, and Yerastian prelatic oaths. (ch. 12)

The first part contains more dialect than the second because the subject matter becomes more technical. It may be difficult enough for some readers to follow it in English; it might become incomprehensible in Scots. This passage contains many typical features found in the dialect: *l* is lost in *a'* 'all', *wad* 'would' and *haud* 'hold'; *v* in *hae* 'have' and *gie* 'give'; and *f* in *o'* 'of'. The reflex of Middle English *o* is written *a* in *wad* 'would', *au* in *haud* 'hold' and *ae* in *sae* 'so'. There are a few dialect words like *gleg-tongued* 'smooth-tongued', *ken* 'know' and *ingan* 'onion', as well as some dialect syntactic usages. The subject *ye* is used; the plural of the present indicative is *-s* in *loses*; and *gay* appears as an intensifier.

Further dialect features may be included when the subject warrants – usually in domestic situations. When Mrs Saddletree reflects on the vanity of human wishes, in part by castigating her servant, her language becomes quite heavy with Scots words and forms, although on other occasions her language can be much more standard.

> 'Grizzie, come up here and take tent to the honest auld man, and see he wants naething. – Ye sillie tawpie' (addressing the maid-servant as she entered), 'what garr'd ye busk up your cockernony that gate? – I think there's been eneugh the day to gie an awfu' warning about your cockups and your fallal duds – see what they a' come to.' (ch. 25)

The dialect words are increased, for even if the reader has never come across them before, the general tone of the abuse is enough to let him guess what their general meaning is likely to be. In many cases the subject matter and the situation may be more important factors in the number of dialect features Scott employs than the class of the speaker.

The Heart of Midlothian is an important novel because it contains more varieties of dialect than that spoken in the Edinburgh region. On Jeanie's trip to London to seek her sister's pardon she arrives at the home of the Stauntons in the Midlands. Here several of the local people speak dialect to a greater or lesser degree. One is simply described as a 'boor', another is Tummas, Staunton's servant, and a third is the beadle. He uses some forms which are found as freely among the Scots speakers: omission of *th* in *wi* 'with' and of *v* in *gie* 'give'; assimilation of *f* in *thysell* 'thyself'; and the representation of *a* before a nasal as *o* in *ony* 'any'. Some syntactic usages like *were no up enow* can be paralleled by speakers from further north. There are, however, inflexions like *does thou* and *I'se be* as well as spellings like *koind* 'kind' and *soa* 'so' which indicate a more southerly language type. The form *measter* 'master' is one which had been found in non-standard representations in the eighteenth century, and may be a general non-standard form which Scott thought would be useful to employ here. In addition the beadle uses a variety of specialized vocabulary which characterizes his language. These words include *donnot* 'foolish and idle person', *gare-brained* 'very heedless', *polrumptious* 'disorderly', *ratan* 'staff' and *snog and snod* 'snug and neat'. These words come from a variety of different origins. *Ratan* is a Scots word meaning 'roll of drums, drumming' and may have been extended by Scott here; *polrumptious* may be one of his own creations; *gare-brained* is an east-country word; *snog and snod* are northern and Scots words which would probably not be used as far south as the Midlands; and *donnot* is also a Scots and northern word, though it may have been found as far south as the Midlands. These words indicate Scott's wide reading and his rather eclectic choice of dialect material. He was not so worried about creating an accurate dialect as giving the impression of a non-standard speaker.

On her way back to Scotland with Archibald, the coach stopped near Carlisle because Jeanie was overcome with the sight of a woman being hanged. During this pause they overhear some 'Cumbrian peasants' discussing the event. Here Scott has characterized the dialect particularly through the use of *ho* 'her' and the representation of [ai] as *oi* as in *woife* 'woman'. Other features are those that one might find in his representation of the Scots dialect. He uses some words not found elsewhere in the rest of the novel like *sture* 'stern', *crining* 'crying' and *tint* 'lost'. But they could readily have appeared like this since they could come from either side of the border. What is remarkable about the language here is simply its density of non-standard features. The dialogue is brief, but it is very heavily non-standard, as perhaps befits the peasants who utter it.

Another dialect is exhibited by Duncan the Captain of Knockdunder, whom the Butlers meet when they settle in their new home provided by the Duke of Argyle. His territory stretches over both the Lowlands and the Highlands, and so Scott no doubt felt he should give him a different form of speech. Although he has many of the features which characterize the Lowland Scots, he also has many of the features which were traditionally ascribed to the Welsh and Irish, and which Scott may have used to suggest the Gaelic affiliations of the Highlanders. Initial *b* becomes *p*, *d* becomes *t*, and *w(h)* becomes *f*. Duncan says *Cot tamn* 'God damn', and *Fat ta deil* 'What the devil', though on some occasions he uses *teil* for *deil* 'devil'. He also uses *sh* for *g* in *shentlemens* 'gentlemen' and *ck* for *ct* in *neglecking*. Long vowels are indicated in *aboot* 'about' and *preceesely* 'precisely' rather than diphthongs, though the sounds intended in *synd* 'send' and *kintra* 'country' are less clear. In this case, as in others, Scott has taken his usual Scots forms as the basis for non-standard speech. When he wishes to indicate a dialect other than that one, he adds a few features in addition to the Scots forms in order to characterize the dialect. These features may in practice have little or nothing to do with the dialect he is trying to represent. They serve only to differentiate its speakers and to add some local colour.

When Scott wrote *Ivanhoe* he was presented with a different problem. This novel is set in England in the early Middle Ages. Scott evidently felt that he ought to archaize in order to give the correct tone to the novel, but he realized that if he did so too extensively he ran the risk of being both unreadable and unintelligible. Some archaisms had been retained in formal eighteenth-century writing, such as the use of *thou* and *thee*, but Scott wanted to be more daring and distinctive in his archaisms. He was very widely read and he brought together words from a variety of sources. Among those he used most were Berners' *Froissart*, Spenser, Shakespeare, other Elizabethans and Percy's *Reliques*. He never forgot what he read and he mingled words from different periods and social origins together quite unashamedly. His linguistic colouring was based on no scholarly foundation. In *Ivanhoe* he uses *thou* and *thee* with the corresponding verb forms such as *art*, *hast*, *mayst* and *wilt*; he also employs the *-eth* ending of the third person singular present indicative as in *altereth*, *flourisheth*. A number of older conjunctions occur as *so* 'if', *an* 'if' and *sith* 'since'. Apart from that most of the archaizing comes in the vocabulary. This can consist of genuine archaisms, apparent colloquialisms and invented words which are meant to blend with the others to give the appropriate tone. They include *gramercy* 'thanks', *scatheless* 'uninjured', *porkers* 'pigs', *skin-cutting* 'wounding' (a word possibly based on Old English compounds), *centrical* 'in the centre' and *byzants*. The effect is not pleasing to modern ears, for the language seems stilted and unnatural.

Although in *Ivanhoe* Scott used his archaic language fairly consistently, at least as far as his English characters are concerned, he was uncertain how to represent the speech of his characters in *The Monastery*, set as it was in the Lowlands during the reign of King Richard I. The characters could speak in the Scots of *The Heart of Midlothian* or with the archaisms of *Ivanhoe*, for he evidently never seriously considered a variety of archaic Scots which might have been too difficult for everyone. The result is that he employed not only standard English, but also both Scots and archaic English within the speech of an individual. This switching is found in the language of Elspeth Glendinning as well as in that of the more homely Hob Miller,and the linguistic chaos is accentuated when Sir Piercie Shatton indulges in a variety of bastard euphuism. This novel is the worst for providing such an undigested variety of different languages. After it Scott fell back increasingly on a variant of standard English even for novels set in Scotland. However he did draw attention to the problems faced by historical and regional novelists, although the former he failed to solve in a satisfactory way.

Scott's successor as a Scottish novelist, James Hogg the Ettrick shepherd (1770-1835), also used the Scots dialect in his work. He did not follow Scott's example in the way he employed it, for he was not so much influenced by realism as by the particular purposes of narrative structure and symbolism. The majority of his characters in *The Private Memoirs and Confession of a Justified Sinner* (1824) use standard English, to which the Scots acts as a counterpoint. Often it is found in use by the lower-class characters such as John Barnet and Samuel Scrape, the former of whom is contrasted with the Rev. Robert Winghim and the latter with Robert, his putative son or the 'sinner'. The dialect speakers are vituperative, vigorous, earthy and honest, or at least they appear so in comparison with the upper-class characters whom they serve. A similar effect is created by the Scots put into the mouth of Baillie Orde, even though he is by no means of inferior rank. It is his daughter who married Lord Dalcastle and became the mother of the 'sinner'. When the lady leaves her husband almost immediately after marrying him to return to her father, the latter treats her severely. His use of dialect suggests a probity and directness not found in his daughter's behaviour. It is symbolic rather than realistic, for this disparity in language between father and daughter is most improbable; it reminds one of the difference between the languages of the King of France and Princess Katherine in *Henry V*. It is used to underline particular points in the novel, not to create a sense of verisimilitude. Yet the regional form is not used by Hogg specifically for comedy; the status of regional varieties (at least some of them) had risen so that they can be used to suggest those virtues which civilization and religion seem to undermine. Sophistication and education no longer carry automatic approval. The Romantic Revolution reversed the trend towards urban predominance and allowed for the growing concern for more rustic virtues. This was a trend that would grow in importance and naturally would affect people's attitudes towards regional varieties of speech. It is hardly surprising that this should happen first in Scotland, partly because of Scott's writings and partly because of the more favourable attitude to the Scots dialect that had been noticeable for many years in England.

Jane Austen, the major English novelist of the period, is quite different in her attitude to language from Scott. She is an author who shows the utmost propriety in language and points out the lapses in grammar and vocabulary made by her characters. Her concern is not with dialect or other regional forms of English. It is therefore unthinkable that Darcy in *Pride and Prejudice* should speak with a northern accent even though his family seat is located in the North, for that would undermine the respect in which he is held. Jane Austen is more concerned with correctness, this being a rather more sophisticated weapon than the blunt hammer of dialect. The latter is suitable for comedy and the grotesque, while the former is more fitting for novels of sensibility and emotion. The differences in language use are not great. In *Northanger Abbey* Catherine Morland has the following exchange with Henry Tilney:

'Not very good, I am afraid. But now, really do you not think *Udolpho* the nicest book in the world?'
'The nicest; by which I suppose you mean the neatest. That must depend upon the binding.'
'Henry,' said Miss Tilney, 'you are very impertinent. Miss Morland, he is

treating you exactly as he does his sister. He is for ever finding fault with me for some incorrectness of language, and now he is taking the same liberty with you. The word 'nicest', as you used it, did not suit him; and you had better change it as soon as you can, or we shall be overpowered with Johnson and Blair all the rest of the way.' (ch. 14)

An appropriate use of words is a desirable accomplishment and meaningless vogue words meet with disapproval. This situation arises through the eighteenth-century insistence on correctness in language use, which continued to exercise a strong influence over the nineteenth century. The development took two forms – the regulation of vocabulary through dictionaries and the regulation of syntax through grammars. The former culminated in Dr Johnson's dictionary of 1755; the latter received its most forceful expression in the grammars of Bishop Lowth (1762) and Lindley Murray (1795) – though Hugh Blair was also a grammarian of note, as the quotation makes clear. The dictionaries suggested to people that certain words belonged to the English language and that those words had a definite and recognizable meaning. They naturally encouraged the view that vogue and cant words were not respectable since such words and usages were not recorded, and so correct language became more conservative and more tied to the written forms. The grammars for their part usually proceeded on the basis that good grammar could best be exhibited by parading examples of bad grammar culled from various authors. This practice directed attention towards mistakes and divided English speakers up into two groups: those who did and those who did not make mistakes when they spoke.

It is not surprising then that in *Emma*, Emma should think that as, in her opinion, Robert Martin was not a suitable match for Harriet Smith he could not be educated and refined. It was consequently with some mortification that she discovered that the letter he wrote to Harriet contained no grammatical lapses, for the proof that the language would provide her of his lack of gentility was missing. Mrs Elton and many of the other characters of her class do not fall into grammatical solecisms as such. Their vulgarity and lack of true refinement are shown in different ways. Thus Mrs Elton is ignorant of the fitting modes of address and uses Italian expressions.

'Insufferable woman!' was her immediate exclamation. 'Worse than I had supposed. Absolutely insufferable! Knightley! – I could not have believed it. Knightley! – never seen him in her life before, and call him

Knightley! – and discover that he is a gentleman! A little upstart, vulgar being, with her Mr E, and her *cara sposa*, and her resources, and all her airs of pert pretention and under-bred finery. (ch. 32)

In *Northanger Abbey* it is the use of such colloquialisms as *quiz* which brand John and Isabella Thorpe as unsuitable companions for Catherine Morland. In all these instances Jane Austen points out the impropriety in language, for the distinctions in language use are so subtle they could easily be overlooked. Indeed Jane Austen is not always consistent, since the respectable characters can also use colloquial expressions.

The attitude to non-standard language was thus entering a new phase. The growth in grammatical propriety made people more conscious of differences in vocabulary and syntax. At the same time regional varieties of English were gaining acceptability, though in the Romantic period only the Scots and Irish varieties found acceptance, as was perhaps natural enough. In the succeeding period this acceptance was extended to local varieties within England itself. This development we must consider in the next chapter.

Chapter 8

THE VICTORIANS

🢒🢒🢒🢒🢒🢒

IN THIS PERIOD it is again the novel which occupies pride of place. The drama remained at a relatively low ebb, though poetry shows some developments in the use of non-standard language. In the novel the most important developments relate to the employment of English (as distinct from British) regional dialects and to the establishment of Cockney as the major comic variety of non-standard language.

Emily Brontë (1818-48) is principally known today for her novel *Wuthering Heights*, a novel of great power and naturalism. In part this effect is achieved from its setting, in which the dialect is a factor. Local speech is largely confined to Joseph, the old servant at the Heights, though occasional dialect forms are found elsewhere. The Brontë sisters lived at Haworth in Yorkshire, where their father, an Irishman by birth, was the parson. The Brontë children were familiar to some extent with the local dialect, though it is likely they mixed more with local tradesmen and the lesser gentry than with the workers in mills or on the land. They are likely to have been most acquainted with a northern modified standard. Indeed, Charlotte, in her preface to the second edition of *Wuthering Heights* (1850), claimed that Emily had no practical knowledge of the speech of the area. Even so, from 1825 the Brontës had employed as a servant an old woman named Tabitha Aykroyd who was a native of Haworth, knew many stories about the area, and spoke in the local dialect. Joseph is modelled on Tabitha, and this is itself a new departure in the novel; it inevitably meant that the dialect speaker was a person of flesh and blood rather than some kind of caricature and the dialect was used to create naturalism and atmosphere. So it may well be that Emily had a rather greater knowledge of the dialect than Charlotte allowed.

The publishing history of *Wuthering Heights* makes it difficult to investigate some aspects of its language with confidence. The first edition (1847) contains many typographical mistakes, partly because Newby the publisher was relatively indifferent to the work at first and partly because he ignored many of Emily's corrections at proof stage.

There are forms which seem impossible in any dialect (like *lught* 'light') as well as standard forms alongside dialect ones (both *never* and *niver*). Whether the standard forms are printing errors caused by compositorial normalization or signs of authorial inconsistency is not known. Because the publisher is known to have been incompetent, it need not follow that the author was consistent. The second edition cannot be used to correct the dialect forms of the first because when Charlotte came to prepare it after Emily's death she decided to emend some of Joseph's dialect forms as she was afraid that southern readers would find them unintelligible. Unfortunately she not only replaced the first edition's forms by standardized ones, she also replaced them by forms with a different variant spelling. It is difficult to decide in many cases what spelling Emily might have preferred for a given word. This is particularly the case because Emily, like other dialect writers, suffered from the handicap of modifying a standard spelling by keeping to the Roman alphabet. English people associate certain sounds with given spellings and these have to be exploited to make the dialect intelligible to those who do not know it. However, by this time some Yorkshire dialect writing had been produced and it may be that certain conventions had developed as to how to represent local sounds, although they would not be widely known.

However well she knew the Haworth dialect, Emily's portrayal of Joseph's language is more comprehensive and professional than anything we have met so far. Even Scott did not go in for such detailed differences. Because she was writing within the framework of standard English, which most of her characters speak, she accepted the limitations this imposed. If a dialect pronunciation of one word resembled the pronunciation of a different word in standard English, she nevertheless used the spelling of the second word to indicate the pronunciation of the first. Normally the context is sufficient to avoid ambiguity in these cases. Thus 'feet' appears as *fit*, the word in standard English which its dialectal pronunciation most closely resembled. In standard English there are many ways of writing a single sound so that [i:] for example can be spelt with *ee* as in *sheep*, *ea* as in *clean*, *i* as in *machine*, etc. Emily took the spelling which she felt to be least ambiguous, in this case *ee*, and used that as her representation of the dialect sound [i:]. She also employed conventions which had grown up in the representation of non-standard sounds such as the use of *h* or *r* after a vowel to indicate length; thus *ah* indicates [a:] as in *daht* 'doubt' and *or* indicates [o:] in *norhter* 'neither'. In general she is content, as is usual in representations of dialect, to vary the spelling of a word only in one particular and to keep the other spelling conventions found in the standard, though they in no way reflect the dialect pronunciation. In this way she does not attempt any kind of phonetic transcription, but she isolates one feature as the distinctive marker between the dialect and the standard. Thus she spells 'house' as *hahse* with her *ah* representing the dialect equivalent of *ou* in the standard. In this word final *e* is pronounced neither in the standard nor in the dialect, for it was a written convention when introduced, and the initial *h* is not a feature of the dialect. The unphonetic retention of these symbols aids the standard reader to understand what word is meant, for *hahse* is more likely to be understood as a variant of 'house' than *ahs* would be. Naturally enough, the fall of *h* in other words might be regarded as the dialect marker and so would be omitted.

We have no contemporary descriptions of the Haworth dialect in the middle of the nineteenth century, though many of the features which Emily isolates are northern and Yorkshire rather than confined to a small region of Yorkshire. It is, as always, difficult to tell precisely what sounds her vowels or diphthongs represent. In some cases ambiguity is caused by her use of different symbols. When she used *ate* for 'eat' it was no doubt because she expected her readers to understand the same sound as in the standard pronunciation of the preterite. But she also used spellings like *cham'er* 'chamber', *maister* 'master' and *nay* 'no', and it is not certain whether these words have the same sound or not. A typical example of Joseph's dialect is this piece:

> 'Nelly', he said, 'we's hae a Crahnr's 'quest enah, at ahr folks. One on 'em's a'most getten his finger cut off wi' hauding t'other froo' sticking hisseln loike a cawlf. That's maister, yah knaw, ut's soa up uh going tuh t'grand 'sizes. He's noan feared uh t'Bench uh judges, norther Paul, nur Peter, nur John, nor Mathew, nor noan on 'em, nut he! He fair likes, he langs tuh set his brazened face agean 'em! And yon bonny lad Heathcliffe, yah mind, he's a rare un! He can girn a laugh as weel's onybody at a raight divil's jest. Does he niver say nowt of his fine living amang us, when he goas tuh t'Grange? (ch. 10)

The influence of the standard can be seen in the heavy use of the apostrophe to alert the reader to something which is missing, seen from the point of view of the standard rather than that of the dialect. Thus we have *Crahnr's 'quest* 'coroner's inquest' and *froo'* 'from'. Standard forms are found in *one* (cf. *un*), *judges* and *Heathcliffe*, where one would expect *Hathecliff*. Variant forms are found in *nur* and *nor*, with the latter from the standard. Inconsistencies are found in *loike* 'like', *likes*, *raight* 'right' and *fine*, where there are two standard spellings and two different realizations of a sound in the dialect. Similarly 'holding' appears as *hauding* without an *l*, though *cawlf* 'calf' still retains it. Features which occur in the passage include *weel* 'well' representing [i:], but elsewhere the short *e* of standard English appears as *i*, as in *niver* 'never' and *divil* 'devil', though in the first word the final *e* is unchanged. Before a nasal or a *w* the *o* of the standard is represented as *a* in *langs* 'longs', *amang* 'among' and *knaw* 'know'; but *a* before a nasal appears as *o* in *onybody* 'anybody'. The *ou* of the standard is changed to *ah* rather arbitrarily as in *ahr* 'our', *enah* 'enough' and *yah* 'you', since these words are hardly likely to have all had the same sound in the dialect. The standard spelling *ai* appears as *ea*, possibly representing a diphthong, in *feard* '(a)fraid' and *agean* 'again(st)'. An *oa* appears in *noan* and *goas*, which may possibly represent a diphthong though it is difficult to be certain. There are fewer changes of consonants than of vowels and diphthongs. The fall of consonant occurs in *hae* 'have' and *a'most* 'almost'. The addition of an inorganic final consonant occurs in *brazened* 'brazen', though one might have expected this to be written *brazend*.

Although such forms are not found in this passage Joseph uses the second singular personal pronoun forms which had disappeared from standard use. He uses *shoo* for 'she' and *ye* for the second plural subject pronoun. An interesting form is *yon* which occurs as a determiner and sets up a threefold pattern with *this* and *that*. Where *that* has the sense of 'close to the person spoken to', *yon* means 'distant from both speaker and person spoken to'. This distinction was still found in Elizabethan English and is characteristic of many dialects. The same goes for the use of *the* as a determiner where standard English would use *those*. The reflexive pronoun ends in *-seln* and is attached to the possessive as in *hisseln* 'himself'. The definite article is usually reduced to *t'* 'the'. Among the verbs may be noted the use of *'s* for 'shall', 'should', a form we have noticed earlier as a characteristic northernism. Joseph says *we's hae* 'we shall have'. He also uses the participial form *getten* for 'got'. The use of *on* as a preposition or an extension of verb where standard English would use a different word is accurate for Yorkshire speech. Among the vocabulary items we may note *at ahr folks* 'at our house', *sticking* 'killing' and *girn* 'show the teeth to indicate emotion'.

This passage is only a small example of Joseph's speech, but it is sufficient to show the density of Emily's dialect representation and its character. She includes far more than the average writer of dialect speech, though she is not consistent or able to avoid the pull of the standard orthography. The dialect is used to suggest coarseness and a latent evil. It is for this reason that it is found in Joseph and the young Hareton, both of whom have been brutalized by Heathcliff. The latter ceases to use dialect as he comes increasingly under the spell of Catherine's love, as though the curse of evil and brutality were broken by her gentleness. The dialect is still a class marker, but it is not used for cheap laughs or to create an eccentric character. Joseph is in many ways diabolical and hypocritical, but he is a character of force and the language he speaks is in no way mealy-mouthed or romantic. He is a minor character in the novel with an important secondary role, for his appearance occurs often at important psychological moments. Characteristically it is he who sets the hounds on to Lockwood and thus suggests the latent violence and inhospitable character of life at the Heights. It is he who plays an important part in the welcome for Isabella Linton after she has eloped with Heathcliff and arrived for the first time at the Heights. He heightens the revulsion felt by the girl for her new home and he forms an important part in the contrast between the horror of the Heights and the gracefulness of her former home. Joseph is blunt and earthy, providing a foil to Heathcliff and he adds a touch of grim humour to the novel because of his very different language. As the love of Hareton and Catherine blossoms, so Joseph becomes less fierce and even perhaps humorous, though he never becomes simply comic.

The dialect used in this novel was important in extending the range to which regional language could be put. But it was still available only for lower-class people such as servants, and it still carried with it certain overtones, in this instance savagery and intolerance. It seemed to the standard speaker rugged and raw, and was thus able to suggest violence and evil in those who spoke it. The dialect is part of the novel's realism, but it ultimately defeats any verisimilitude because the gap between the dialect speakers and the standard speakers is too large. Dialect has been rehabilitated, but it is still the language of the poor. Naturally this is the working poor of the North, because with the Industrial Revolution it was there that most poor people were congregated and it was there that violence erupted most frequently in the nineteenth century.

This violence forms the background to Mrs Gaskell's *North and South* (1855), but although she and Emily Brontë both deal with the North of England, their novels and their portrayal of dialect are quite different in tone and intention. They are alike in that the regional dialect is used as a class marker, for the Higgins family in *North and South* are mill workers who are born and bred in the North. Nicholas Higgins says that he comes *fro' Burnley-ways*. Although Margaret Hale and her family come from Hampshire, they are not contrasted with all northerners. The Thorntons speak an English which is as standard as that spoken by the Hales. The social divisions are both of class and of region. The language spoken by the Higgins family is not a strong dialect; in representation it cannot compare with that spoken by Joseph. These are Nicholas Higgin's first words in the novel:

> Thank yo', miss. Bessy'll think a deal o' them flowers; that hoo will; and I shall think a deal o' yor kindness. Yo're not of this country, I reckon. (ch. 8)

This is virtually a return to the traditional way of representing non-standard speech. The language is essentially standard with only a few dialect markers. There is much less reliance upon differences in sound, and much more upon those of vocabulary and grammar. The ab-breviated forms *'ll* 'will/shall' and *o'* 'of' may be as much colloquial as dialect. The representations *yo'* and *yo're* are ambiguous since it is not clear whether they indicate different pronunciations or not. They seem to be as indicative of low-class as of regional origins. In vocabulary one can note usages like *a deal* 'much, a lot', *country* 'region' and *reckon* 'think'. These words are not restricted to South Lancashire. The same applies to the use of *them* as a determiner. The most striking feature is *hoo* 'she', which is a regular element in Nicholas's language, though even that is not very specific in its localization. The dialect gives a col-our to the novel, but it is a pale representation. It is gentler and more restrained than the dialect found in *Wuthering Heights*, as is true of the novel as a whole. It lacks realism, but for its time it marked an ad-vance in that it confirmed that English regional dialects could be used in a serious way. Perhaps because of Bessy's fate there is a feeling that the dialect adds a touch of pathos and simplicity to the novel.

In *Cranford* (1853), Mrs Gaskell also used some dialect, but in this novel there is more occasional low-class usage than dialect as such. Cranford represents Knutsford, Cheshire, but the language of the non-standard speakers rarely shows any regional affiliation. Jenny, the maid, uses expressions like *them railways* with *them* as a determiner. Mr Holbrook uses an old-fashioned pronunciation for some names and Miss Matty's parents' letters contain archaic spellings. The largest amount of non-standard language is used by the carter who reports Captain Brown's death:

> 'Please, mum, it is true. I see'd it myself,' and he shuddered at the recollection. 'The captain was a-reading some new book as he was deep in, a-waiting for the down train; and there was a little lass as wanted to come to its mammy, and gave its sister the slip, and came toddling over the line. And he looked up sudden, at the sound of the train coming, and see'd the child, and he darted on the line and cotched it up, and his foot slipped, and the train came over him in no time.' (ch. 2)

Here most of the features are non-standard like *mum, see'd*, the prefix *a-*, the use of *sudden* as an adverb, and *as* used as a relative pronoun. There are only occasional attempts to render a different pronunciation as in *cotched* and *mammy*, and these are insufficient to localize the pronunciation. This book does, however, show how popular non-standard language had become for the representation of low-class characters even where there is no element of humour.

George Eliot used dialect extensively in *Adam Bede* (1859) and in this aspect her novel reaches back to the example of Scott. Adam Bede himself and many of his workmates and relatives are dialect speakers, and thus dialect occurs throughout the novel. It is not used sporadically for particular effects as is true of *Wuthering Heights*; it was employed to convey realism and was part of the process whereby the novel gains verisimilitude. The action is set in Staffordshire and Derbyshire, and in a letter to W. W. Skeat the author claimed she had followed the dialect as closely as she could, given the need for a novelist to make what is written intelligible to readers who are familiar only with standard English. Indeed it was with this need for intelligibility in mind that she let G. H. Lewes standardize some of the dialect in the novel during its proof stage. Some of her friends such as George Bulwer-Lytton thought that her style was excellent except when it was 'provincial'. It was no doubt Scott's example which gave her the resolution to carry through this use of non-standard language. It must be said that she was genuinely interested in philological matters: she had read Max Müller's *Lectures on the Science of Language* and she was familiar with several languages. She evidently possessed a sensitive ear and a retentive memory for variant sounds.

Yet her intention in *Adam Bede* was artistic rather than strictly linguistic. Dinah Morris, the Methodist woman preacher, does not use dialect even though she comes from the same social milieu as Adam. In her case biblical and Wesleyan English take precedence over dialect.

Adam's workmates in the opening chapter speak varying degrees of dialect as though they are being partly distinguished through the way they speak. There is no attempt at consistency or uniformity in the representation of dialect. Consider the following passage:

> 'Hoorray!' shouted a small lithe fellow called Wiry Ben, running forward and seizing the door. 'We'll hang up th'door at fur end o' th' shop an' write on't 'Seth Bede, the Methody, his work! Here, Jim, lend's hould o' th' red pot.'
> 'Nonsense!' said Adam. 'Let it alone, Ben Cranage. You'll mayhap be making such a slip yourself some day; you'll laugh o' th' other side o' your mouth then.' (ch. 1)

Adam's language is more standard than Ben's. He has elided forms like *o'*, idiomatic expressions like *you'll be asking*, and words like *mayhap*. But Ben uses dialect pronunciations such as *fur* 'far', probably representing [ə:], *hould* 'hold', probably indicating a diphthongal pronunciation, and *hoorray*. In addition there are idiomatic usages like *lend's hould* 'give me', *his work* and *at fur end* and he also includes elided forms.

Elsewhere dialect forms can be introduced more frequently in the language of some characters, notably Lisbeth and Mrs Poyser. Even in these cases George Eliot does not introduce many unusual dialect words, preferring to make her point through syntax and the occasional altered spelling. It is not only the country folk who use dialect. Mr Casson uses a form of Cockney, and in his role as former butler he scorns the language of those around him. He thinks he speaks better than they do. This is how he expresses his feelings on the matter:

> He's allays put up his hoss here, sir, iver since before I hed the Donnithorne Arms. I'm not this countryman, you may tell by my tongue, sir. They're cur'ous talkers i' this country, sir; the gentry's hard work to hunderstand 'em. I was brought hup among the gentry, sir, an' got the turn o' their tongue when I was a bye. Why, what do you think the folks here says for 'hevn't you?' – the gentry, you know, says, 'hevn't you' – well, the people about here says 'hanna yey'. It's what they call the dileck as is spoke hereabout, sir. That's what I've heared Squire Donnithorne say many a time; it's the dileck, says he. (ch. 2)

Some of the characteristic features of Cockney, which we shall look at in more detail shortly, are here. But the passage shows that George Eliot was sensitive to the regional pronunciations of the country and wanted to make her readers aware of them too. In Mr Casson she underlines the snobbery that can build up round variant speech and the ease with which people can misjudge those who speak differently.

In *Silas Marner* George Eliot uses dialect speech as well, though in this case the approach is more traditional. The major characters in the novel speak standard English and it is the minor characters who are localized in North Warwickshire. The butcher and the farrier at the pub speak dialect, whereas Silas and the Squire's family usually speak the standard with only an occasional provincialism.

These three women novelists made dialect respectable again. They extended Scott's example to England and, not surprisingly, this extension happened first with reference to the North. The manufacturing industries produced local communities there which were increasingly conscious of their identity and of their difference. It is ironic in some ways that two of the novelists, Emily Brontë and George Eliot, should set their novels in rural settings into which the industrial environment rarely impinges. Only *North and South* uses the setting of a mill-town, though Mrs Gaskell's other novels are set in more genteel localities. From this time onwards a vigorous dialect literature grew up in Yorkshire and Lancashire, associated in part with the development of local journalism and cheap newsprint. These writings, which were largely of an uplifting kind, had little impact outside the communities for which they were produced, but they began to attract the attention of some educationalists so that by the end of the century there were voices raised against the erosion of the dialects through the teaching of standard English. The influence on literary writing of these local pieces was limited. In the rest of the country there was little dialect writing, for the dialects in the East, West and South were ignored by writers.

One exception to this is Tennyson, who wrote seven poems in the Lincolnshire dialect. He was born at Somerby in the South Lincolnshire Wolds, though in later life he spent most of his time in the South. His dialect poems were written after he left Lincolnshire and so they represent what he recollected of the dialect. It is hardly surprising that there are inconsistencies as well as features from other dialects in his representation. Thus he varied between *oi (oy)* and *ai (ay)* in his representation of what Tennyson called long *i*, i.e. Modern English [ai]. He introduced from different dialects such forms as *she* for 'her' and *hond* for 'hand', which have no place in this dialect. There are many features of the dialect which he does try to reproduce such as the diphthong in *mea* and *shea* corresponding to Modern English [i:], and the long vowel which he wrote with a *u* and which corresponds to

Modern English [o:] as in *curn* 'corn'. The following is an example of the dialect from *Northern Farmer, Old Style*.

> Parson's a beän loikewoise, an' a sittin' 'ere o' my bed.
> 'The amoighty's a taäkin o' you to 'issén, my friend,' a said,
> An' a towd ma my sinds, an's toithe were due, an' I gied it in hond;
> I done my duty boy 'um, as I 'a done boy the lond.

Whatever the merits of the dialect representation, the significance of the poems lies in the fact that an established poet is prepared to use dialect at all. Naturally poems written by Tennyson had more chance of being widely read than those written by the average dialect poet. As it happens these poems are rural in subject, for Lincolnshire was one of the least industrialized counties. Apart from these few poems Tennyson used archaism rather than dialect or other forms of non-standard language. Other poets of his age are alike in this. Only Browning tried to experiment with dialogue by omitting some of the grammatical words. In that way he evolved a language which was not an attempt to recreate a non-standard variety; it was a peculiar type of literary style.

Cockney, as a form of London speech, is essentially an urban dialect, but it had evolved as a type of low-class speech because any educated Londoner would naturally be expected to speak standard English. In the eighteenth century Cockney had developed as the primary non-standard language, but its usefulness was not so much as a marker of class but as a vehicle for humour. This aspect remained an important characteristic of the dialect in its later manifestations. A foremost example of Cockney at the beginning of the Victorian period is provided by Jorrocks, the hero of such novels as *Handley Cross*. Jorrocks is a man of substance even though a native of London, and his particular delight is hunting, which his wealth enables him to satisfy. As he is offered the position of the Master of Foxhounds at Handley Cross, much of the story takes place outside London. Consequently Jorrocks can be contrasted with the other characters. He is given the typical characteristics of the Cockney dialect, though these add to the humour and geniality of the man; they in no way imply criticism or scorn. The dialect is part of the good-natured humour of the piece. His linguistic quirks include the omission or addition of initial *h* as in *'unting* and *hanimal*, the interchange of *w* and *v* as in *werry* 'very' and *wales* 'vales', the dropping of the *g* in the *ng* group when final as in *stoppin'* and other occasional forms such as *'oss* 'horse', *zactly* 'exactly', *marmeylad* 'marmalade' and *bouy* 'boy'. He uses little syntactic variation or specialized vocabulary.

Although Charles Dickens introduced many varieties of non-standard language into his writings, it is his representation of the Cockney dialect which brought him fame and for which he is principally remembered. His interest in speech probably sprang from his experience as a reporter and shorthand writer; he served in this capacity at Doctors' Commons and in the law courts. The continual recording of actual speech made him sensitive to the different varieties of English then in use. While he may have been familiar with a greater range of English than many other writers, it does not follow that he was any more concerned with creating accurate representations of the varieties he puts into the mouths of his characters. As Dickens first attracted public acclaim with *Pickwick Papers* (1836) we may first consider his representation of Cockney as spoken by the Wellers. Sam Weller is a traditional character, for he falls into that literary type of the devoted servant who acts as a foil to his master. He is flashy, witty and brave, as the tradition demands. He also speaks Cockney, for it is part of the tradition that the servant should be the source of humour in the literary work; and Cockney helped Dickens to provide such humour. Hitherto Cockney speakers had largely been drawn as caricatures and often they had done little more than corrupt standard English into a non-standard form by the veneer of various non-standard spelling conventions. Dickens's Cockney speakers have more life and vigour because they are given a variety of appropriate colloquialisms, slang expressions and turns of phrase suitable for their particular status. Sam Weller is no different in this, and he thus has to interpret some of what he says for the benefit of his master (and also of the reader). Even so, the use of non-standard spelling to indicate a dialectal pronunciation remains the principal means of indicating Cockney speech with Dickens, though it is closely associated with grammatical departures from the norm. The standard language had become so regulated by the nineteenth century, and the influence of education was becoming so pervasive, that any deviations from the recommended correct forms were marked as non-standard.

Weller uses most of the features regarded as characteristic of Cockney. He confuses *v* and *w*, though the substitution of *v* for *w* as in *vith* is rather more common than that of *w* for *v* as in *wery*. The assimilation of *rs* to *ss* as in *'oss* and *nuss* 'nurse' is common, as is the omission of the final *g* in the group *ng* such as *shillin'*. Omission of vowels in unaccented syllables occurs commonly as in *reg'lar*, and the consonants *t* and *d* are likewise omitted in certain consonantal groups as in *mas'rs* 'masters'. There are in addition various spellings which indicate Cockney pronunciation such as *biled* 'boiled'. Not infrequently Dickens gives Weller a variant spelling which in fact indicates the normal spoken form of a word, as in *wos* 'was', though the reader is clearly asked to understand this as being another feature of Weller's deviant speech. Weller also has many syntactic variants, though these are less easy to categorize and are not confined to Cockney speech since they occur in many non-standard varieties. These include the use of double negatives, lack of congruence between subject and verb, verb forms such as *know'd* for *known*, adverbial forms without *-ly*, and unusual comparative and superlative forms of adjectives. The following is a good example of the way father and son speak.

> 'Wery good power o' suction, Sammy,' said Mr Weller the elder looking into the pot, when his first-born had set it down half empty. 'You'd ha' made an uncommon fine oyster, Sammy, if you'd been born in that station o' life.'
>
> 'Yes, I des-say, I should ha' managed to pick up a respectable livin',' replied Sam, applying himself to the cold beef, with considerable vigour.
>
> 'I'm wery sorry, Sammy,' said the elder Mr Weller, shaking up the ale, by describing small circles with the pot, preparatory to drinking. 'I'm wery sorry, Sammy, to hear from your lips, as you let yourself be gammoned by that 'ere mulberry man. I always thought, up to three days ago, that the names of Veller and gammon could never come into contract, Sammy, never.'
>
> 'Always exceptin' the case of a widder, of course,' said Sam. (ch. 23)

In this passage one can see that Dickens is content to indicate the dialect in general terms, for there are many instances where the appropriate Cockney form is not introduced, as in *always* rather than *alvays*. The dialect features are relatively lightly scattered through the text. Dickens did, however, use hyphens as in *des-say* to indicate stress, the joining of words in speech or even a longer pause over a sound, when he felt this necessary.

Many of these features are found also in the speech of Mrs Gamp in *Martin Chuzzlewit* (1843-4), which is perhaps hardly surprising since the Wellers had brought him such fame and popularity. But Mrs Gamp does have other peculiarities. She substitutes *g* for *s, z* or *t*, as in *surprige* 'surprise'. She also uses more malapropisms as well as many pious allusions such as to the *wale of grief*. These points are important in showing that Dickens was intent on creating individual speakers who had their own speech peculiarities; he did not want to create a succession of Cockneys who all talked in the same way. He realized that individual features of non-standard speech could be isolated to create the idiolect of particular characters, even though this meant that these characters were not speaking a complete Cockney.

Dickens is an author who made extensive use of diacritic marks of one sort or another. Often they are introduced to point the humour of a passage, for Dickens was greatly interested in linguistic play. Often the marks indicate a colloquialism or an idiosyncratic stress pattern rather than a variety of non-standard language. Thus when Joe Gargery in *Great Expectations* says: 'Pip. I do assure *you* this is as-TON-ishing!' (ch. 13), we understand that the dashes and the capitals indicate a drawing out of the word with heavy stress in the middle to suit the requirements of the emotional effect of that particular passage. Elsewhere, as in his *American Notes*, Dickens used the dash to indicate a non-English stress pattern, a pattern which he accentuated by introducing marks over some vowels as in *en-gine* and *pre-ju-dice*. What these marks mean is often difficult to decide precisely, as is the case with *mountaïnous*. Dickens was one of the first English writers to realize the potential of American speech, which no doubt came from his visits to America and his familiarity with American writings. Throughout *American Notes* there are traces of local varieties of speech, even though most Americans are allowed to speak in a standard variety. The black driver of a coach can speak like this:

> 'We shall get you through, sa, like a fiddle, and hope a please you when we get you through, sa. Old 'ooman at home, sa,' chuckling very much ... So he stops short; cries (to the horse again), 'Easy. Easy den. Ease. Steady. Hi. Jiddy. Pill. Ally. Loo,' but never 'Lee!' until we are reduced to the very last extremity. (ch.9)

Here we have various spellings used to suggest the pronunciation of a black American. But the language of the brown forester from Mississippi is represented almost entirely through syntactic variations.

> 'This may suit *you*, this may, but it don't suit me. This may be all very well with Down Easters, and men of Boston raising, but it won't suit my figure nohow; and no two ways about *that*; and so I tell you ... It don't glimmer where *I* live, the sun don't. No. I'm a brown forester, I am. I ain't a Johnny Cake.' (ch.10)

Dickens's linguistic exuberance has much in common with that of eighteenth-century writers: he employs many punning effects and malapropisms. He also uses language for more serious purposes, for its many varieties enable him to differentiate between the characters of the individuals who throng his novels. In serial publication the language could act as a linking device between chapters. Usually non-standard language is still confined to the lower-class people. It includes slang, though it is the slang of the underworld more than that of genteel society. Dickens's example was important in the history of the novel; especially as the function of dialogue began now to be appreciated fully. Dialogue was breaking free from the stranglehold of correctness, which came to be reserved increasingly for narrative sections. His non-standard language impressed many contemporaries with its realism and it helped to show that a man's true worth cannot be gauged by the class of society he is born into. Modern commentators have been less impressed by the realism of Dicken's non-standard language: his portrayal of Lancashire dialect in *Hard Times* has been shown to be far from accurate. But Dickens, like most other writers, was interested in using dialect for character delineation more than in giving an accurate representation for its own sake. Even so, he did try to be as accurate as possible, for he acquired contemporary descriptions of any dialect he was going to use. We should of course remember that the nineteenth century was the great age of recording dialect words and phrases, for there was a strong interest in the preserving of dialects and in understanding what they could tell about the history of English. This interest in local speech was in part a reaction against the purity of the standard; and writers who wanted to escape from the restrictions of correctness in order to experiment had to look to non-standard varieties of English. Within those varieties slang was a more useful vehicle than dialectal pronunciation since it did not carry the same prejudice. Each class had its own slang, as we saw in *Tom and Jerry*, and consequently slang in itself could not damn a man as uneducated or provincial; indeed, the reverse was usually the case. To use slang was to be in the know, to be up with the current fashion.

Dickens was not the only writer to use a wide variety of non-standard language at this time. One of the lesser writers of the period, William Ainsworth, uses as many varieties in his novels. *Jack Sheppard*, published in 1839, contains speakers of thieves' cant, a Jew, a Dutchman, and an Irishman among others. The most interesting non-standard variety is perhaps the thieves' cant spoken by the Londoners. This is used as a secret language to prevent other people from understanding what is being planned; it is also used as a kind of passport into the thieves' society. When Mr Woods is in the Mint he shows he is not a member of the thieves' fraternity because he does not understand their language, although they had come to help him against what they thought were bailiffs. At another point in the novel Jack Sheppard is able to help Thames Darrell because 'I overheard Jonathan Wild's instructions to Quilt Arnold, and though he spoke in slang, and in an undertone, my quick ears, and my acquaintance with the thieves' lingo, enabled me to make out every word he uttered.' (Epoch II, ch.12). Naturally Ainsworth cannot reproduce the thieves' cant in full or else the reader would be as mystified as some of the other characters. He introduces the occasional cant word into the thieves' speech in such a way that its meaning can usually be understood. They include *all's bowman* 'all's ready', *covey* 'chap', *bandag* 'bailiff', *trap, shoulder-clapper* 'constable', *flash* 'slang', *kimbaw* 'question' and *post the cole* 'pay up'. With the other characters Ainsworth follows the traditional method of representing dialect. In the novel the non-standard speakers tend towards the comic and grotesque. His book differs from earlier representations only in the extension of dialects. Jews had not figured largely in literature hitherto as speakers with a special accent. In fact Abraham the Jew in *Jack Sheppard* has many features of the Cockney in his speech. He confuses *v* and *w*, he uses faulty inflexions, and he also uses *sh* where standard language has *s* as in *shave* 'save'.

In this period the work of Thackeray is particularly interesting for he did not restrict slang to the idiomatic usages of the lower classes. In his writings slang appears frequently in the mouths of upper-class speakers. Even so it is more often found used by young men, for women are supposed to be ignorant of it and older men have evidently not acquired it. Slang is thus very much the preserve of the young unmarried men who are represented as having their own social group. Consequently when slang is used it often meets with an enquiry from someone outside that social group as to the meaning of the word in question. In this way Thackeray is able to explain the word and also to indicate its quality. For the most part the slang consists of single lexical items like *stunner* used of a young lady or of a short idiomatic phrase like *on tick* used of credit; together such words form the vogue vocabulary of their time. Such a vocabulary was finding a wider audience through such periodicals as *Punch*, to which Thackeray himself contributed, and his 'The Snobs of England' series contained many slang words and expressions. Thackeray used slang in his novels to distinguish his characters. For the most part he writes of the higher echelons of society, a group which naturally contains many who want to make their mark as well as many who want to rise further. A knowledge of the appropriate language is desirable in such cases and the language they use can be an important pointer to their character. Since dialects and malapropisms would be unsuitable vehicles for linguistic censure, it is hardly surprising that Thackeray should rely upon slang. Through it he is able to indulge in social comment and the ridiculing of affectation. It might also be noted that those who use slang often have certain verbal forms which are no longer part of the standard language. It was perfectly acceptable for a young man to say *ain't she* and *don't she* for 'isn't she' and 'doesn't she' respectively. Similarly many colloquial pronunciations like *p'raps* 'perhaps' may be found as part of their language. Such forms are not however very common, because it would be easy to overstep the boundary between acceptable and unacceptable non-standard language.

The early Victorians established non-standard language as an important tool in the hands of the novelist, but in poetry and drama it remained relatively unused. The novelists, inspired in part by the realism of the French novel and in part by the growing interest in the deprived classes, wanted to portray the life of the regions and of the less fortunate. Hence non-standard language tended to lose its comic overtones, though that aspect was not completely abolished. Naturally it tended to be used for the less educated members of society, though its use among the more fashionable also began to be represented. Whereas the dialects were represented more by differences in pronunciation, which were characterized by variants from standard spelling, upper-class language was represented more by slang than by pronunciation.

Chapter 9

THE EARLY MODERN PERIOD

ඖඖඖඖඖඖ

As THE NINETEENTH CENTURY proceeded the use of regional varieties of language became more accepted in novels of rural life, but dialect representations still attracted unfavourable comments from critics. The gradual acceptance of local speech forms in England may have been expedited by parallel trends in America where once literature had thrown off the constraints of the English literary tradition there was a blossoming in the use of language. There the size of the country, the varied nationalities of the immigrants and the absence of any indigenous tradition or standard made regional writing inevitable. At first this freedom was frowned on by more traditional American authors, but the success of such novels as *Huckleberry Finn* converted a grudging acceptance to a patriotic welcome. During the nineteenth century, American prose style underwent important modifications which were influenced in part by the new attitude towards the regions which developed in Europe through the Romantic Revolution. The change was away from the abstract philosophical style of the eighteenth century to a more concrete and earthy style. This was partly the product of the regional varieties of language found in the nineteenth-century novel, for this writing was felt to be truer to life than the abstract style it superseded. The development towards a more socially conscious and realistic novel in Europe also encouraged the new style. It was part of the new trend that all writing, whether in dialogue or not, became simpler, and this was particularly the case where there was a fictional narrator through whom the author related the story, for it would not be appropriate for such a narrator to use an abstract style. Writers were willing to adopt a more colloquial style which increasingly broke away from the correctness associated with the traditional standard. However, this creates a problem in our trying to detect what was non-standard, for as the narrative style became more colloquial so the gap between it and non-standard writing decreased. Thus the failure to observe the dictates of correct grammar may no longer be a sign of non-standard language. While this development was more marked in America than in England, the effect of this new attitude to style was increasingly felt as the twentieth century progressed.

Non-standard writing continues in this period to appear most frequently in the novel. Poetry remained conventional in language until after the First World War when it adopted more colloquial and regional varieties. The subject matter moves away then from the rural ideal to the urban environment as in T. S. Eliot's *The Waste Land*. In that poem we find lines from popular songs as well as snatches of ordinary conversation. The latter may extend over a considerable number of lines, as in the conversation between the two women in the pub at the end of part II. Although some of the vocabulary is colloquial like *demobbed*, there is no attempt to introduce phonetic spellings or dialect forms. The poem does not aim to reproduce non-standard language for it is more an ordinary language which is invoked, though the boundary between the two is not easy to decide. What we see in poetry is the loosening of linguistic restrictions, though not specifically in the direction of non-standard language. The linguistic experiments of the poets took another direction.

The main exception to this is Rudyard Kipling, whose *Barrack-Room Ballads* took the country by storm when they started to appear in 1890. The ballads are dramatic monologues put into the mouths of fictitious characters, drawn from the ranks of the common soldiers. As a rule they come from the London working class. Literary Cockney is thus the language of the ballads. Kipling treated this in much the same way as novelists treated regional dialects and so he helped to raise Cockney in stature. Features from Cockney that he constantly uses include the dropping of initial *h* and the omission of final *g* in present participial forms and of final *d* in a few words like *and*. Many unstressed syllables are represented by *er* as in *ter* 'to' whereas others are contracted through loss of vowel or consonant as in *s'pose*. Some words are given a different spelling to indicate a sound which is supposedly Cockney, though many such spellings had become traditional as *'arf* 'half', *yuss* 'yes' and *wot* 'what'. Double negatives and irregular verb forms also occur, as do occasional grammatical solecisms. Kipling could not introduce four-letter words at this time and so he was forced to rely on euphemisms like *blasted* and expletives like *hoi*. There is little that is new in this representation of Cockney except that it occurs in poetry and became very popular. As can be seen from the following extract from *Mandalay* the use of dialect was only occasional, so that standard and occasional forms exist cheek by jowl.

But that's all shove be'ind me – long ago an' fur away,
An' there ain't no 'busses runnin' from the Bank to Mandalay;
An' I'm learnin' 'ere in London what the ten-year soldier tells:
'If you've 'eard the East a-callin', you won't never 'eed naught else.'
    No! you won't 'eed nothin' else
    But them spicy garlic smells,
    An' the sunshine an' the palm-trees an' the tinkly
      temple-bells;
    On the road to Mandalay ...

In drama there were not many new developments either, for it was not a very rich period for new dramatic talent. Bernard Shaw dominates the period and he was, of course, interested in both language and spelling. His main use of non-standard language is through Cockney. This appeared in several plays like *Pygmalion* and *Major Barbara*. Shaw differs from Kipling in that he introduces Cockney consistently into the language of a given character and he attempts to realize Cockney sounds through his own spelling conventions. Thus we get the following exchange in *Major Barbara*:

BILL.   Youre Todger Firemawl, are you?
TODGER.   Sergeant Fairmile, at your service, sir.
BILL.   You took awy maw judy, did you? Nime of Mog Ebbijam.
MOG.   Bill!! Dont you know me?
BILL.   Blaow me! Its er voice. Wot ev you dan t'yseeawf? Wotz e dan to you?
MOG.   Sergeant: it's Bill Walker, that was my bloke. And I'm so changed he doesnt know me.
TODGER.   We'll make the same change in you, Bill. Is that what youve come for?
BILL.   Awv cam to ev me fice chynged rawt enaff; an' youre the menn that's gaoin to chynge it. Tike thet. [*He spits in Todger's face.*] Nah, eah's maw jawr. Itt it. Itt it your best. Brike it.

There are a few slang words like *judy* and *bloke*, but Shaw has put special effort into Cockney diphthongs and triphthongs, though his representation of 'yourself' as *yseeawf* might cause difficulties to many readers. His spelling is not strictly phonetic, since he keeps the *k* of *know* and the *c* of *fice*. Indeed the *e* in *fice* and *brike* is a traditional spelling convention to indicate that the proceeding syllable contains a long vowel or diphthong. It is not clear whether the *i* and *y* in *fice* *chynged* indicate the same sound or not. The unusual spelling of some words draws attention to the whole representation of the dialect and encourages the reader (and the actor) to think of this as true Cockney. Many of the traditional Cockney traits reappear such as the fall of initial *h* and of final *g*. The Cockney speaker is still very much the lower-class character, though he is no longer necessarily comic, and social conscience increasingly makes itself felt in such characters as Bill.

This is also the period of the great Irish dramatists like J. M. Synge, who use an Irish variety in many plays. But it is not easy to describe this variety as non-standard any more: it is the language of Ireland and it can be employed for patriotic reasons in the struggle against the English. It may be non-standard seen from England, but it is not deviant in Ireland, even though it is found more commonly among the rural population and the urban masses because the upper classes had been more subject to the influence of standard English.

In the novel there are new extensions of non-standard language although the more traditional rustic variety continued in the work of writers like Thomas Hardy. In his works it is not only the minor characters forming the chorus who speak dialect, for some of the major ones like Michael Henchard in *The Mayor of Casterbridge* do so too. Hardy was attacked by some critics for inconsistency in his portrayal of dialect. Such inconsistency, as we have seen throughout this book, is characteristic of all non-standard language representation, for writers wished to point out certain features of a character rather than to create a photographic reality in linguistic usage. Hardy himself in a letter to *The Athenaeum* of 30 November 1878 on 'Dialect in Novels' recognized that true representation of dialect was not suitable in a novel:

> An author may be said to fairly convey the spirit of intelligent peasant talk if he retains the idiom, compass, and characteristic expressions, although he may not encumber the page with obsolete pronunciations of the purely English words, and with mispronunciations of those derived from Latin and Greek ... If a writer attempts to exhibit on paper the precise accents of a rustic speaker, he disturbs the proper balance of a true representation by unduly insisting upon the grotesque element.

It is noteworthy that for Hardy, as for most other people, dialect and peasants go together, although some of his dialect speakers are better than peasants. In his revisions to his novels Hardy both added and deleted dialect features, but in no instance does it seem that he was motivated by a desire for consistency or accuracy in his dialect port-rayal. To Hardy dialect was a vehicle to indicate social class and irony.

A typical example of the local Egdon dialect is that found in the first appearance of the peasants in *The Return of the Native*.

> 'A fair stave, Grandfer Cantle; but I am afeard 'tis too much for the mouldy weasand of such a old man as you,' he said to the wrinkled reveller. 'Dostn't wish th'wast three sixes again, Grandfer, as you was when you first learnt to sing it?'
>
> 'Hey?' said Grandfer Cantle, stopping in his dance.
>
> 'Dostn't wish wast young again, I say? There's a hole in thy poor bellows nowadays seemingly.' (Bk I ch.3)

Hardy has introduced a few words like *stave* and *weasand* as well as the expression *three sixes* 'eighteen' to suggest the dialect, though the lat-ter may be a Hardy invention. Although the 2nd person singular forms of the verbs and pronouns occur, they are mixed with the plural 'you' forms as well. There is a little elision to indicate a colloquial style, but it is not obtrusive. All in all the dialect gives some flavour to the piece, but does not hinder intelligibility. On other occasions Hardy had more dialect features such as the use of *a* for Middle English *ē* as in *clane* 'clean' and the voiced forms of initial *s* and *f* as in *volk* 'folk'. These features are never excessive.

The minor characters present little problem for a novelist as far as dialect is concerned, which is why non-standard language had been largely confined to them, because they speak in their own way among themselves and to their superiors. The major characters present a dif-ferent problem because of the greater role they play in the novels. The use of dialect by such major characters will be marked and it will tend to set them off against the other characters in the novel. They may naturally appear to be boorish if they speak dialect among more refin-ed people, though at other times they may through their language suggest qualities which have been lost by more educated people. Hardy therefore varied the amount of dialect spoken by his major characters according to the way he wanted the reader to respond to them at any given point. Naturally this is not an exercise in realism, but a use of dialect for literary ends. Hardy is a good novelist in which to see this aspect of non-standard language since we have evidence of how he revised his novels. Thus he removed a heavily non-standard speech given by Henchard as mayor in chapter five of *The Mayor of Casterbridge*, perhaps because Henchard was then at the peak of his career and was so distanced from the local people around him whom he had apparently outgrown. It also made him seem very different and imposing in the eyes of the women outside. However, the dialect spoken by Gabriel Oak is increased in *Far From the Madding Crowd* in scenes where he speaks to Bathsheba to warn her against Troy. Here his local origins and all they represent are brought into sharper focus through his dialect and are pitted against the stranger and his superficial attractions. Dialect was a marker of class and status, and as such it could cause pride and shame. Henchard is angry with Elizabeth Jane for her occasional relapse into dialect, although he himself used nonstandard language more regularly. Her linguistic improprieties (seen from his point of view) gave him another handle with which to criticize her when he was angry with her. All these uses by Hardy of dialect are important in extending the range of non-standard language. It was no longer a mere vehicle for comedy, but it became an important tool in the hands of the novelist.

Naturally not all novelists used dialect in such an imaginative way from this time on, for there developed a rural tradition in the novel in which sentimentality and romanticism were often important elements. For novelists in this tradition, a tradition which some of them traced back to Hardy, dialect was an evocative medium to create the countryside. For others dialect was part of the strength of nature, its primitive and robust character. The latter is true of Edward C. Booth (1873-1954), whose novels are set in Holderness and whose characters use the local dialect very extensively. The sentimentality is found more in the works of 'John Trevena', the pen name for Ernest G. Henham (1870-1946), who wrote about Devon, though he could also exploit the harshness of the country and its inhabitants. Such novelists may introduce new dialects into literature, but they hardly extend the range to which non-standard language is put.

As the nineteenth century progressed writers increasingly turned their minds to the urban working class, and it was inevitable that more attention would be focused on the inhabitants of the great manufacturing cities of the Midlands and the North. The dialect used in these areas had the advantage that it had not been associated with comedy, as Cockney and the south-western rustic dialect had been. This was quite fortuitous and is attributable to its late appearance in literary works. It could not, naturally enough, escape the associations that went with all non-standard speech, particularly those of lack of sophistication and education. The dialects of the North and the North

Midlands became linked with the industrial working class and so came to be regarded as hard and uncompromising. For many it seemed to epitomize unremitting toil, attempts to escape from the industrial background, and a feeling of being closer to 'real life'.

This can be seen in the works of Arnold Bennett and D. H. Lawrence, and we may consider the latter first since he has many points in common with Hardy. In his *Sons and Lovers*, dialect is used intermittently for it is needed only on occasions to make a particular point; sometimes it appears to be used to suggest contradictory attitudes. Mr Morel is a dialect speaker. In his exchanges with his wife his speech suggests all that is unsatisfactory with working-class life: violence, a failure to understand the more emotional and cultural aspects of life, and an innate conservatism. However, in his dealings with the pit managers, the speech underlines what is good in that way of life: an independence of spirit which will not be browbeaten and a pride in a job well done. Some of this can be seen in:

'Th'gaffer come down to our stall this morning, an' 'e says, "You know, Walter, this 'ere'll not do. What about these props?" An' I says to him, "Why, what art talkin' about? What d'st mean about th'props!" "It'll never do, this 'ere," 'e says. "You'll be havin' th'roof in, one o' these days." An' I says, "Tha'd better stan' on a bit o' clunch, then, an' hold it up wi' thy 'ead." So 'e wor that mad, 'e cossed an' 'e swore, an' t'other chaps they did laugh.' Morel was a good mimic. He imitated the manager's fat, squeaky voice, with its attempt at good English. (ch.1)

In this passage it is the standard language which is made to seem effete and alien. The dialect itself is indicated more through elision and the occasional vocabulary and morphological item. Not much attention is given to variant phonological features.

Paul himself reacts to the local dialect because it seems to him to embody all that is ugly and violent in his surroundings. He says to his mother:

'They're hateful, and common, and hateful, they are, and I'm not going any more. Mr Braithwaite drops his "h's", an' Mr Winterbottom says "You was". (ch.4)

Yet even here Paul expresses his opinion in a colloquial way which has some elements from the local area, such as the repetition of *they are*. More importantly, when he is with his mother he can relapse into dialect and colloquialism at moments of emotional tenderness, for the dialect suggests a sincerity and warmth which the usual standard language seems incapable of expressing.

In Arnold Bennett's *Clayhanger* there is much the same use of dialect in that it divides the older from the younger generation. Darius Clayhanger is a self-made printer who escaped from the workhouse through the generosity and protection of a Sunday school teacher. He retains an element of the dialect in his speech, though it is never obtrusive. It becomes more marked in passages when he is exerting himself against his children and when the author wishes to contrast the generations. He can say 'Ye'd only be good glad if I killed mysen' (III.12.1) with *ye* for 'you' and *mysen* for 'myself'. He uses *childer* 'children', *mun* 'must', *her* as the pronoun subject, and second singular present tense forms like *hast*. He also uses the same variant pronunciations like *mester* 'mister' that are put into the mouths of the less elevated locals. Edwin, his son, and his daughters never relapse into dialect and thus remain distanced emotionally and psychologically from their father. If Edwin differs from his father, he also differs from his friends the Orgreaves, who have a much freer use of language. Charlie Orgreave, or 'the Sunday' as he was known to Edwin, and his brothers indulge in mild forms of slang and colloquialism, though they never use truly non-standard language. Bennett points out that Charlie is less provincial in his language than Edwin:

> The Sunday's accent was less local; there was a hint of a short 'e' sound in the 'a', and a briskness about the consonants, that Edwin could never have compassed. The Sunday's accent was as carelessly superior as his clothes. Evidently the Sunday had someone at home who had not learned the art of speech in the Five Towns. (I.1.3)

This is stated in the narrative; it is never expressed through the dialogue. There is nothing to distinguish the Sunday's accent from Edwin's. It would not have been easy for Bennett to indicate this subtle difference between the two friends without losing something of the sympathy that he was intent on acquiring for Edwin.

The local people of the Five Towns occasionally appear and use a modified version of the dialect. The speeches they utter are usually brief and the dialect forms sporadic. Thus the boy who delivers a message for Mr Peake says:

> 'If ye please, Mester Peake's sent me. He canna come in this afternoon – he's got a bit o' ratting on – and will Mester Clayhanger step across to

th'Dragon tonight after eight, with that there peeper as he knows on?'
(I.8.5)

There is no attempt here to be consistent or comprehensive. A flavour
of the locality is all that Arnold Bennett is intent on.

Authors like Hardy, Lawrence and Bennett form the mainstream in
the use of non-standard language in that they rely on a modified form
of dialect as had been done for many years. Other authors at the time
were more experimental in their use of language, mainly because attitudes towards linguistic propriety were becoming freer. Echoes of
Shakespeare and other Elizabethan writers are increasingly encountered. In H. G. Wells's *The History of Mr Polly* several characters
speak with the traditional Cockney-type language, although their
origins are not specifically localized. Apart from indicating the continuing popularity of this variety, little more needs to be said about it.
A more important feature of the novel is its use of slang and of punning verbal creations. Mr Polly is at first a salesman in a gentleman's
outfitters. He and his friends use the slang of the trade such as *crib*
'position' and *refs* 'references for a job' as well as the slang of young
people of the time. Thus he can refer to *piping my eye* as a slang expression for 'crying'. Sometimes the boys speak a kind of telegraph
language, for Mr Polly 'specialised in slang and misuse of language'
(ch.1). Thus he can say:

'In the warehouse, O' Man. All among the table-cloths and blankets.
Carlyle. He's reading aloud. Doing the High Froth. Spuming! Windmill-
ing! Waw, waw! Its a sight worth seeing. He'll bark his blessed knuckles
one of these days on the fixtures, O' Man.' (ch.1)

His misuse of language takes the form of inventing new words or
perverting existing ones into new shapes to give them a new range of
associations. Thus 'lunatic' becomes *lune-attic* and 'alliteration'
becomes *allitrition*. Heavier linguistic innovations include *wreckery-
ation*, *intrudacious*, *rectrospectatiousness*, *absquatulate* and *med-
itatious*. He also invents new phrases as when he 'spent a pleasant Sunday afternoon in a back seat inventing such phrases as:

"Soulful Owner of the Exorbiant Largenial Development." An Adam's Ap-
ple being in question.' (ch.3)

This reminds one of earlier forms of linguistic exuberance and thus
Wells helped to extend the range of what was possible in the novel.

A similar way of extending the non-standard language was by using schoolboy slang and pronunciation. This Kipling did in his *Stalky & Co* (1899). Some slang of this type is found in *Tom Brown's Schooldays* by Tom Hughes, but Kipling introduced far more and helped to popularize the idea of schoolboys speaking a different language. In some ways the slang exhibits many features of eighteenth-century or earlier speech patterns as though schoolboy speech had not been subjected to the same process of standardization found in the adult language. This may in part be due to the literary nature of some of the language used by the boys. Forms with aphaeresis like *'pon* 'upon', *'trocious* 'atrocious' and *'tention* 'attention' could well have been found in an eighteenth-century play. We also find omission of the subject pronoun, occasionally indeed with its verb as well, so that *'member* does service for 'Do you remember', and expressions like *Bagged it from my pater* for 'I bagged it from my pater' are common enough. In addition the boys use adjectives for intensifiers as in earlier forms of English, where adverbials were by Kipling's time virtually obligatory. Thus they say *it made me horrid sick* and *something unusual dam' mean*. There are naturally many elided forms, some of which like *'Twon't* seem rather too literary for schoolboys even at the turn of the century. Others like *you'll* an *you'd* are more natural.

The boys tend to use exaggerated pronunciation of some words which may in many instances simply indicate an unusual stress pattern. Thus they say *fee-rocious* 'ferocious', *fa-ags* 'fags' and *day-vilish* 'devilish'. The exact pronunciation in these cases cannot be decided with any certainty. Characteristic of their language is naturally the slang words of schoolboys. Some of this has become common today, partly through the spread of education, but no one would find *lark* or *mug up* necessarily characteristic of schoolboys any more. Other words like *wuzzy* 'a hide made in the furse' and *Chingangook*, a term of affectionate abuse, are specialized forms with a limited currency. Words for anger are common such as *paddy-wack, bait* and *wax*, as are those implying enthusiasm and excellence as *downy* 'clever', *egregious* 'excellent', *frabjous* 'wonderful' and *giddy* 'elated' among others. It is typical of the boys that they use a lot of alliteration in such expressions as the *giddy garden goat* to give their language a more colloquial and humorous touch, for it is in these young men that one finds the same exuberance in language that is today associated more with the Elizabethans. It is partly for this reason that they lard their English with Latin and French words. Stalky says: 'Of course, but I'm not smokin' *aujourd'hui. Parceque je* jolly wel *pense* that we'll be *suivi.*'

172

There is naturally an element of exhibitionism in such language which has largely been eliminated from the speech of adults. This slang is therefore a very specialized type of language which is suitable only in portrayals of certain types of school at a certain time. Its use here does underline how writers were more and more conscious of the need to achieve greater verisimilitude and how they reacted to that need.

A different problem faced Kipling when he came to write *Kim* (1901), for this is a novel set in India. Kim himself is a boy with an Irish father but who was brought up in the native way. Hence he can switch from being English to being Indian – and this is something that needs to be indicated in the novel. But India embraces a vast range of different nationalities, religions and races. The problem facing Kipling was not dissimilar to that facing historical novelists: how to create a realistic background to the action when that background and the vocabulary which goes with it are likely to be unfamiliar to the average reader. Kipling inevitably arrived at a compromise. Some Indian words are introduced to give a local colour, but when they occur they are glossed in brackets immediately afterwards or else they are explained by one of the characters in the novel. The Indian words are normally italicized so that they stand out as foreign words. Thus *mallum* is glossed '(Do you understand?)', *not-cut* is '(rogue)' and *Belait* is '(Europe)'. Some words are used so frequently in the text that they are explained only on their first occurrence. Thus *chela* 'a disciple of a lama' and *madrissah* 'a school for white children' occur constantly and are assumed to be familiar to the reader, though they are always put in italics. In addition the flowery style of vernacular speech is transliterated, as it were, into English so that an Indian flavour is given to the novel. When Kim has seen the face of the old queen in the carriage, the novelist remarks:

> It was by no means lovely, but as the man gathered up the reins he called it a Moon of Paradise, a Disturber of Integrity, and a few other fantastic epithets which doubled her up with mirth. (ch.4)

In addition the dialogue is often made stilted and archaic to distance it from the English of Kipling's own day. The lama and other older people who are presented as venerable and not wholly living in this world use language of this kind. Thus the lama might say: 'It repents me that I did not give a rupee to the shrine.' Similarly he says 'What profit to kill men?' where the omission of the verb helps to make the speech appear old-fashioned. This is a not uncommon characteristic of this type of language so that an old Indian soldier says: 'What need of a river save to water at before sundown?' These characteristics may occasionally be reinforced by a supposed Indian pronunciation of an English word. Thus *te-rain* is sometimes used for 'train'. In general difference in pronunciation is not used except when the author wishes to distinguish Irish or Cockney accents among the ordinary soldiers of the Indian army. The practical difficulties in trying to represent the various Indian accents were no doubt considered insuperable.

One linguistic feature is important in the novel, though its precise interpretation is not made clear by the author. The second singular of the personal pronoun with the appropriate verbal ending in *-(e)st* occurs constantly. It is used particularly by the lama and at first the reader assumes that it is an aspect of the archaic, semi-religious manner of speaking used by him. It is only when we get to chapter seven that we learn more of its implication. When Kim is talking to Colonel Creighton he says:

> 'Not when I brought thee' – Kim actually dared to use the *tum* of equal – 'a white stallion's pedigree that night?'

Here it is suggested that white men when talking among themselves would use the *thou/thee* forms if they were of equal rank, though the explanation which makes use of *tum* suggests that this was a usage influenced by local conditions rather than a revival or survival of the older use of the English second personal pronoun. A little later in the same chapter when Kim is in the carriage which is taking him from the station to his school, the driver says:

> 'My order is to take thee to school.' The driver used the 'thou', which is rudeness when applied to a white man. In the clearest and most fluent vernacular Kim pointed out his error.

One assumes that the driver had been speaking English to Kim and that this use of *thou/thee* was a characteristic of Indian English. Its use was a status marker, though that usage could be breached by those like the lama who were beyond the level of such petty mortal concerns. In this novel then there are some linguistic clues to the Indian setting, but they are not obtrusive and they are explained carefully so that the reader is not confused. The result is a suggestion of realism rather than any full-blooded attempt to create verisimilitude.

An impetus to greater change in the use of non-standard language was provided by the First World War, which encouraged a freeing of linguistic inhibitions so that slang and other forms of colloquialism became more acceptable. Whereas previously the language of the younger generations was represented as standard and that of the older generation as deviant because it was archaic or provincial, from now on it is the language of the younger generation which is seen as out of line because its members speak a fashionable slang whereas the older generation uses the standard. The use of slang is found among the upper classes for they are less inhibited by notions of correctness in language, and the upper classes begin to emerge once again as a distinct class of speakers at this time. Their speech can also be characterized by certain distinctive pronunciations. A further effect of the Great War was to make different varieties of English, both within England and outside, better known because the war had brought so many people of such diverse backgrounds together. This may have encouraged writers to widen the scope of non-standard speakers in that some authors portray a wide variety of different dialects.

Many of these characteristics can be detected in the novels and plays of Galsworthy, though it is true that a few of them do ante-date the Great War. The range of dialects he portrays is large: it includes people from Devon, Oxfordshire, Worcestershire, Monmouthshire, Yorkshire, Northumberland, Scotland, Ireland, London, Liverpool, Glasgow and America. He also portrays people with different social, rather than regional, varieties. The speakers of dialect still come for the most part from the lower classes. In Devon for example they consist of farmers and sailors. In London they are the maids, clerks and other workmen and artisans. However, whereas in Devon the dialect speakers have only one language, Cockney speakers can adapt their language to the standard if occasion warrants. Nevertheless, the further north one goes the more likely it is that more educated speakers will use the local variety. Thus in *Exmouth* Miss Card, the private secretary to Sir John in Bableigh, speaks a form of the Yorkshire dialect which is hardly distinguishable from that of the workers. Indeed a Cockney commercial traveller exclaims in desperation 'Why the hell can't she speak the King's English?' Galsworthy correctly recognized that the further north one goes in England the more likely it is that regional pronunciation is not a marker of class. Despite the example of Miss Card, it is an interesting feature that in his novels women are less likely to speak dialect than men.

The representation of dialect in Galsworthy is no more consistent than it is in most other novelists. He does not try to create a realistic portrayal of the speech of an area, though he introduces more non-standard features than many writers. Many of the features in any given dialect portrayal can be found in that of another dialect, for they are often more distinctively non-standard than specifically characteristic only of a small area. This applies to many of the syntactic features. In the Devon dialect these include the occurrence of adverbs without the ending -*ly*, whether in an intensifier slot or not: *proper rough, she rode beautiful*. *Like* can be added to adjectives or just tacked on to the end of a clause: *nervy-like, there wasn't room like*. The pronouns have not been regularized so that subject and object forms freely interchange: *I've a-burried she, us calls it*. *These* and *those* are replaced by *them*, and the relative pronoun *which* and *that* by *as*. All these features are found in the representation of other dialects, and few of them would necessarily today conjure up a Devon speaker. The same goes for the frequent omission of a syllable as in *'lumination* and *yest'day* as well as for the common representation of unstressed syllables by *er*.

The Devon dialect consists of a fairly wide scatter of non-standard forms which are found among the speakers of other dialects together with a certain number of representations of differences in pronunciation. Even these are not in themselves confined to one dialect. Galsworthy may suggest some features which he thinks mark out the dialect, as when in *The Patrician* he says of the Devon dialect: 'a stream of talk would issue, all harsh *a*'s and sodden soft *u*'s.' Not only is it difficult to know precisely what is meant by these sounds, they do not find expression through different spellings in the text. For Devon he uses the traditional voicing of initial *f* and *s* together with other occasional items like *oi* for [ai] in *woi* 'why' and *e* for *i* in *ded* 'did' and *fenesh* 'finish'.

The more interesting aspect of Galsworthy's portrayal of variant language is the speech of the upper classes. This is basically represented through a single feature – the fall of final *g*. This idiosyncracy is commented on in *Maid in Waiting* where Clare and Dinny Cherrel are talking of the pronunciation of their aunt, Lady Mont:

'Where on earth did Aunt Em learn to drop her g's?'
'Father told me once that she was at a school where an undropped "g" was worse than a dropped "h". They were bringin' in a county fashion then, huntin' people, you know.' (ch.31)

This had been a characteristic of the standard language which was noted by orthoepists at the end of the eighteenth and beginning of the nineteenth centuries. It had gradually been eliminated as a result of the influence of spelling, but this development had not influenced upper-class speech. Galsworthy remarked on the phenomenon frequently. He noted in *The Island Pharisees* of Mrs Dennant's pronunciation:

> Her accent in speaking showed her heritage; it was a kind of drawl which disregarded vulgar merits such as tone, leaned on some syllables, and despised the final -*g*, the peculiar accent, in fact, of aristocracy.

In his novels a whole range of speakers avail themselves of this particular trait.

An equally important feature of upper-class language is the use of slang. It is by no means found exclusively in this class, though it is more noticeable among its speakers partly because the author draws attention to it and partly because it is often the sole feature which makes their language non-standard. In speakers of dialect such as Cockney the use of slang expressions is only part of their non-standard linguistic repertoire, and not usually the most noteworthy. In the *Forsyte Saga* we can see how the older generation like Old Jolyon and Soames avoid slangy expressions. The younger generation on the other hand indulge in it so freely that their parents remark on it. Lady Mont complained to Dinny and Michael that they used the 'oddest expressions'. In Galsworthy's works the Great War is an important watershed in the use of slang because it becomes much more marked in the post-War novels. Indeed it is so frequent that it is in danger of becoming standard rather than non-standard. For Galsworthy, though, it remained non-standard and thus an important marker of difference between the generations. He thus frequently dwells on a particular word or expression which offends the older characters. In *To Let* Soames is made to reflect: 'What was that odious word? – Flapper! ... Fleur was *not* a flapper, *not* one of those slangy, ill-bred females.' (Part I ch.2) Similarly in *Maid in Waiting* Lady Mont misunderstands the word *hunch* which is new to her and thinks that Dinny has said *hump*. Dinny has to explain what the word means.

The popularity of these methods of portraying upper-class speech can be gauged from their constant reappearance in comic novels. In Evelyn Waugh's *Decline and Fall* Lady Circumference drops her final g's as freely as any upper-class character in Galsworthy. 'That grass is shockin' bad on the terrace' is typical of her utterances. She also employs an occasional *ain't* for 'is not' as in 'Rain ain't doin' the turnip crop any good'. Mrs Beste-Chetwynd, however, resorts to fashionable slang such as *dotty, to be crazy about, isn't he divine,* and *how too shattering for you.* In P. G. Wodehouse's *The Code of the Woosters* Bertie Wooster has no special pronunciation which is marked in the text but his language is characterized by the slang typical of the upper-class young man about town. He and his friends use words like *chump, binge, my little chickadee, frightful, hornswoggling highbinder, push off, buzz along, hep.* Some of these expressions have since become more common, while others have disappeared altogether. Even those that remain retain a colloquial feel and a few are still restricted to certain classes.

An interesting example of the growing interest in different varieties of English is provided by Conrad. He was not English by birth and he had spent a lot of time in the Far East where many of his stories are set. Generally he has few portrayals of non-standard English speech, but he feels constrained to introduce some examples because his novels contain so many non-native speakers of English. Arabs, Malays, Dutch, German and Chinese interact with English people of different regional origins in his novels. Most of them are not characterized by a separate language, for Conrad is content for the most part to add the occasional non-English word to give some colour to a man's speech. At times he gives slightly more non-standard language as with Jukes in *Typhoon* who speaks pidgin to the Chinese or with Hudig in *Almayer's Folly* whose Dutch origins are emphasized in such words as 'Ver' you gome vrom? Bali, eh? Got bonies? I vant bonies! Vant all you got.' (ch.1) In *Nostromo* there are several Italians who use the odd Italian expression or even occasionally an archaism. Mrs Viola can say: 'Oh! Gian' Battista, why art thou not here?' (ch.3), though elsewhere she does not use the second singular form of the pronoun and verb. Words like *avanti, padrona, casa* and *misericordia divina* appear in their speech. Similarly, because the novel is set in South America, the occasional Spanish word is found, and Martin Decoud uses French expressions. The need to convey some linguistic impression of the nationalities of his characters was clearly felt pressing by Conrad, even though the impression is a very fragmented one: standard English is thus occasionally interrupted by a foreign word or an archaism.

It is only in *The Nigger of the Narcissus* that Conrad really tried to present a range of English regional speech, though he had insufficient knowledge of the English dialects to do this convincingly. Presumably he wanted to suggest that the Narcissus was a microcosm of English society and so he tried to differentiate the characters through their language. It is likely that much of what he included was borrowed from other writers. Interestingly enough there is no attempt to make the nigger himself, James Wait, speak non-standard English; if anything his language is superior to that of any other member of the crew. The major speakers of dialect are the Cockney Donkin and the Irishman Belfast, and these two dialects represent the traditional stereotypes found so frequently in earlier writers. Conrad himself made use of the Cockney dialect in some other novels, such as *The Secret Agent*, but it was not used for a major character again. Donkin drops initial *h* and final *g*. However, in *nothink* final *g* is not omitted, but it is replaced by *k* to represent the voiced form. As a complement to omitting initial *h*, he can add an inorganic *h* before vowels as in *hout* and *Hirish*. Only mild expletives like *blooming* occur. Some words are found in a clipped form like *'cos* for 'because'. Double negatives and such forms as *a'n't* for 'is not' also appear sporadically. A typical piece of his language is:

> 'My dorg at 'ome wouldn't 'ave it. It's fit enouf for you an' me. 'Ere's a big ship's fo'c'sle .... Giv' us a bit of 'baccy, mate' he breathed out confidential-ly, 'I 'aven't 'ad smoke or chew for the last month. I am rampin' mad for it.' (ch.1)

Conrad uses the apostrophe and variant spellings in *giv'* and *enouf* to suggest a non-standard speaker, though such representations could as easily be made for the standard pronunciation. Belfast has some of the same characteristics as Donkin. He also drops initial *h* and final *g*. He uses forms like *sorr* 'sir', *yer* 'your', and *sooperfloos* 'superfluous'. The verb *seez I* for 'I said' consists of a diphthong which might be [Iə] and the ending -*s* or -*z* for the first person singular of the past tense. A word like *anyhow* 'anyway' is characteristic of his lexis. He also in-dulges freely in abuse. But there is in fact little that is specifically Irish in this. Indeed his language is not very easily distinguished from Donkin's. Despite his relative unfamiliarity with regional dialects Conrad evidently felt that he should introduce them into his novel. The pull to make the language realistic was evidently strong.

Other forms of slang are represented from time to time in novels. Thieves' cant appears in the novels by John Curtis which include *The Gilt Kid* (1936), *You're in the Racket* (1937) and *They Drive by Night* (1938). In them we can find slang words and expressions like *do a blag* 'steal', *screw* 'burgle a house', *chat* 'house', *to be on fly-paper* 'to be justifiable under the Prevention of Crimes Act (1909)', *the nick* 'prison' and *queer place* 'prison'. Although novels of this type may have had a temporary success, they soon lost popular appeal in part because of difficulties of the language. Thieves' cant is a specialized language and not many elements from it enter the everyday language. It differs from the kind of language spoken by Bertie Wooster, because that fashionable language is imitated by some and has a much greater currency. People want to understand it, and more of them are likely to have come across it through their own education. Thieves' cant remains a kind of secret language and its usefulness in literature is therefore very limited.

Dialect retained its usefulness and was exploited by many writers particularly for comic scenes. In J. B. Priestley's *The Good Companions* people from different parts of the country join up with a troupe of actors and travel round with the show. However, not all those who use a variant pronunciation are represented by means of different spelling. Hugh McFarlane, who marries the heroine, Elizabeth Trant, speaks with a Scots accent, but this is not indicated through the spelling of his dialogue. It is merely referred to once in passing:

> 'You're going to stay here until that arm's mended and you've had a nice rest and your nerves are quiet again.' He still called them "nairrves". He still brought out those huge vowels and smashing consonants. (Bk 3, ch.5)

This reticence to represent McFarlane's language through variant spellings indicates an unwillingness to compromise him, for non-standard English still carries an unfortunate implication of lack of education and professional ability. This may be particularly so in a novel where non-standard English is used specifically for working-class people or to mark the affectations of actors and others.

Jess Oakroyd who comes from Bruddersford is represented as speaking a West Riding accent, though this is not portrayed consistently or fully. When Jess speaks for the first time, Priestly comments:

> This "Na", which must once have been "Now", is the recognised salutation in Bruddersford, and the fact that it sounds more like a word of caution than a word of greeting is by no means surprising. You have to be careful in Bruddersford. (Bk.1 ch.1)

The accent comes to stand for some of the strong, silent qualities of the West Riding work people. It is significant that it is not found in

Mrs Oakroyd, their son Leonard or his friend Albert. Mrs Oakroyd still drops her *h*'s and has a few features of the dialect like the use of *t'* for the definite article. But Leonard and Albert have consciously tried to replace their accent with what they consider to be the approved standard. Leonard says *rorther* 'rather' and Albert says *quaite* 'quite' and *meself* 'myself'. Jess Oakroyd speaks the dialect in a strong form. Standard writing *ou* is replaced either by *ow* in *thowt* 'thought' and *owt* 'ought', which probably represents [au] or by *ah* in *pahnd*, probably indicating [a:]. The modern diphthong [ai] is written either *ee* or *i* as in *seet* 'sight' and *bi* 'by' which no doubt represents [i:]. The West Riding diphthong found in *school* and *foot* is written *ooi*. Standard *ever* appears as *ivver*, and *over* as *ower*. Oakroyd uses reflexive pronouns ending in *-sen* such as *hissen* and *thisen*. *Our* appears as *wer*. A fair amount of elision is indicated, such as *'a'* for 'have'. Certain Yorkshire words and expressions are also found: *they'd nobbut* 'they had only', *think on* 'think about', *ner* 'than' and *lake* 'play'. In general this is a reasonable representation of the dialect which has been modified for the purposes of the novel and the understanding of standard speakers.

Some of the other accents indicated are more comic, for they carry the mark of affectation. Thus the accent adopted by Mr Jerry Jerningham is put on for effect:

> It is Mr Jerry Jerningham, who now raises his beautiful head to voice a protest. 'Look hare, Jaymy, thet's all raight about the two weeks' meney. Quaite generous, and all thet.' (Here we must break in to say that though there is no more graceful and exquisite young man in the Midlands than Mr Jerningham, his accent, a comparatively recent acquisition, unfortunately demands this kind of spelling. It is one thing to look at Mr Jerningham, and quite another thing to listen to him. The thousands who have crowded in from Shaftesbury Avenue since then to see Jerry Jerningham will not recognise this accent, for the simple reason that he afterwards dropped it and then picked up another during his successful season on Broadway.) (Bk.2, ch.1)

It does not seem necessary to examine this speech in detail, though it indicates how non-standard language was still used to exploit character and raise a laugh.

Other forms of non-standard language in the novel include the portrayal of a man's speech when drunk. Here his *s*'s are represented by *sh*, and the words he utters are truncated or even occasionally garbled. The slurring of sounds is also indicated by the use of *r*'s.

Although the First World War loosened inhibitions about the language, there are few new developments to record in this period in the use of non-standard language. It is time now to see how far this is also true of the period following the Second World War which is the subject of the final chapter.

Chapter 10

MODERN TIMES

𝔊𝔊𝔊𝔊𝔊𝔊

IT IS A TRUISM to say that the world is changing quickly today. Not unnaturally language has been as much affected as any other social force. Like the Great War, the Second World War brought people of many different classes together and encouraged the ideal that the world should be made a better place for all people to live in. The result was a spate of reforms in education, planning, housing and other areas of society. The old empire was broken up and many countries gained their independence to join the British Commonwealth. Full employment at home led many employers to seek labour abroad, particularly in the countries of the new commonwealth, and so there was a massive immigration of people of different racial origins into England. At the same time the revival of regionalism and the desire to eliminate racial prejudice led to attempts to revalue different regional varieties of English. This attempt was motivated in part by the idea of social justice in helping the socially disadvantaged. All language was seen to be inherently acceptable. On the other hand, the growth of a youth culture created new social varieties of English which were national or even international in their currency. New habits such as drug-taking and the renewed interest in esoteric cults spawned their own special vocabularies. Most importantly there was the continuing lessening of the bonds of linguistic propriety so what was unacceptable one year became tolerated the next. This trend was expedited by the growth in communication and travel, of which the rise of television was particularly significant. It created an interest in different regions and sections of society and made the languages of different groups more familiar.

Even so, these developments had much less impact on the use of non-standard language in literature than might have been expected, though naturally they extended the range of linguistic varieties available to writers. Writers who wanted to discriminate between their characters still found the use of non-standard language a useful tool which was readily comprehensible to their readers. Whatever the good intentions of those who wanted to eradicate the prejudices associated with different linguistic types, the novelist and dramatist found the varieties too useful to be jettisoned without more ado. But the new attitudes affected the type of people who might be depicted using non-standard language. For modern poetry the lyric poem is all supreme and rarely needs the effects which can be produced by non-standard language. The poets continued to stretch language in other directions. Occasionally they had recourse to some non-standard features, but this was rarely in the creation of a particular character who is set apart from other characters, for even longer poems today hardly bother to make that kind of contrast. Auden in his *A Bad Night*, which is subtitled 'A Lexical Exercise', drew on a wide range of the lexicon, particularly dialect, to exhibit his expertise. Thus the poem contains such words as *hirple* 'hobble' and *stoachy* 'dirty'; but the whole is hardly an example of non-standard language as we have defined it. Poetry, like most language, became more colloquial and so we often find the rhythms of ordinary speech breaking in. Sometimes the effect is deliberately created, as in Larkin's *Poetry of Departures* in the volume *The Less Deceived* where expressions such as *He chucked up everything* and *Take that you bastard* are introduced into the poem (in italics) to indicate the conversational style of people talking. Other poets, like the Liverpool poets, use a vocabulary that is slangy. Words like *yobbo* and *mojos* occur in their works commonly. Even they do not use a regional variety, and there is nothing ostensibly Liverpudlian about the Liverpool poets. They are modern in their informality and slangy style which they use to catch the rhythms of ordinary speech, but this is rarely set in contrast with a more standard usage.

In the drama there was after the War some attempt to portray the realities of life in what was known as 'kitchen-sink drama'. This often meant a concern for the members of the working classes or of immigrant communities in their struggle to make ends meet or to make some sense out of the world in which they found themselves. In Arnold Wesker's trilogy, which includes *Chicken Soup with Barley*, *Roots* and *I'm Talking about Jerusalem*, the main protagonists are a Jewish family who live in London's East End. Although one character says of Ronnie Kahn, the son of the family, 'Nobody could understand how an East End boy could speak with such a posh accent.' (Act III sc.1), Ronnie's language in its written form does not betray any Jewish or East End origins or even for that matter any trace of the 'posh' quality which this character comments on. For the most part all the characters in the play use standard English with an occasional syntactic irregularity despite their ethnic origins and place of domicile. The only exception is Harry Kahn, the father, who relapses into some Yiddish as he is about to suffer his first stroke ('Vie iss sie der mamma'; Act II sc.1) and who sometimes uses an adolescent colloquialism in his senility after his stroke ('Gimme. S'mine. S'mine. I wan' that envelope'; Act II sc.2). In this play it is possible that the background of the action which concerns the fight of communism against the fascists may have inhibited the use of non-standard language in that it might suggest some intellectual weakness among the supporters of the party. It might be difficult to persuade an English audience that a man who spoke with an East End accent was intellectually serious in his view rather than merely comic.

The situation in *Roots*, the second play of the trilogy, is quite different. This play is set in Norfolk where the family of a country girl, Beatie Bryant, who has lived in London for a time, gather to meet her young man, Ronnie Kahn, though he never in the end makes an appearance there. The members of this Norfolk family all to some extent use non-standard English which is a representation of the Norfolk dialect. Thus when the play opens Jenny Beales, Beatie's sister, speaks to her child: 'Shut you up Daphne and get you to sleep now.' Although there are here no changes in spelling to indicate a dialect pronunciation, the syntax with its use of a subject pronoun with the imperative is distinctly non-standard. It had been a feature of the standard language till the seventeenth century, when it had disappeared to remain only in many dialects. There are, however, indications of non-standard pronunciation, though few are distinctively East Anglian. Most typical is the omission of a final consonant particularly when it is proceeded by an *n*, a feature which some would regard as colloquial rather than dialectal. Thus Jimmy Beales can say 'They don' wan' nothin' ' (Act I). The spellings *ole* and *owle* 'old' are doubtless variations of this same fall of final consonant. Initial sounds can also be lost as in *'cos* 'because' and *'ont* 'wont'. Some words are given a different vowel sound as *blust* 'blast', *yit* 'yet' and *git* 'get', *hevn't* 'haven't' and *hed* 'had', and *me* 'my'. There are words which are characteristic of the area like *bor* 'young man (also used as a term of affection)' and *gal* 'young woman (also used as a term of affection)' as well as more general dialect words like *a'tween* 'between'. Syntactically one may note such forms as *he've hed* 'he's had', *longer'n* 'longer than' and *driv* 'drove'. This play is very much about the power of language and the need to develop the ability to talk so that one can rise above one's social origins. When Beatie first comes back to Norfolk she says 'Funny that! Soon ever I'm home again I'm like I always was – it don' even seem I bin away. I do the same lazy things an' I talk the same. Funny that!' (Act I). And a little later she quotes Ronnie as saying 'Go on, pick a subject. Talk. Use the language. Do you know what language is?' Towards the end of the play when Ronnie does not turn up, Beatie does in fact start to talk and use the language. Finally she seems to have broken out from her limited horizons and lack of understanding as represented by her family and the way they speak. It is for this reason that dialect was used in this play. The differences in the attitudes of the first two plays of the trilogy clearly demanded a different use of language.

In the final play of the trilogy, *I'm Talking about Jerusalem*, there is not much non-standard language, though some of the characters have their own ways of speaking, some of which verge on the non-standard. Thus Sarah Kahn, the mother, who makes a short appearance, has the syntactic feature of putting the complement first in the sentence, as in 'Not even a road here there isn't' (Act I), which also has two negatives in it. No doubt this usage is meant to represent her Jewish origins. The removal men use a colloquial form of language at first which is characterized by the dropping of many vowel sounds, as in 'I'd've clipped him round the ear if he'd've called me lunatic' (Act I). As the act progresses they begin to use a few more non-standard features, which include the dropping of some subject pronouns, occasional *me* as a subject, lack of congruence in *we was*, dropping of final *g* in *bleedin'*, colloquial pronunciation in *gotta* 'got to', and slang words or pronunciations in *missus* and *cock* 'chap'. Clearly the removal men are intended to be understood as Londoners, but they are by no means Cockney. They represent the traditional urban attitude towards the country, where Dave and Ada have gone to set up a new home. They are somewhat lower class, though they appear to own their removal business. In general their representation of language is somewhat ambiguous, and they may represent those who are moving up the social ladder. Ada and her husband Dave use standard English, though after living in Norfolk for some years they begin to pick up a few local words, such as *riled* which, when Ada uses it, is remarked upon by Dave as a Norfolk intrusion into her speech. The colonel, for whom Dave works, is a military man and a landowner, but he is not given any special form of language. Local Norfolk people do not make any appearance in the play, and so the problem of how a local member of the working class might be represented is not raised. Dave's apprentice, Sam, is not necessarily local, and he certainly does not use a local form of speech, though he has a few colloquialisms.

In these plays Wesker uses dialect as he needs to, though as he is not much concerned with language he does not employ much non-standard language. It may be that he did not want to create the stereotyped caricatures which too much non-standard language can so easily lead to. Many of his characters use a certain amount of collo-quialism, though the slang is still fairly restrained. In fact, what is most noticeable, is the traditional aspects of non-standard usage found in these plays. No doubt Wesker relied upon the actors interpreting more of the local atmosphere through the accents they adopted. Wesker himself is content to indicate a few touches of non-standard language and that is sufficient. His reliance upon the actors is made more manifest in a play like *The Kitchen* in which, in an introductory note about the characters, many of whom are foreigners, he indicates which of them have accents so that the actors can know how to repre-sent them. The accents are not represented orthographically in the play, though a few lexical and syntactic features are introduced for those characters who speak English least perfectly.

A playwright who has made extensive use of non-standard English is Edward Bond, whose plays have enjoyed some popularity recently. An interesting example to start with is *Bingo*, which concerns the last years of Shakespeare's life in Stratford during which the powerful land-owners attempted to enclose some of the common. The people who appear in the play do not use archaisms. There is, as already implied, a division between the landowners and the working people with Shakespeare in the middle. They all share some features of non-standard language such as *mornin'* 'morning', though in general Shakespeare and the landowners use standard English. Ben Jonson, who also makes an appearance, also uses standard English, though his style is clipped and abrupt, and he also uses rather slangy words like *shit*. Indeed, in the modern period the use of swear words and so-called four-letter words has grown tremendously, partly in an attempt to suggest the real language of men. The lower classes in the play are represented by the old woman who keeps house for Shakespeare, her husband and her son, and the young woman who is hanged during the play's performance. All these people are given a rustic-type dialect which in the circumstances may be understood to represent the speech of Warwickshire locals.

There are few lexical items which belong to this language. The use of apostrophes indicates the dropping of certain sounds, though on oc-casions it is difficult to know what the resulting sound was supposed to be. What is meant by *yo' 'you'* is uncertain other than that it is clearly non-standard. Other abbreviated forms include *diggin'* 'digging', *an'* 'and', *ol'* 'old', *t'Judith* 'to Judith', *'n* 'than', *'un* 'him' and *'em* 'them'. One might also note *they'm* 'they are' and *yo'm* 'you are'. Syntactically the object pronouns like *her* and *us* are used as subjects, the 3rd person present indicative form can be without final *-s*, *say* for 'says', and *they* can do duty for 'the, those, their'. The forms *on* and *a* are used indiscriminately for 'on, about, of', and *-a* attached to verbs like *ought* can mean the simple or the perfect infinitive. Certain pronunciations are characteristic of these rustic speakers. The spelling *oi* replaces the standard *i* sounded [ai] in *roight* 'right', *toime* 'time' and *loike* 'like'. Initial *h* is replaced by *y* in *yand* 'hand' and *yead* 'head'; but *yont* can mean 'wont, dont, haven't, am not'. Internally *e* or *ea* is replaced by *i* in *sit* 'set', *frit* 'fret', *git* 'get' and *thrid* 'thread'. The *a* of 'have' appears as *e* in *hev*. Other forms include *skart* 'skirt' and *larn* 'learn', *hwome* 'home', *thass* 'that's', *arter* 'after' and *okkard* 'awkward'. The word 'victuals' is represented as *fettles*.

Some of these features were probably introduced to indicate a country or lower-class speech since they are close to current colloquialisms. Others may have been intended as more localized items, but the whole is not convincing. However, it may be best to delay considering the implications of this language until we have looked at some other examples from Bond's plays.

The location of *The Sea* is not specified, but it is clearly on the coast somewhere. Nevertheless some of the lower-class characters in this play have many of the same features of language as those in *Bingo*. The use of apostrophes to indicate omitted sounds is more or less the same in this play as the former one. Thus we find *watchin'* 'watching, *ol'* 'old', *lor'* 'lord', *an'* 'and', *t'be* 'to be', *'em* 'them' and *n'more* 'no more'. Many of the same syntactic features reappear as well; the 3rd person singular of the present indicative is often without final *-s*. Forms like *arter* 'after' and *hev* 'have' are also the same. The representation of 'head' as *hid* echoes forms like *frit* and *thrid* in *Bingo*. There are some differences, though. The form *yont* in *Bingo* here appears as *on't*, though how significant this is remains uncertain. Bond may simply have adopted a different spelling convention. The same may apply to *yoo* 'you' instead of *yo'*. The forms *yoor* 'your' and *yood* 'you would' also occur. The form *en't* 'are not' is found in *The Sea*, but others like *they'm* as in *Bingo* are not.

This kind of non-standard language occurs again in *The Fool* which is located in different parts of the country. A typical sentence which reveals many of the features is *On't hev t'kip grabbin'*. This includes the form *on't* for 'I wont', *hev* for 'have', *t'kip* for 'to keep', with the *i* writing here replacing *ee* or [i:] rather than *e*, and the omission of final *g*. Other plays have similar characteristics. When these various plays are put together there seems little doubt that Bond has created an artificial non-standard language which is designed to suggest in the theatre the language of lower-class people. Perhaps the rustics in *Bingo* have a few extra features like initial *y* for *h*, initial *f* for *v*, and forms like *yont* to suggest rusticity. These forms probably play on our inherited attitudes towards certain sounds and what sounds rustic. The others are general colloquialisms and non-standard pronunciations and syntactic usages which are rarely particularly localized. Indeed, Bond may not have wished to give too close a localization to his language since his characters are meant to stand for something more than the individuals they are. They are part of the struggle between rich and poor, possessed and dispossessed, and they must show the characteristics of their class without becoming too closely rooted in particular events and situations. This use of a rustic artificial language is important and reminds one of the situation which existed in the sixteenth and seventeenth centuries, when dramatists were quite prepared to use the traditional non-standard language for particular dramatic effects. It may be that Bond was consciously imitating this earlier language.

These conclusions do not seem to be invalidated by a consideration of the language in *Saved*, one of Bond's earliest and best-known plays. The participants here all use a form of non-standard language and although the precise locality of the action is not identified, it is clearly a large urban environment, possibly London. Many of the same features we have seen in the other plays occur here too. More noticeable in this play are the fall of initial *h* in words like *'is* 'his' and *'orn* 'horn', the representation of 'you' as *yer* and 'my' as *me*, and the use of *a* and *er* to represent the schwa sound of unstressed syllables. The assimilation of *t's* to *ss* in *whass* 'what's' and *juss* 'just' is frequent. Equally characteristic of this play is a much wider use of slang and swear words. They include words like *caper* 'game', *crap* 'nonsense', *pecky* 'hungry', *reckon* 'like', *doin' a ton* 'going at a hundred miles an hour, very fast', *snout* 'cigarette' and *knocked off* 'had intercourse with'. These lexical items are not specific to one part of the country since they are part of the colloquial slang common to many regions which has been popularized by television. To many people in the audience the immediate reaction would be to identify this language with London (depending on the accent adopted by the actors) since it has many similarities with traditional representations of Cockney. But in view of the similarities it shares with the language in many of Bond's plays, one may conclude that Bond has divided English up into two major types: standard and non-standard. These varieties are more class-specific than regional in his plays. Although some plays may introduce features into the non-standard variety which may seem to localize the speakers, it is doubtful whether this was intentional on his part. It seems more likely that his orthographic realizations have changed from time to time. To Bond language is part of the class scene, and class is supra-regional.

Although many plays continue to appear in a literary prose, the general tendency has been towards a kind of clipped colloquialism. The use of swear words, occasional incorrect pronunciations or syntactic usages, and slang is common enough. In some regions local forms have been deliberately fostered, as in Scotland, to portray the real life of the people. For the most part in England the use of non-standard English has been limited to the class warfare plays, and the type of non-standard language used has been very restricted. This is because the dramatists have not been interested in the language or even perhaps the people as such; they have been more intent on making wider political and social points. Drama, as always, has preferred the broad stroke of the brush rather than loving attention to detail.

With the novel the situation since the Second World War has been marked by the growth of what is now called Commonwealth literature. Many former colonies have produced fine writers, many of whom have achieved quite a following in England. Some, like Wole Soyinka, have written plays and poems as well as novels, though for the most part it is the novels of such writers which have had the greatest impact on English readers. These writers may be divided into two major groups: those for whom English is their first language, though it may have been learned in some local variety such as a creole as in the West Indies; and those for whom it is a second language. For the latter there has always been a tension between the need to develop a national identity by writing in a or the vernacular language and the desire to reach a wider audience which the use of an international language gives. Furthermore English, with its long literary tradition, is a language with echoes which can be exploited by writers, and because these echoes are literary they are widely known. Even so, many writers from countries where English is a second language feel or have felt a sense of betrayal in using English because of the compromises which its use imposes on any depiction of non-English attitudes and ideas for an English-speaking audience. However, the situation for those writers for whom English is a first language also has its problems in places like the West Indies where different creole varieties are used in the different islands. Because the individual islands were colonized at different times by people from varying parts of the British Isles and because they have been subject to different West African influences depending upon which African tribe provided the majority of the slaves, the various vernaculars have differed as much among themselves as some English dialects do. Writers in the West Indies can therefore face the same problems that confront regional writers in England itself. To use the local variety to excess could lead to a writer becoming inaccessible not only in England but also in other islands of the West Indies.

It is possible for the West Indian writer, like the writer of a regional dialect in England, to choose one of three strategies. The first is to use standard English throughout with the occasional local word. The second is to use standard English for narrative and the local vernacular for dialogue. The third is to use a modified form of the vernacular for the whole work. The latter solution is rarely attempted, though it is found in Vic Reid's *New Day* (1949). The second solution is the one which many writers adopt because it allows the writer to place people in their local environment without cutting them off entirely from the wide audience which the use of English allows. Among authors who have successfully adopted this procedure is V. S. Naipaul.

His *The Suffrage of Elvira* deals with an election in Trinidad in which Surujput Harbans is one of the candidates. The majority of the speakers in the novel use the local variety of English, though it is always understood that there is a purer and more correct form to which some of them aspire. The eldest son of Mr Baksh called Foam, who is appointed Harbans's campaign manager, lost a job to another boy, Lorkhoor, because his command of English was far from perfect while Lorkhoor's is described and portrayed as faultless. Certainly he can write poems in standard English which were published in the local paper. The local variety of English is represented through changes in syntax. There are few phonological variations to speak of, though forms like *wuss* 'worse' and *chu'ch* occur. There are also very few local words, though *obeah* 'magic' and *doolahin* 'bride' are used. There are Muslims, Hindus and Spaniards on the island and so the local variety of English is the lingua franca. In general, as is true of many creoles, this variety exhibits a much simpler syntax than standard English. The present tense does duty for the past as well, for an adjunct or the context makes the tense clear: *already I spend* means 'I have already spent', and *since he come* means 'since he came'. The present tense omits the -*s* for the third person as in *The boy answer for me*. Similarly *is* is the universal form of the present tense of the verb 'to be'. There is a form *ain't* which is used almost as a kind of universal negative auxiliary as in *I ain't want no campaign manager* 'I don't want a campaign manager', and *they just ain't have* 'they just don't have'. Auxiliaries in declarative and interrogative sentences are usually omitted. Thus we find *The boy going to work for you, You talking like Foam mother* and *We really want a loudspeaker van?* The verb 'to be' can also be omitted in simple declarative sentences as in *I for you*. If it is included, then the subject pronoun may be omitted as in *Is true, Is a nice one*. *Go* can be used as a quasi-auxiliary, though if so it occurs in the simple form as in *You go want* rather than as in the standard 'You are going to need'. In nouns the possessive -*s* ending is omitted to give forms like *Foam mother* and *the boy head*. Repetition of adjectives is the commonest way of intensifying them so that *big big* means 'very big'. Among new pronouns may be noted new dual and plural forms of 'you' in *both-you* and *all-you*.

This variety is used throughout the novel with care. It represents a modified form of the language used there to make it acceptable within a literary medium to an English audience. For the most part the language is used in much the same way by all the speakers no matter what their ethnic or religious affiliation. It is used for local colour rather than to differentiate between the various characters.

As an example of those novelists for whom English is their second language we may take Wole Soyinka, whose *The Interpreters* is one of the more famous Nigerian novels to be written since the Second World War. Nigeria contains many ethnic groups each with its own language, and this situation can cause jealousy and even conflict as the Biafran War revealed only too well. The English in their colonial period created a system of secondary and tertiary education based on the model in England, and this system has been left virtually intact by the new rulers. Consequently many Nigerian authors have chosen to write in English, though this has not been without its complications. For the subject matter of these novels is usually life in Nigeria, but many aspects of Nigerian religions and cultures are unknown to the average English reader. The problem has been to know how much to include and this applies to some extent to the language as well. How many local words can one use in this kind of situation? Soyinka's novel deals with the problems of the new democracy in which the ideals of the

Western-educated young come up against the traditions and mercenary cynicism of the old. Most of these Western educated people speak standard English and no attempt is made to give this English a Nigerian accent. The people speaking could be English as much as Nigerian, except that occasionally a Yoruba word will be included or a local saying will be given in English but its subject matter or syntax will proclaim it to be Nigerian. These words are often included in italics to underline their local origin. Thus it appears that a *Gambari* is a Nigerian from the northern part of the country since Dehinwa's mother is so worried about rumours that her daughter is going out with one. On the other hand an expression like 'the hungry clerk dons coat over his narrow belt and who will say his belly is flat?' (I.5) proclaims its Nigerian origins because of its syntax and its unfamiliarity to an English reader. Some characters appear to speak only a native language, though naturally these have only a very minor role in the poem. An example is the boy at the night-club who tells Egbo that Simi is waiting for him in the taxi.

The varieties of English in the novel include pidgin and different forms of corrupt standard English. Pidgin is clearly represented as the lingua franca of the less-educated people in Nigeria, such as Mathias the messenger of the *Independent Herald*, waiters and taxi-drivers. A typical example of Mathias's language is 'Oga, sometimes den go want me for other office. Messenger job for newspaper office no get siddon time.' (I.5) This language has many of the features found in the creole of Naipaul's novel, but there are some differences. Mathias uses *den* as an indefinite pronoun. The verb forms are simplified with the present serving also for the past, the absence of inflexional endings, and the general disappearance of auxiliaries. There is no *does not* with the *get*. There is the same *go* type of auxiliary in *go want*, though here it is almost superfluous. There are no articles whether direct or indirect. The negative is formed with *no* instead of 'not'. The words 'sit down' have been corrupted into *siddon*. This sentence alone cannot exemplify all the features of Mathias's speech, but it reveals its general features. These are repeated by most other pidgin speakers.

The pidgin speakers may be said to use a natural language in that they are not trying to achieve a different utterance since the pidgin is their accepted norm of communication. Other speakers are trying to achieve standard English but fail to do so for a variety of reasons. Some of the older ones like Chief Winsala exhibit a few syntactic peculiarities as though they suffer some interference from their own language in trying to speak English. There is, however, no indication of an accent or inability to pronounce English. Thus Winsala can say:

'You know, I like the American, they are not like the English, too much cunny for English man, so so diplomacy but they are much more so wicked even when they are saying Yes please and No thank you ha ha ha ha ha.' (I.5) This speech pattern suggests the older man who has not quite familiarized himself with English idiom or current expressions; he is still influenced too much by his first language. But this method of speech is not to be understood as humorous or ignorant. The same cannot be said for Professor Oguazor, whose fault is that he knows English too well and has tried to imitate some of its supposed elegancies. For Professor Oguazor that means adopting, whether consciously or not, a high-class English accent, which is here represented by the falling of many vowel and diphthong sounds under a general *e* sound. Thus the professor says *Cem en der* 'Come on dear' (I.10) and *Ceroline der, the ledies herv been wetting for you* 'Caroline dear, the ladies have been waiting for you' (I.10). Here the humorous corruption of 'waiting' to *wetting* is in a long-standing literary tradition which deflates pomposity by humour through corruptions which can be understood in a different sense. A different form of corruption is provided by Peter, an Americanized German. He speaks as follows: 'Yeah, wall, not really. I'm German but I use 'merican passport. Just gonna get m'self a zrink. So soree couldn't come down wi' ze others to Lagos, burra had a date wiz a Minister.' (I.10) This talk consists of American, German and drunken corruptions of the language, though its particular constituents have been put together for the sake of the character by Soyinka. It is not necessary to dwell on it.

We have, then, in Soyinka, two forms of acceptable English, a high-class or the standard and a low-class or pidgin. People who use one or the other form are marked off simply by education or lack of it; neither variety is marked by affectation or humour. Other speakers use English in a corrupt form and this corruption in itself is a clue to the characters themselves. The languages so created are in part artificial, but they are intended to help the characterization and moral purpose of the novel. In that respect Soyinka is in the English tradition of the use of non-standard language.

Among the writers of Commonwealth literature there are naturally many who were born in or who have emigrated to the older white Commonwealth countries and who no doubt assume that their English is as standard as anybody's in the mother country. For writers of this type there is the question of representing varieties within their own country, though these will for the most part represent varieties in England. Thus Patrick White in *The Tree of Man* introduces an Irishwoman, Mrs O'Dowd, whose language is a mixture of Irish features with some more general non-standard ones. Thus when she says 'Ah, it's terrible, the men, when all is said and done, an him officiatun, and the fowls not fed' (I.6), the latter half of the sentence has Irish-influenced syntax, but the ending in *-un* 'ing' is more an example of abbreviating the final syllable common to many non-standard speakers. It is a characteristic of many Australians in the novel whatever their ethnic origin. Many of the speakers in this part of the outback use some forms of non-standard language such as double negatives, lack of congruence between subject and verb, and corrupt pronunciation of unstressed syllables. There is little that is particularly Australian about these things; for the most part parallels in literary works written in England could readily be found. For places like Australia there is likely not to be much difference from England in respect of non-standard language. One finds it in the less educated and those who live furthest away from the intellectual and educational centres.

In addition to the native writers of Commonwealth literature there are English writers who have chosen to write about a Commonwealth country. They are in much the same position as writers of historical novels in that they have to choose what varieties of language they will use. In the case of a country like India the number of languages and varieties of English are immense, as can be seen from a novel like John Master's *Bhowani Junction*. Usually most speakers use standard English, particularly those who have any major role to play in the novel. But there are those who use a high-class accent such as Brigadier Nigel ffoulkes-Jones who drops his final *g's* as well as any other member of the upper classes. On the other hand a former private in the British army who is now a gang leader on the railway uses traditional Cockney forms which include dropping initial *h*, use of *ain't, nor* for 'than' and syncopation of medial syllables. Both these varieties are traditional in English novels. The Anglo-Indian, that is the person who is half-Indian and half-English, is characterized by his stress on the final *-y* of words which is represented *-ee* as in *onlee*, and by his pronunciation of 'the' as *thee*. But this form is general only among the minor characters or at times of crisis with the major ones. It does not occur when Patrick Taylor is the narrator, though he does relapse into it on a few occasions, particularly when he is at some disadvantage as against one or other of the main participants in the action, as in chapter 30. The Indians themselves are usually represented as speaking good English, for it is not part of the novelist's intention to suggest any inferiority in intelligence or planning among them. Again a few lesser characters may use a non-standard variety, which is more usually represented through syntax than through pronunciation. Thus Bhansi Lall, one of the station-masters, can say things like 'I am seeing nothing! Look, station is *there*, and rail was pulled *here*, round curve, under embankment. How can *I* be seeing that villainy.' (ch.1) It is his use of the continuous tenses which marks out Bhansi Lall as an Indian, though otherwise his English is good enough. Some Indians are said to talk pidgin, but this is hardly represented in the novel. Many Indians talk in their own languages, though this is given in standard English. The only exception to this is the Gurkhas, whose speech is occasionally represented in Gurkhali. The other Indian languages are ignored except that the odd word is introduced into the narration or dialogue for the sake of local colour. Considering the setting of the novel and the number of different minor characters involved, the amount of non-standard language is really very small. It helps to provide a certain amount of atmosphere, but it is not used for characterization or really for class discrimination.

With novels written in England there is not quite so much non-standard language as one might have expected. The expansion certainly comes from abroad. Slang and colloquialism continue to increase, though these are hardly non-standard any more. Even a novelist like Ivy Compton-Burnett whose characters speak a formal, not to say stilted, English introduces some slang from time to time. Expressions like *to-do, shindy* and *phiz* occur in her work. Otherwise the main area of non-standard speech is the lower-class character. As in the drama there is in the novel much less interest in distinguishing between different varieties of non-standard speech. The care to discriminate between the different regions found in J. B. Priestley is not repeated after the War. This is in part because the language of the working class is increasingly seen as working class rather than as regional. Hence it tends to be generalized. The home areas of some of the characters in the novels are not clearly identified, as though this was something unimportant. Increasingly, too, the non-standard speakers are young or even adolescent, and they are seen to belong to a national or international culture rather than to a local one. Schoolboy slang gives way to a more generalized adolescent slang such as is found in Salinger's *The Catcher in the Rye*.

Joby Weston, the adolescent hero of Stan Barstow's *Joby*, is just at the point in his education when he is leaving junior school to go to grammar school. But there is little of the old school slang about his speech, although one or two words may be adolescent rather than general for his part of the world. He uses abbreviations like *aft* 'afternoon' and words like *keff* 'old man', *spice* 'sweets' and *rammy* 'strong'. Joby and his parents and friends all use a dialect to some extent, though it varies in the novel. But this dialect is fairly generalized working-class rather than strictly regional. Some elements are simply respellings of words in ways to indicate a pronunciation which is common enough, but the spelling suggests something non-standard. Thus 'Fascists' appear as *Fashists*. Vowels and consonants are omitted at both beginning and end of words, as in *'ud* 'would', *'ull* 'will', *'Itler* 'Hitler', *'at* 'that', *an'* 'and', *t'* 'the', *o'* 'of' and *kiddin'* 'kidding'. 'We shall' appears as *wes'll*, 'have' as *ha'* and 'them' as *'em*. Unstressed syllables appear often as *er* as in *feller* 'fellow', and there are general colloquial pronunciations like *summat* 'something' and *shurrup* 'shut up'. 'My' appears as *me* and 'may be' as *mebbe;* 'nothing' is usually *nowt*. A few more specific northernisms are *happen* 'perhaps' and *aye* 'yes'. There are few syntactic differences from colloquial English. Indeed, throughout the novel, the dialect, if we may call it that, is not much exploited. Most of its features are widespread and thus non-localized. The actual setting of the novel is not particularized except through the names of schools and the fact that one man works for the Calder Valley Transport Company. A discerning reader will assume from these that the novel is set in West Yorkshire, but the dialect is not made aggressively local. Perhaps dialect had become too 'folksy' in its image, and so modern novelists find it easier to use a less particularized form, thus achieving the necessary verisimilitude without any suggestion of comedy or being patronizing.

A similar situation prevails in Sillitoe's *The Loneliness of the Long-Distance Runner*. Here the hero, who is in a borstal institution, is given a language which sets him off from the more fortunate members of society; there is in this short novel a 'them' and 'us' mentality. The particular origins of the hero are unimportant, and so they are not localized. What is important is that he belongs to a particular culture which is different from and has its own rules which set it apart from the middle-class society which is the norm now in Western Europe. The language used by the hero is a general non-standard form which has no local features which might identify it with one place rather than another. One assumes that it is an urban environment. There are slang words like *nicker* and *clambed* 'starved'. A few words have non-standard spellings such as *boggery* 'buggery', *mam* 'mum' and *nowt* 'nothing'. There are also many elided forms like *we'd* and non-standard determiners like *them bastards*. For the most part, though, the language is characterized by a certain formless syntax in which several thoughts are woven together in a single sentence, a feature which helps to give the impression of semi-conscious thought. An example is:

> Mike was a nipper compared to me, but underneath the scruffy draught-board jersey he wore were muscles as hard as iron, and you wouldn't think to see him walking down the street with glasses on and hands in pockets that he'd harm a fly, but I never liked to get on the wrong side of him in a fight because he's the sort that don't say a word for weeks on end – sits plugged in front of the telly, or reads a cowboy book, or just sleeps – when suddenly BIFF – half-kills somebody for almost nothing at all, such as beating him in a race for the last Football Post on a Saturday night, pushing in before him at a bus stop, or bumping into him when he was day-dreaming about Dolly-on-the-Tub next door.

There is not much that is specifically non-standard here, and even the concatenation of the sentences is more colloquial than anything more specific. But it helps to create the picture of somebody who is different from 'them' and who has to get his own back.

Sillitoe used rather more examples of non-standard language in his *Key to the Door* which deals with some poorer sections of the community in the Nottingham area. Many of the same features recur. Initial and final consonants are dropped and their absence is indicated through the apostrophe. Double negatives occur and the form *ain't* as the negative present tense form of the verb 'to be' is regular. Words like 'something' occur as *summat*. The fall of *l* before *d* is found in *owd* 'old' and *showders* 'shoulders'. The former of these is quite common in other non-standard representations as we saw in *Roots* and it is doubtful whether the *w* has any significance other than to indicate a non-standard form. An *r* before a consonant can be assimilated to that consonant as in *woth* 'worth'. The pronoun 'you' appears fairly regularly as *yer*, though sometimes as *yo'*. Both these features can readily be paralleled in other non-standard writings. The northern *'appen* 'perhaps' occurs occasionally and some speakers say *tek* for 'take' and *feyther* for 'father'. Occasionally two or three dialect forms occur together as in *Wheer yer bin*, though this is unusual. In general the language is not too far away from the standard. There are certain features which are widely current in colloquial language that occur frequently and these are supplemented by a few more localized forms such as *feyther*.

In modern times the non-standard language has lost some of its comic overtones in England at least, as authors have tried to use it for local colour and as part of the background to class. Consequently, the attempt to represent the working class as serious people with their own culture has made non-standard language less useful for comedy. However, it does remain a ready tool for comedy, as the example of writers like Soyinka reveals, and as our experience of comedians and others on television reminds us. It is a useful tool, which cannot be exploited too much because of its latent comedy. How the use of non-standard language will develop in literature is impossible to predict because that is dependent upon changes in language and society that have yet to happen. It is likely to remain a significant tool in the writer's kit, but how it is exploited remains to some extent outside his control, for it depends upon a wider attitude to language in the society in which he lives.

SELECT BIBLIOGRAPHY

ⓢⓢⓢⓢⓢⓢ

(i) *Editions used.*

This section of the Bibliography contains only those works which have been quoted in the book in editions which I have had to refer to by page number or which have an individual or new system of reference. Other works are quoted from standard editions and the reader should have little difficulty in locating the examples given.

The Canterbury Tales by Geoffrey Chaucer, edited from the Hengwrt Manuscript by N. F. Blake (London: Arnold, 1980).

Caxton's Own Prose, ed. N. F. Blake (London: Deutsch, 1973).

The Chester Mystery Cycle, ed. R. M. Lumiansky and David Mills (Early English Text Society s.s. 3, 1974).

The Novels of Thomas Delony, ed. M. E. Lawlis (Bloomington: Indiana University Press, 1961).

Maria Edgeworth: Castle Rackrent, ed. G. Watson (Oxford: Clarendon, 1964).

Fulgens & Lucres, ed. F. S. Boas and A. W. Reed (Oxford: Clarendon, 1926).

The Works of Stephen Hawes. Facsimile Reproduction with an Introduction by F. J. Spring (Delmar, New York: Scholars' Facsimiles and Reprints, 1975).

A Hundred Merry Tales and Other English Jestbooks of the Fifteenth and Sixteenth Centuries, ed. P. M. Zall (Lincoln: University of Nebraska, 1963).

The Macro Plays, ed. M. Eccles (Early English Text Society o.s. 262, 1969).

The Works of Sir Thomas Malory, 2nd edn by E. Vinaver (Oxford: Clarendon, 1967).

Thomas Middleton: The Family of Love, ed. S. Shepherd (Nottingham: Drama Texts, 1979).

Respublica, ed. W. W. Greg (Early English Text Society o.s. 226, 1952).

John Skelton: Poems, ed. R. S. Kinsman (Oxford: Clarendon, 1969).

Tobias Smollett: The Expedition of Humphry Clinker, ed. Lewis M. Knapp (London: Oxford University Press, 1966).

Swift's Polite Conversation, ed. E. Partridge (London: Deutsch, 1963).

Select Bibliography

The Wakefield Pageants in the Towneley Cycle, ed. A. C. Cawley (Manchester: Manchester University Press, 1958).

(ii) *Select secondary material.*

Alston, R. C. 'English Dialects, Scottish Dialects, Cant and Vulgar English,' *A Bibliography of the English Language from the Invention of Printing to the Year 1800*, vol. 9 (London: Scolar, 1971; reprinted with corrections 1979).

Axon, W. E. A. 'George Eliot's Use of Dialect,' *English Dialect Society Miscellanies* 19 (1876-87), 37-44.

Ayres, H. M. 'A Specimen of Vulgar English of the Mid-Sixteenth Century,' *Studies in Philology*, ed. K. Malone and M. B. Ruud (Minneapolis: University of Minnesota Press, 1929), 397-400.

Bentley, P. E. *The English Regional Novel* (London: Allen and Unwin, 1941).

Blake, N. F. 'The Northernisms in the Reeve's Tale,' *Lore and Language* 3:1 (1979), 1-8.

Boggs, W. A. 'A Win Jenkins' Lexicon,' *Bulletin of the New York Public Library* 68 (1964), 323-30.

_____. 'Dialectal Ingenuity in *Humphry Clinker*,' *Papers in English Language and Literature* 1 (1965), 327-37.

Bridgman, R. *The Colloquial Style in America* (New York: Oxford University Press, 1966).

Brook, G. L. *The Language of Dickens* (London: Deutsch, 1970).

Costello, D. P. 'The Language of *The Catcher in the Rye*,' *American Speech* 34 (1959), 172-81.

Craigie, W. A. 'Dialect in Literature,' *Essays by Divers Hands* 17 (1938), 69-91.

Dean, C. 'Joseph's Speech in *Wuthering Heights*,' *Notes and Queries* 7 (1960), 73-6.

Diller, Hans-Jürgen, *Redeformen des Englischen Misterienspiels* (Munich: Fink, 1973).

Eckhardt, E. *Die Dialekt- und Ausländertypen des älteren Englischen Dramas*, 2 parts (Louvain: Uystpruyst, 1910-11).

Evans, G. Lloyd *The Language of Modern Drama* (London: Dent, 1977).

Franklyn, J. *The Cockney: A Survey of London Life and Language* (London: Deutsch, 1953).

Funke, O. 'Zur "Erlebten Rede" bei Galsworthy,' *Englische Studien* 64 (1929), 450-74.

Gerard, D. E. 'A Glossary of Eastwood Dialect Words used by D. H. Lawrence in his Poems, Plays and Fiction,' *D. H. Lawrence Review* 1 (1968), 215-37.

Gerson, S. *Sound and Symbol in the Dialogue of the Works of Charles Dickens* (Stockholm: Almqvist and Wiksell, 1967).

Haddock, N. 'Thomas Shadwell and "The Lancashire Witches",' *Journal of the Lancashire Dialect Society* 25 (1976), 19-24.

Hudson, K. 'Shakespeare's Use of Colloquial Language,' *Shakespeare Survey* 23 (1970), 39-48.

Ives, S. 'Dialect Differentiation in the Stories of Joel Chandler Harris,' *Readings in Applied Linguistics*, ed. H. B. Allen (New York: Appleton-Century-Crofts, 1958), 413-19.

_____. 'A Theory of Literary Dialect,' *Tulane Studies in English* 2 (1950), 137-82.

Keating, P. J. *The Working Classes in Victorian Fiction* (London: Routledge and Kegan Paul, 1971).

King, A. H. *The Language of Satirised Characters in Poëtaster* (Lund: Gleerup, 1941).

Kökeritz, H. 'A Record of Late 18th-Century Cockney,' *Language* 25 (1949), 190-4.

_____. 'Shakespeare's Use of Dialect,' *Transactions of the Yorkshire Dialect Society* 9: 51 (1951), 10-25.

Leclaire, L. *A General Analytical Bibliography of the Regional Novelists of the British Isles 1800-1950* (Paris: Les Belles Lettres, 1954).

Leonard, S. A. *The Doctrine of Correctness in English Usage 1700-1800* (Madison: University of Wisconsin Press, 1929).

Le Page, R. B. 'Dialect in West Indian Literature,' *Journal of Commonwealth Literature* 7 (1969), 1-7.

McIntosh, A. '*As You Like It*: A Grammatical Clue to Character,' *A Review of English Literature* 4 (1963), 68-81.

Mark, H. *Der Verwendung der Mundart und des Slang in den Werken von John Galsworthy* (Breslau: Priebatsch 1936).

Matthews, W. *Cockney Past and Present* (London: Routledge and Kegan Paul, 1938).

Neumann, J. H. 'Chesterfield and the Standard of Usage in English,' *Modern Language Quarterly* 7 (1946), 463-75.

Owens, R. J. 'The Effect of George Eliot's Linguistic Interests on her Work,' *Notes and Queries* 203 (1958), 311-13.

Page, N. 'Eccentric Speech in Dickens,' *Critical Survey* 4 (1969), 96-100.

_____ . 'Convention and Consistency in Dickens' Cockney Dialects,' *English Studies* 51 (1970), 339-44.

_____ . 'Trollope's Conversational Mode,' *English Studies in Africa* 15 (1972), 33-7.

_____ . *Speech in the English Novel* (London: Longmans, 1973).

Partridge, A. C. *Orthography in Shakespeare and Elizabethan Drama: A Study of Colloquial Contractions, Elisions, Prosody and Punctuation* (London: Arnold, 1964).

Partridge, E. *Dictionary of Slang and Unconventional English*, 2 vols (London: Routledge and Kegan Paul, 1974).

_____ . *Slang Today and Yesterday* 4th edn (London: Routledge and Kegan Paul, 1970).

Petyt, K. M. *Emily Brontë and the Haworth Dialect* (Yorkshire Dialect Society, 1970).

Phillipps, K. C. *Jane Austen's English* (London: Deutsch, 1970).

Pound, L. 'The American Dialect of Charles Dickens,' *American Speech* 22 (1947), 124-30.

Quirk, R. 'Shakespeare and the English Language,' *New Companion to Shakespeare Studies* ed. K. Muir and S. Schoenbaum (Cambridge: Cambridge University Press, 1971), 67-82.

_____ . *Charles Dickens and Appropriate Language* (Durham, 1959).

_____ . 'Some Observations on the Language of Dickens,' *Review of English Literature* 2 (1961), 19-28.

Rinehart, H. '*Jonathan Wild* and the Cant Dictionary,' *Philological Quarterly* 48 (1969), 220-5.

Salmon, V. 'Elizabethan Colloquial English in the Falstaff Plays,' *Leeds Studies in English* n.s. 1 (1967), 105-40.

_____ . 'The Representation of Colloquial Speech in *The Canterbury Tales*,' *Style and Text: Studies Presented to N. E. Enkvist* (Stockholm: Språkförlaget Skriptor AB and Åbo Akademi, 1975), 263-77.

Schmidt, F. 'A Study in English School-life and School-boy Slang as Represented by Kipling's *Stalky & Co*,' *Englische Studien* 39 (1908), 240-74.

Smith, K. E. *The Dialect Muse* (Wetherby: Ruined Cottage Publications, 1979).

Thielke, K. *Slang und Umgangssprache in der Englischen Prosa der Gegenwart (1919-1937)* (Emsdetten: Lechte, 1938).

Tilling, P. M. 'Local Dialect and the Poet: A Comparison of the Findings in the *Survey of English Dialects* with Dialect in Tennyson's

Lincolnshire Poems,' *Patterns in the Folk Speech of the British Isles,* ed. M. F. Wakelin (London: Athlone, 1972), 88-108.

Tillyard, E. M. W. 'Scott's Linguistic Vagaries,' *Études Anglaises* 11 (1958), 112-18.

Trease, G. 'Language in the Historical Novel,' *English* 12 (1959), 126-9.

Underwood, G. N. 'Linguistic Realism in Roderick Random,' *JEGP* 69 (1970), 32-40.

Vicinus, M. *The Industrial Muse* (London: Croom Helm 1974).

Waddington-Feather, J. 'Emily Brontë's Use of Dialect in *Wuthering Heights,'* *Brontë Society Transactions* 15 (1966), 12-19.

Watson, G. *Literary English Since Shakespeare* (New York: Oxford University Press, 1970).

Watson, K. 'Dinah Morris and Mrs Evans: A Comparative Study of Methodist Diction,' *Review of English Studies* n.s. 22 (1971), 282-94.

Weekly, E. 'Mrs Gamp and the King's English,' in his *Adjectives and Other Words* (London: Murray, 1930), 138-61.

Weimann, R. 'Rede-Konventionen des Vice von *Mankind* bis *Hamlet,'* *Zeitschrift für Anglistik und Amerikanistik* 15 (1967), 117-51.

————. (trans. R. Schwartz), *Shakespeare and the Popular Tradition in the Theater* (Baltimore: Johns Hopkins University Press, 1978).

Whitehall, H. 'Thomas Shadwell and the Lancashire Dialect,' *Essays and Studies in English and Comparative Literature* (University of Michigan) 10 (1933), 261-78.

Wilson, F. P. 'Shakespeare and the Diction of Common Life,' *Shakespearian and Other Studies* (Oxford: Clarendon, 1969), 100-29.

Wright, J. *The English Dialect Dictionary*, 6 vols (London: Frewde, 1898-1905).

Wyld, H. C. 'Class Dialect and Standard Language,' *A Miscellany Presented to J. M. Mackay* ed. O. Elton (Liverpool: University Press, 1914), 283-91.

————. *A History of Modern Colloquial English*, 3rd edn (Oxford: Blackwell, 1936).

INDEX

Index

213

Index

217